VIA GARIBALDI

Garibaldi's Italy. (Adapted from a work by Gigillo83 under Creative Commons Attribution 3.0 Unported)

VIA GARIBALDI
ON THE TRAIL OF ITALY'S HERO

JIM HOLDEN

For Austin, Daphne and Raymond

First published 2026

Amberley Publishing
The Hill, Stroud
Gloucestershire, GL5 4EP

www.amberley-books.com

Copyright © Jim Holden, 2026

The right of Jim Holden to be identified as the Author of this work has been asserted in accordance with the Copyright, Designs and Patents Act 1988.

ISBN 978 1 3981 2718 0 (hardback)
ISBN 978 1 3981 2719 7 (ebook)

All rights reserved. No part of this book may be reprinted or reproduced or utilised in any form or by any electronic, mechanical or other means, now known or hereafter invented, including photocopying and recording, or in any information storage or retrieval system, without the permission in writing from the Publishers.

British Library Cataloguing in Publication Data.
A catalogue record for this book is available from the British Library.

1 2 3 4 5 6 7 8 9 10

Typesetting by SJmagic DESIGN SERVICES, India.
Printed in the UK.

Appointed GPSR EU Representative: Easy Access System Europe Oü, 16879218
Address: Mustamäe tee 50, 10621, Tallinn, Estonia
Contact Details: gpsr.requests@easproject.com, +358 40 500 3575

CONTENTS

	Timeline	7
	A note on language	9
1	Prologue: London	11
2	Nice/Nizza	22
3	Genoa/Genova	37
4	Rome/Gianicolo	55
5	Cesenatico/Ravenna	78
6	Sardinia/Caprera	95
7	Como/Milan	111
8	Marsala	129
9	Palermo	147
10	Naples/Napoli	165

11 Turin/Torino	185
12 Aspromonte	202
13 Venice/Florence	221
14 Rome/Mentana	241
15 Epilogue: Caprera	263
Bibliography	277
Acknowledgements	280
Index	282

TIMELINE

1807   Born on 4 July in Nice/Nizza.
1825   First trip to Rome sailing with his father Domenico.
1833   Sails to Taganrog in Russia where he joins the Young Italy Movement.
1834   Takes part in failed revolution in Genoa and forced into exile.
1836   Joins the rebel Rio Grande forces seeking independence from Brazil.
1839   Meets his future wife Anita (Anna Ribeiro da Silva) in Brazil.
1841   Moves to Montevideo and put in charge of Uruguayan navy.
1843   Creates the red shirt uniform for his Italian Legion in Uruguay.
1846   Wins battle at Salto against Argentine army.
1848   Returns to Europe to fight in First War of Italian Independence.

1849 Heroic defence of the independent Roman Republic, and dramatic escape during which Anita dies near Ravenna.
1850 Exile in New York where he works as a candle maker.
1852 Sails round the world as a merchant seaman from Peru to China and Australia.
1854 First visit to England, where he becomes engaged to Emma Roberts.
1855 Buys the island of Caprera to create his long-term home.
1859 Wins battles at San Fermo and Varese in the Second War of Italian Independence.
1860 Leads the Expedition of The Thousand which conquers Sicily and Naples, paving the way for Italian unification.
1861 Declines an offer from Abraham Lincoln to fight as a general in the American Civil War.
1862 Famously wounded at Aspromonte in a failed attempt to capture Rome for the new united nation of Italy.
1864 Visits London to a rapturous welcome, meeting Florence Nightingale, Charles Dickens and Alfred Lord Tennyson.
1866 Wins the Battle of Bezzecca in the Third War of Italian Independence as Italy attempts to gain control of Venice.
1867 Defeated in the Battle of Mentana in another failed attempt to capture Rome.
1870 Rome finally becomes part of Italy.
1871 Joins French army and wins Battle of Dijon in the Franco-Prussian war.
1874 Elected to Italian Parliament and promotes plan to divert the River Tiber outside the city of Rome.
1882 Dies on 2 June at his home in Caprera.

A NOTE ON LANGUAGE

In a book such as this, written in English about another country, there are bound to be issues of language. I have taken a flexible rather than dogmatic approach, going with what feels natural and appropriate.

On place names I have tended to stick with the English version, such as Milan rather than Milano, and Florence rather then Firenze. But with others, such as Nice or Nizza, switching between both is an important aspect of the story. There are also a few examples of preference for the Italian name, such as calling it the Gianicolo hill in Rome rather than the old-fashioned English version of Janiculum. Livorno is also preferred to the outdated name of Leghorn. I have kept the names of leading characters of the Risorgimento in their original Italian. Thus, the first king of the united Italy is always described here as Vittorio Emanuele II rather than Victor Emmanuel II.

I have opted in several places to use the Italian word to describe something, when there is no direct English translation. However, this is always followed by an explanation and rough equivalent of the term used. When visitors come to Italy they will hear these words widely spoken, and it seems to me sensible to use them here.

I

PROLOGUE: LONDON

'The people of England have gone quite mad about Garibaldi.'

Queen Victoria

Pall Mall may seem a curious place to begin a journey on the trail of Giuseppe Garibaldi, the swashbuckling national hero of Italy, but the world has many curious delights, and this is one of them. There really was nowhere better to start than strolling past the statue of Florence Nightingale and the grand private clubs and the splendour of St James's Palace, following the route taken by Garibaldi when he came to London in the spring of 1864. He was the most famous man in the world at the time, prompting half a million people to crowd onto the streets and celebrate his arrival. It took seven hours for his horse and carriage to travel three miles from the railway station to the mansion where he stayed during his visit. Lancaster House, as the building is now called, is just off the end of Pall Mall, and also firmly off limits to the public.

It didn't take long to discover I could not go down the small access road and follow Garibaldi inside. No entry said the sign. No entry said the armed policemen blocking my path. No entry to the mansion which has hosted two G7 global political summits and continues to house the vast Government wine cellar. No entry to an opulent interior so majestic it is often used as a stand-in location for Buckingham Palace in movies like *The King's Speech*. No entry, too, for those eager to see one unique treasure inside – a small stone bust, carved in relief, of Giuseppe Garibaldi.

Across the world there are countless fine statues dedicated to his memory – from New York to Paris and Montevideo to Milan. The little bust here inside Lancaster House is the only tribute in Britain. It is now a hidden gem of history, more's the pity, just as the remarkable story of Garibaldi's life has been hidden away for too long in this country.

When I mention the name Garibaldi to people the invariable reply is: 'Oh yes, the biscuit.' He was rather more than that. He was the warrior general who forged the modern nation of Italy. He was the first maestro of guerrilla warfare, the forward thinker who crusaded for female emancipation, the sailor who voyaged across the oceans to Australia, China and Peru, the humble hero who lived modestly on his remote island farm when he wasn't fighting independence wars. Garibaldi has been compared to Che Guevara, Nelson Mandela and George Washington – and maybe there is something of each in him. It seems a great shame to me that the casual visitor cannot see the only formal honour to Garibaldi which exists in London, even acknowledging the necessary rigours of our security-conscious age.

'Unfortunately, Lancaster House is not open to the general public,' said the official email reply to my subsequent request to take a look. 'We know this will come as disappointing news. We wish you all the best.'

Thank you and goodnight? Well, not quite. The quaint courtesy extended to sending a photo of the bust, and the plaque beneath. These were commissioned by the Duke of Sutherland, who owned the mansion known as Stafford House back then, and who had invited Garibaldi to stay as his guest. The plaque is written entirely in Italian and entreats his compatriots living in London to keep the memory of the hero alive in the city forever. It is a little slice of Italy, and really this is not so surprising in the vicinity of Pall Mall. This apparently very English street name derives from an old Italian game called *Pallamaglio*, an early version of croquet, which became popular with King Charles II in the seventeenth century. He played it on a street that was christened in consequence Pall Mall.

So, yes, there was nowhere better to begin my journey in search of Giuseppe Garibaldi and try to discover the myths and legends that surround one of history's most charismatic figures. He was the first celebrity icon of the new mass media emerging in the Victorian era when he came to London, a unique figure in that he was admired by both the working-class masses who cheered him on the streets and the aristocrat politicians who feted him in the corridors of power. The duchesses who sent him swooning love letters were fond of Garibaldi, too. During the visit in 1864 he met Florence Nightingale, Charles Dickens, poet laureate Lord Tennyson, Prime Minister Palmerston, and the Prince of Wales. He went to factories and addressed radical meetings, yet on the same day he would attend an aristocratic party or the opera. Everyone was bewitched by him, barring a couple of unamused outliers. Karl Marx said the infatuation with Garibaldi was a 'miserable spectre of imbecility', while Queen Victoria was so worried about revolutionary fervour being stirred in England that she plotted to get him out of the country as quickly as possible.

A few other reminders of his visit linger in England. There is a Garibaldi Street in Plumstead, east London, and a Garibaldi School in Mansfield. You can drink in Garibaldi pubs in Northampton, Woking, Stourbridge, St Albans and Bourne End. The sign for the latter features the independence warrior wearing a red shirt and bowler hat. The shirt, at least, is authentic. It was a feature of Garibaldi's troops across Italy and South America to wear bright, blazing red shirts in battle to intimidate the enemy.

This idea was also taken up by the Nottingham Forest football team when it was formed in 1865. They bought 12 tasselled caps in 'Garibaldi red', and so the club colours were born. They were the first team to chase a ball around a field in red tops, but many others have followed. There is a direct link also to Arsenal, who were formed in 1886 and were gifted Garibaldi red shirts by Nottingham Forest to wear during matches. The history remains resonant for modern supporters of Forest, who launched a Forza Garibaldi movement in 2016 to reinvigorate support for the club. At every match now they unfurl a banner which reads: 'The Garibaldi that we wear with pride was made in 1865'. TV coverage sends the sentimental message all round the world.

Garibaldi's name is commemorated in many ways in many countries, and even in outer space. The state fish of California, a volcano, mountain range and lake in Canada,

Prologue: London

three goldmines in Australia, and a best-selling beer in Argentina all bear the moniker. There is Garibaldi aftershave and Garibaldi wine, made in both Italy and Brazil. The 4317 Garibaldi asteroid orbits between Mars and Jupiter. Then, of course, there is the biscuit, the thin sweet sandwich filled with raisins, created by the Peek Freans company of Bermondsey. Why did they call it a Garibaldi biscuit? One answer, the dramatic version, is that the new product was inspired by tales of Garibaldi and his troops feeding themselves on the battlefield with slices of dried bread which had been soaked in horses' blood and filled with berries. The truth, a commercial brainwave, was that the immense popularity of General Garibaldi would make it a top seller. The biscuit was an instant success and remains a supermarket staple in England 160 years later. It is virtually unknown in Italy. The name of Garibaldi, by contrast, is inescapable.

In every village, town, and city of the Italian peninsula there is a Via Garibaldi; there were more than 6,000 at the latest count. Discover a place without a Via Garibaldi, and that will only mean there is instead a Piazza Garibaldi, a Corso Garibaldi, a Giardino Garibaldi, or a Teatro Garibaldi. In the small town of Piazza Armerina in central Sicily there are all five – a *via, piazza, corso, giardino* and *teatro* (street, square, avenue, garden and theatre), not, to mention an *enoteca* (wine bar), ristorante and a B&B. Around the nation there are hundreds of statues and busts, and many thousands more tributes and dedications on walls and buildings.

My favourite is in Palermo, a large stone plaque which sits above the great door of Palazzo Villafranca. It has the ubiquitous language of glory, describing how Garibaldi and his men ended the tyranny of Sicily, and then it reads: 'In this illustrious house, for only two hours, I lay down my weary limbs: G Garibaldi.' Yes, even the house where he just had a brief rest receives the full-on treatment – even the Italians laugh about that.

Many other illustrious characters grace the history of Italy, the land of Dante, Leonardo Da Vinci, Machiavelli, Marconi, Michelangelo, Verdi, Volta and Christopher Columbus. None of them come close to the public recognition given to Garibaldi, and one cannot live in Italy for too long before beginning to wonder what all the fuss is about. I moved to Rome in the autumn of 2020, and swiftly decided I needed an answer to the question: Why him? Why Garibaldi?

There are so many avenues to follow, so many contradictions to unravel. How can the same man be claimed by all Italians as their inspiration – the communists, the fascists, and the liberals? It was the Garibaldi brigade of partisans who captured dictator Benito Mussolini towards the end of the Second World War; it was the Mussolini regime which built several of the memorials to Garibaldi in Rome. Still today, left-wing radicals and right-wing zealots each like to claim his legacy as their own. When the actor Luca Zingaretti, who plays Inspector Montalbano in a much-loved TV detective series, was asked which person in history he would like to be, the reply was: 'Garibaldi. Garibaldi – for his free spirit, his unpredictability, his passion, his heroism, and at the same time for his sense of being disinterested.'

We have become accustomed to think of Italy as a natural country – the leg and boot with the stiletto heel sticking out into the Mediterranean. It has been that way all our lifetimes, but as a nation it did not exist until 1861, and Rome only became the

Prologue: London

capital in 1870. For more than a thousand years following the end of the ancient Roman Empire it had been divided into many small chunks ruled by local nobles, foreign invaders, or the Pope.

The dream of Italian unity was long held amid the turbulence of so many centuries of repression. Niccolo Machiavelli expressed it with stirring passion in the final chapter of his great work, *The Prince*, written in 1532, delivering 'an exhortation to liberate Italy from the barbarian yoke ... a plea for someone to lead the way'. Although others were heavily involved, the leader above all proved to be Garibaldi. It was his daring actions that forged unification – winning impossible battles, conquering territory, driving out despots. He fought in the thick of war as the bullets flew; several times wounded and several times imprisoned. His personal courage and his unquenchable fervour had the power to inspire ordinary people to heroism. His long flowing hair, his fiery red shirt worn under a poncho and his white horse made him an instantly recognisable warrior. We are talking about a man of whom the English historian A.J.P. Taylor wrote: 'He is the only admirable figure of modern history.' We are talking about the man who made Italy.

Start a conversation with Italians about the unity of their nation today and you will be told of the paradox of a definitively sovereign state that is also defiantly local in the outlook of its population. Each village, district, town, and city is the unit closest to the heart of people. And the fiercest rivalry is with the neighbouring village, district, town, or city. Then each of these combines to defend the honour of their region, of which there are twenty in Italy. Each person feels Umbrian or Calabrian or Ligurian far more than feeling they are a citizen of Italy. At the same time, they do feel unmistakably 'Italian'.

They love, live, breathe, eat, and drink the same things: from fashion, fine art, football and fast cars to scooters, pizza, pasta, and beaches. They adore their coruscating national anthem, the words to which were written by Garibaldi's adjutant Goffredo Mamelli. You will often hear them complaining about the rotten state of Italy: the dangerous roads, corrupt officials and incompetent politicians. Yet they are also swift to tell you why so much that is Italian is the best in the world: the architecture, churches, paintings, automobiles, clothing, design, landscape, wine, history, coffee, ski slopes, thermal baths, volcanos (alive and dormant), cuisine and opera. They are extremely proud to be Italian, and everyone can see and hear unity when the national team wins football tournaments like the World Cup and the anthem is sung with incomparable fervour.

You will discover, too, an inordinate pride in the quality and quantity of UNESCO world heritage sites spread across Italy. The official number is sixty, just above the second-placed country, China. Italians will then tell you this hides the truth they in fact they are far ahead of anyone else. For example, Palermo's marvels are grouped together as one site, yet they encompass ten very different structures, two of them in other towns entirely.

There is another matter on which Italians are also united, the military genius of Giuseppe Garibaldi. Such is his legend that even the most educated and knowledgeable people will tell you The General never lost a battle. The verdict is too optimistic. Garibaldi fought in 53 separate conflicts through 40 years of combat. The final count, calculated like a league season in sport, reads: Won 34, Drawn 4, Lost 15. That's not a bad record, and several of the defeats were contests against impossible odds. Perhaps that's why even the losses are considered moral triumphs. Perhaps that's why belief in the invincibility of Garibaldi remains widespread. Perhaps, too, the myth endures because he symbolises a spirit of rebellion that seems to be a natural way of living for Italians. Argue first, arrange later, arrive later still. Official rules and regulations, and red traffic lights, are often an optional extra.

The rebel nature is likely to have been a huge part of Garibaldi's popular appeal in Britain. Not only was he portrayed as a recklessly courageous warrior in battle, but he also cut a dashing figure with his his red shirt, his feathered cap and his poncho. His fierce hostility to the Pope was another major factor in Protestant England, along with tales of fighting in revolutionary wars in South America during the 1830s and 40s when he won the nickname of the Hero of Two Worlds. The legend was strong, whether deserved or not.

When he travelled to England in 1864, the invitation had come from two entirely different groups. There were liberal aristocrats like Lord Shaftesbury and the Duke and Duchess of Sutherland, who wanted to parade him around London society. Then there was another Italian hero, Giuseppe Mazzini, and his fellow revolutionary exiles, who implored him to make speeches at trades union meetings to galvanise radical sentiment among working people. Both groups claimed Garibaldi as their own.

The scenes at his arrival in London were extraordinary. A military band played the Garibaldi hymn written to celebrate his bloody battles for Italian unity, while tumultuous crowds crammed the route of the journey along Wandsworth Road, across Westminster Bridge, down Parliament Street, across Trafalgar Square, and finally along Pall Mall. There is a painting of the commotion in Trafalgar Square with Garibaldi standing in his horse-drawn carriage waving his hat to the masses. Among the ocean of people, thousands are waving red scarfs and handkerchiefs. *The Times* newspaper reported that this was 'most emphatically a people's welcome, a working men's reception from first to last'. A handful of policemen were present only for traffic duty. There was no disorder. When the carriage eventually arrived at Stafford House, it fell apart as Garibaldi climbed out. The sides had been lifted out of their hinges by the pressure of the crowd. The same pressure had kept it from crumbling to pieces on the way.

Queen Victoria was less than enthused. She wrote in her diary:

> The people of England have really gone quite mad about Garibaldi, who made a sort of triumphal entry into London yesterday, driving in the Duke of Sutherland's state carriage and being received by the good (I must say foolish) Duchess at the foot of the stairs! A tremendous crowd, but of the lowest riff-raff! Honest, disinterested, and brave, Garibaldi certainly is, but a revolutionist leader!

The Duchess of Sutherland and the Dowager Duchess both fell head over heels for Garibaldi and wrote love letters to him when he had returned to Caprera. The latter was particularly smitten, she even allowed Garibaldi into her boudoir during a visit to her grand house at Cliveden.

The Prince of Wales, the future King Edward VII, insisted on meeting Garibaldi, to the intense irritation of his mother. He was impressed, saying of Italy's hero: 'He has such a dignified and noble appearance, and such a quiet and gentle way of speaking, especially never of himself, that nobody (sic) who sees him cannot fail to be attracted by him.' By contrast, Karl Marx refused a request from the organisation of German Socialists in London to present a personal message of greeting to Garibaldi. He had no time for what he called a romantic revolutionary.

Garibaldi's eventual trip home began with a visit to Cornwall to see his old friend Colonel John Peard, who had volunteered to fight in Sicily in 1860 during some of the decisive battles that unified Italy. Peard lived in a manor house close to the port of Fowey in Cornwall, and in the town museum today they proudly display one of Garibaldi's cloaks he wore in battle. Eight years later, Garibaldi commissioned a new home to be built nearby for Peard called Trenython Manor. It was his personal gift, and is now, in the way of things, a luxury hotel.

The lustre of Garibaldi's name has gradually faded since then in England, but 150 years later a celebration dinner was held in 2014 at Lancaster House to mark the anniversary of the General's famous visit. It was a grand affair, attended by the London mayor at the time, Boris Johnson, by the then Italian prime minister Matteo Renzi, and by one of Italy's greatest football heroes, Marco Tardelli, scorer of a memorable goal in the 1982 World Cup final. Why did they invite the sportsman? Well, the inspiration for Tardelli's sporting career began in his hometown of Pisa, playing as a junior at the club's modest stadium. The name is forever in his heart – the Arena Garibaldi.

2

NICE/NIZZA

'What could be better than sailing over the ocean, hardening ourselves in the rough life of sailors, in conflict with the elements and with danger?'

Giuseppe Garibaldi

A fine morning sun warmed the bones and an occasional sharp gust of wind blew through the outside tables sending paper napkins flying everywhere as I took the time-honoured breakfast of coffee with croissants at a busy bar on the harbourfront of Nice. Hundreds of little boats were moored all around, bobbing up and down on the swell as the breeze strengthened. It looked like a good sailing day, and also a good searching day. Here on this quayside is where Giuseppe Garibaldi was born and raised, where his restless thirst for adventure took shape, where he learned to play and swim and fight and dream.

The city stayed forever in his heart, and as I sipped my coffee I wondered how much, if at all, Nice still returns the affection for him more than two centuries later. It took a few minutes to find out. The very first thing that caught my eye walking in the area known as Port Lympia was a plaque fixed halfway up a wall. The stone was bleach white, the engraving immaculate, the message an invitation to remember a small slice of history – which many other visitors did when I was there. '*Qui di fronte era la casa dov'ebbe i natali il 4 Luglio 1807 – Giuseppe Garibaldi.*' 'Opposite here was the house where he was born on 4 July.' The plaque was pristine, lovingly maintained, a strong initial clue this city reveres the memory of a famous son.

There was another clue in the use of the past tense. 'Here was the house' it said. There was no building to inspect now. Opposite the plaque there was only the flock of tightly packed sailing boats swaying on the water, and beyond them the breakfast bar on the other side of the harbour. Garibaldi's precise birthplace, the home where he spent the first years of his life, had long since disappeared. The area was excavated at the end of the nineteenth century to enlarge the harbour, making it a haven for pleasure cruisers and ferries, as well as fishing boats and merchant vessels. In any case, there was never an official address for the house where Garibaldi was born. All we know is that it was located close to what was then the water's edge, in an alleyway described in the local Nizzardo idiom as *Cuou de Buou* – the Tail of the Ox. This was home to his father Domenico Garibaldi, a sailor and trader, his mother Rosa Raimondi, along with two sisters and three brothers.

The Garibaldis were proud of their roots in the region of Liguria just along the riviera coastline. They hailed from the seaside towns of Chiavari and Loana, as well as the

Val Graveglia, a valley in the hills above Genoa. This area of several small villages is also informally but proudly known as Val Garibaldo. A commemorative stone there features the face of a youthful Giuseppe Garibaldi, while another has the birth certificate of his grandfather Angelo carved into the stone to prove that this was the true 'cradle of the Garibaldi family'. The current local mayor also shares the surname.

During grandfather Angelo's lifetime Nice was an 'Italian' city, part of the Kingdom of Piedmont/Sardinia, but when the family moved there in 1794 it had recently been captured by France. By 1807 it was under the rule of Napoleon Bonaparte, and Giuseppe Garibaldi was born as a French citizen.

I found evidence for this in the little church of St Martin and St Augustin tucked away in a side street not far from the tourist trail of the Port Lympia waterfront. On display just to the left of the main door were the handwritten clerical records of the baptism of a boy on 19 July 1808. He was officially named Joseph Marie Garibaldi, and it was not until 1814, when Nice was handed back to the Kingdom of Piedmont/Sardinia as part of the re-arrangement of Europe following the defeat of Napoleon, that he became better known as Giuseppe Garibaldi.

Not that this mattered much in practice. What everyone always called him was Peppino, the routine diminutive of Giuseppe. The boy grew up on the streets around the church, but mostly on the waterfront itself. He swam in the harbour, learned how to sail small boats and climb the rigging with his friends; he trawled for oysters and read books under olive trees. He clambered up the hill that separates the quayside from the district of Old Nice and would walk to the nearby mountains with a borrowed gun and a game bag.

One of the legends surrounding the young Garibaldi is that he dived into a river one day, aged eight, to save a woman from drowning. It is not hard to imagine this as a formative moment, to experience the intense feeling of being a hero, and with it the first sign of an ability to affect the world around him. (It is equally plausible that the story is a fiction.) Although he was known as Peppino, there was nothing small about his nature. The outdoor life was preferable to being at school. He skipped lessons as often as possible, and on one occasion he and some friends sailed off in his father's boat in search of adventure, causing panic until they were found.

In 1815, the Garibaldi family moved to a new harbourside home situated in Quai Lunel, a road which still exists, and where you see the plaque. They lived at No.3 in a building known as Aburarum House, but that number no longer exists following a restructuring of the quayside road. My guess is that the most likely spot is the current No.20 along the modern Quai Lunel, a five-storey house which has been there since 1751. Garibaldi would surely be amazed at the scene now. The ground floor was a smart restaurant, and diners looked out on a luxurious super-yacht. Hundreds of small sailing boats jostled for space on the waterfront alongside the billionaire's toy, and there was also a modern ferry terminal for trips to Corsica. The water sparkled with wealth in the sunshine, while almost every building on the quayside was a bar or restaurant, serving dishes from Lebanon, Turkey, and India as well as coffee and croissants. The scene reflected the complicated heritage of the city of Nice, or as Garibaldi always called it, Nizza.

He grew up intensely proud of Nizza as an Italian city, spoke in the Nizzardo dialect, with French as a second language – and in later life his accent, spelling and grammar all revealed his origins here. Garibaldi insisted all his life that Nizza was as integral to a united Italy as cities like Venice, Rome, and Florence; and a little history is required to appreciate why. For more than five hundred years from 1388 the city was mostly part of the territory of Savoy, one of the many ever-changing independent 'Italian' states, this one stretching from the shores of Lake Geneva to the city of Genoa, and by the late 18th century also incorporating Piedmont and Sardinia. The armies of the French Revolution captured Nice in 1792, and it was from the city that Napoleon launched his rise to power a year later. After the fall of Napoleon in 1815, the Congress of Vienna divided up the spoils of war across the Italian peninsula, and one outcome was the restoration of Nizza to the control of what was now called the kingdom of Piedmont/Sardinia. The city stayed that way until 1860, when further international political manoeuvres saw Nice return to French territory, a switch confirmed by a stage-managed plebiscite that enraged Garibaldi.

This dual identity of Nice/Nizza was evident wherever I went in the city. Many of the older buildings were clearly Italianate, and the labyrinth of alleyways that comprise Old Nice were reminiscent of those in hundreds of Italian towns large and small. It was perhaps most evident in the food of the city, the traditional 'Cuisine Nicoise' advertised in many restaurants as a badge of honour. When I ordered a roast lamb one evening it came on a plate alongside a generous helping of pasta and pesto. Halfway through the meal the waiter arrived with another giant vat of pesto from the kitchen, quite certain I would want some more. I mentioned this meal to several friends in Rome and the mixture of anguish and disgust on their faces was a sight to behold. They told me it was an unforgivable crime against culinary and common decency to serve roast meat with pasta, and that the addition of pesto was beyond shame.

Other delights were deemed acceptable. The street food dish of *socca* was a chickpea fritter virtually identical to the *farinata* of Genoa, while the ubiquitous *pissaladière* was an obvious cousin of pizza. Some restaurants had a sign proudly boasting: 'Parlarem Nissart aqui', which means 'we speak Nissart here' – although I couldn't tell.

Nissart is certainly recognised as the second official language of the city. It is a blend of French and Italian, and whether you say good morning as bonjour, buongiorno or boana jonada you are likely to be understood. Many of the street signs are in both French and Nissart. The latter is probably very similar to the Nizzardo dialect that Garibaldi grew up speaking.

One significant emblem of the confusion of identity in this city lay in its oldest square. It was 200 metres walk up the road from Quai Lunel, and my obvious next port of call. The name of the square has forever been changing between languages and national heroes. It measures 123 metres by 92 metres, bigger than a football pitch, with grand Italian-style palazzi on all four sides and was created in 1773 at the end of what is now the Avenue de la Republique, and what has always been the road out of town towards Turin and the Alps beyond that. The original name was Piazza Vittorio to honour a King of Piedmont/Sardinia who came to visit and inspect troops in the square. Following the French Revolution, it became Place de la République, and by the time Garibaldi was born it had been re-named as Place Napoleon. When the city returned to rule by Piedmont/Sardinia it became Piazza D'Armi (Place D'Armes) and for twenty-four years from 1836 it was Piazza San Agostino (Saint Augustine). Another change occurred in 1860 when the city became French again, reverting to Place Napoleon for a second time. Few people know this curious history. Everybody knows the square by the name it has kept since 1870 – Place Garibaldi – the name that stuck.

The mayor of Nice suggested the change at a time when an ageing Garibaldi was fighting one last time on a battlefield, on the side of the French army in the Franco-Prussian war. The idea was received with popular acclaim by the people of the city. Garibaldi was not only a man in the news again in 1870, he was the most famous son of Nice and a hero to the whole world, not just in the two nations identified with his hometown. It has been his square now for more than 150 years and counting – another crushing defeat for Napoleon.

Place Garibaldi lay in the heart of the city, a magnet for all, from children enjoying the permanent merry-go-round in one corner to the tramps sleeping rough in the doorways at night. It was also crammed with cafes, bars and restaurants. The Cafe de Turin is renowned for fresh seafood, particularly its oysters, and they offered a 'Plate Garibaldi' on the menu at the fancy price of 120 Euros. This would buy 18 Fine Claire No.2 oysters, 4 papillons, 8 amandes, 4 palourdes, 6 moules d'espagnes, 4 grosses crevettes, 14 petites crevettes, 400g bulots, 110g grises, 4 langoustines, 1 tourteau and 1 tarama de crabe. And no need to eat for the next week.

I decided to swerve this extravagance and headed for the huge statue in the middle of the square – the first of many monuments to Giuseppe Garibaldi I would encounter on my journey. He stood high in battledress, his left arm resting on his sword. There was a neckerchief but no hat, and his coat was hanging half-off over one shoulder. His eyes were turned in the direction of Turin, the capital of Piedmont/Sardinia, home of the scheming politicians and the king who gave away Nice to the French, which was no accident. Nor was the decision to have Garibaldi depicted with his right fist clenched in anger, an expression of his contempt for the diplomatic horse-trading of 1860 that lost Nizza.

The statue told other stories, too. Underneath there was a bronze carving of two women holding flags as they watched over the cradle of a small child perched between them. This depicts the boy Garibaldi in the place of his birth. The woman on the left represented France and her flagpole had a rooster on the top. The woman on the right was Italy, her flag adorned by a Roman she-wolf. Above were two lines of inscription: 'A Garibaldi, Sa Ville Natale' – To Garibaldi, His Native Town. There were two bronze lions commemorating Garibaldi's sons Menotti and Ricciotti, each leaning on a cannon. One said 1860, a reference to the most important year of battles in the quest for Italian unification. The other said 1870, when Garibaldi was fighting in the Franco-Prussian war. Below the lions were two stone medallions showing the faces of Garibaldi's grandsons, Constant and Bruno, with the coat of arms of Nice between them. The attention to detail was typical of an Italian desire for many layers of symbolism on their monuments.

The city had another tribute to Garibaldi, a very modern and democratic affair. I drove out along the famous Promenade Des Anglais seafront and its art-deco hotels before heading a little inland to the stunning Allianz Riviera sports stadium, home of the local OGC Nice football team. It was built ahead of the 2016 European Championships, and club supporters were invited to choose the names of the stands in a popular vote. The result was that the giant eastern section on one side of the pitch became the Garibaldi stand.

Close to the stadium was the River Var, where the eight-year-old Peppino had saved a woman from drowning. He was the strongest of swimmers, thoroughly at home on the sea, which was hardly surprising given his father Domenico was a sailor who owned *La Santa Reparata*, a 29-ton vessel. Garibaldi's parents had wanted their little boy to become a priest, lawyer, or doctor, but there was no chance of that. By the age of fourteen his name was inscribed on the official register of seamen in Nice, and his first voyage was a six-month trip to Odessa in 1824 to collect grain from the Ukraine. The exhilaration he felt is clear enough in this passage from his memoirs: 'What could be better than sailing over the ocean, hardening ourselves in the rough life of sailors, in conflict with the elements and with danger?'

The next trip was accompanying his father to Rome, the first time he saw the Eternal City, a visit he never forgot. The final leg of the journey was taking a cargo of wine up the river Tiber in a small boat drawn by oxen. Many years later Garibaldi recalled the moment: 'The Rome that I beheld with the youthful eyes of my imagination was the Rome of the future – the Rome that I never despaired of even when I was shipwrecked, dying, banished to the farthest depths of the American forests – the dominant thought and inspiration of my whole life.' It was the first stirring of what became Garibaldi's obsession; to make Rome the capital of a united Italy.

There are no portraits of him from this time. He wasn't famous, just another young man growing into adulthood, determined to find adventures where he could. We do have an account of what he looked like, though, as written in the official register of the merchant shipping of Nice: 'Height: 5ft 7ins. Hair: chestnut. Eyebrows: fair. Eyes: light brown. Forehead: high. Nose: regular. Mouth: average. Chin: round. Beard: fair. Face: oval. Complexion: good. Special marks: none' Much more than this, what contemporaries noted was a character of courtesy, sincerity, and dignity. Sparks of anger were few, but when they came they were prompted by perceived injustice and insult.

He soon became a first mate on the merchant vessels he worked on. These took him to North Africa and Gibraltar and out in the Atlantic Ocean to the Canaries, but the greatest danger was in the Aegean Sea where pirates were a constant threat. In 1827, Garibaldi's boat was attacked three times in three days and he was robbed of everything, even the clothes he wore. The humiliation he felt at being ordered not to fight back against the pirates was compounded by being stuck in the region the whole winter because of ice. Eventually, his vessel made it to Constantinople in the summer of 1828, but Garibaldi fell ill and was left behind.

What followed was the least known, and very surprising, period of his life. He settled down for almost three years to a tranquil existence as a teacher of French and mathematics to a family from the Italian community in the city. Why? Did he fall in love with the widow, Signora Timoni, whose children he taught? We simply don't know. What is certain is that by the spring of 1831 Garibaldi was back in Nizza, ready to resume as a merchant trader. Sometimes he was the first mate, and on occasion the captain of his ship. On one trip in the Aegean Sea, they were again attacked by pirates, but this time opted for victorious combat against the raiders. When he logged all his battles, this was No.1 on the list. 'I learned,' he said, 'that it is always better to fight when one is attacked than to yield without a struggle.'

His most important voyage in this period began at Marseille in January 1833, a journey ostensibly to take oranges to the Russian port city of Taganrog, but one that catapulted him into a new life. He was exposed to liberal and radical cultural ideas, and he found the political cause that was to dominate his life. He was the first mate of the *Clorinda*, and on board were a group called the Saint-Simonians led by Emile Barrault. They had been sent into exile by France after being found guilty in a show trial of offences against public decency.

The movement had been started by the Count de Saint-Simon and preached a peaceful socialism inspired by the initial idealism of the French Revolution of 1789. They proposed equal distribution of wealth and the ownership of goods in common. When the count died, a new leader called Enfantin added a cultural edge to the political idealism for this new 'religion', perhaps a cult. It advocated equality of the sexes, the liberation of women from the chains of marriage, and pursued a doctrine of free love. Garibaldi became friends with Barrault and was instantly attracted to the ideas of the Saint-Simonians, both political and social. He forever kept a copy of Saint-Simon's book *Le Nouveau Christianisme*, and it remains on display in the museum at his house at Caprera.

It explains so much about Garibaldi's endless adventures – his constant desire to fight for freedom, and the expansive, guilt-free way he conducted his personal and sexual affairs. Throughout his life he revelled in the company of women, and they were attracted to him, from duchesses and countesses of European high society to the nursemaid of his children, who became his third and final wife. His attitude to women is revealed in the words he wrote to one of his contemporary biographers, Jesse White Mario: 'How very foolish for a man to kill himself for a woman when the world is full of women. When a woman takes my fancy, I say: "Do you love me? I love you. You don't love me? More fool you!"' The selfishness, the vanity and the peacock ego of the classic male is clear enough, but Garibaldi was also among the very few men of his time who campaigned for female emancipation and for women to be given the vote. That only came about in Italy more than sixty years after his death.

The political education begun on board ship listening to Barrault did not end when the Saint-Simonians disembarked at Constantinople and the ship continued to the small port city of Taganrog in Russia to deliver the oranges. It was here that Garibaldi found his destiny. Taganrog lies close to Russia's border with Ukraine on the far eastern edge of the Sea of Azov. On his first visit there, a few months earlier, a boisterous Garibaldi had been briefly arrested by the local police for making a public nuisance with his singing and drinking. This time he was in more serious mood, going to the Italian seamen's club where he heard a speech about a new organisation called Young Italy, about the ideas of its founder Giuseppe Mazzini and, above all, about the desire to liberate Italy from foreign rulers.

What historians now call the Risorgimento, the 'rising again' of Italy, was in its infancy. After the fall of Napoleon, the various parts of the peninsula were divided up, with Austria taking much of the north and the Papal States covering much of the centre. The south was mostly in the hands of the Bourbons. They were all harsh regimes, with only a handful of mild and relatively independent regions like Tuscany, Parma and Piedmont-Sardinia. The repression inevitably inspired dissent, and a secret society called the Carbonari was founded. It was one of the first ever underground movements, the inspiration for so many that have followed. Its attempts at revolution were haphazard, though, and one of its members, Mazzini, broke away in 1831 to create his own organisation of Young Italy. He was the most influential political thinker among radicals in the nineteenth century, his aim to unite his nation of Italy and make it a republic with an internationalist outlook.

Prince Metternich, the forceful chancellor of Austria, famously called Italy 'merely a geographical expression', contemptuously implying that it could never be a proper nation like others. It was a memorable phrase, but mistaken. Even with its diverse regions and dialects, there has always been a shared Italian cultural identity and a recognisably Italian language that bonds people together. Mazzini argued this with persuasive intellect, and Giuseppe Verdi wrote operas aiming to prove it. Garibaldi felt it only with an intense instinct, but he was a captive listener when another young sailor, Giovanni Battista Cuneo, was making his speech in the faraway Taganrog seamen's club. Garibaldi, aged twenty-six, was an instant convert, and wrote in his memoirs:

> I am sure that Columbus did not feel so much satisfaction at the discovery of America, as I felt on meeting someone who was working for the redemption of our country. I had found my aim in life. I threw myself wholeheartedly into the national struggle and made it my own.

A seminal moment in the history of Italy is remembered in Taganrog, where a monument in honour of Garibaldi stands on a stretch of waterfront now called the Pushkin Embankment, which is likely to be the area where the *Clorinda* berthed with its cargo of oranges.

When Garibaldi returned from this trip he went first to Marseille where he was initiated into the Young Italy movement in the autumn of 1833 and declared himself ready to serve the cause. For a few weeks afterwards, he visited his family in Nizza before a first dramatic assignment with Young Italy. He was unknown then, but never afterwards. When Garibaldi came back to the city in 1848, artists queued up to capture his portrait. I went to see one of the most famous paintings, which was hanging in the gallery of the Musee Massena, situated close to the Promenade des Anglais, amid a display of memorabilia from his life and that of Napoleon.

The painting depicts Garibaldi standing on the clifftops above Nice, wearing a red shirt and jeans. He is still young, the hair is still chestnut, and it pictures him directly after he returned from his adventures in South America. There is a map under his right hand, his finger placed on Nizza, sending an unmistakable message – this is my town. There was a modern expression of this, too. Our smartphones of the twenty-first century invariably have a weather app on the home screen which details your location wherever in the world you happen to be, London, Rome, New York. When I was in this city, and not just in the main square, it didn't say Nice, or even Nizza. No, my phone said the location was Garibaldi. I couldn't help but smile.

3

GENOA/GENOVA

'Garibaldi is sentenced to ignominious death as an enemy of the State, and liable to all the pains and penalties imposed against bandits of the first degree.'

Genoa court judgement.

THE signs recommending a stroll along *Via del Jeans* were everywhere when I arrived in Genoa, luring visitors into the tumbling alleyways that make up the historic centre of Italy's most important port, and demanding celebration of the city's pride in being the birthplace of blue jeans. Of course I had to take a look. The maze of *vicoli* (lanes and alleys) close to the harbour has always been the heart of Genoa, a home to rebels and thinkers, drinkers, streetwalkers and beggars for centuries – a haven of mischief and mayhem where it's easy to hide and even easier to get lost. I turned a couple of corners and suddenly there was angry shouting from windows high above the narrow lane, a palpable tension in the air, and a tiny bar where the locals didn't seem the type to welcome the presence of outsiders. It felt as if I'd wandered back to the time of Garibaldi, who in January 1834 plotted his first act of revolution for a united Italy in these very alleyways and that kind of bar. When the rebellion failed, he left as a man on the run with a death sentence hanging over him. I had the luxury of Google maps directing me back to the jolly street of jeans.

This turned out to be a special temporary 'widespread jeans exhibition', located in several places around the city to explore the history of denim and underline its continuing importance in twenty-first century fashion. It featured many treasures, but for me the finest was undoubtedly a work of art I came across in the Museo del Risorgimento. This was a fabulous creation by the contemporary English artist Ian Berry, whose speciality is pieces made entirely in denim. He had been commissioned to recreate a famous painting of Garibaldi – the moment when he symbolically planted the tricolour flag of Italy into the ground during one of his victorious battles to unify the nation (see front of jacket). The effect of Berry's work was more than striking. It was astonishing, a masterpiece of conception and craft. He had used different shades and textures of blue jeans sewn together in patchwork to produce a miracle for the eyes. Even the frame was denim. Garibaldi was a suitable subject. He was forever in blue jeans.

He was wearing them in the painting I had seen in Nice, and also in another vivid exhibition at this museum in Genoa where three large rooms were devoted entirely to comic books celebrating the history of the Risorgimento. In one of them Garibaldi was depicted in his jeans in all-action American style, given the rebel film star looks of James Dean, alongside Anita drawn as a Sophia Loren wife. Another section was a

Disney cartoon caper with Mickey Mouse and Donald Duck on board ship with Garibaldi as their dashing captain. It was a telling illustration of how deep into Italian culture the legend of Garibaldi is embedded.

There couldn't have been a better location than Genoa for these exhibits. Blue jeans comes from *bleu de Gene'*, the French description for the trousers that were first made in this Italian city – a strong, coarse, cross-weaved cotton dyed with indigo blue traded from India in the sixteenth century. Garibaldi wore them first as a young man at sea; jeans were the choice of many sailors, and the gauchos he encountered during his time in South America also had something similar. They became his uniform many years before blue jeans with metal rivets to strengthen them were patented in the 1870s by Levi Strauss. The trousers worn by Garibaldi in battles, which feature on the painting recreated by Ian Berry, still exist today. They are the star exhibit in the Central Museum of the Risorgimento in Rome, and are proudly proclaimed as the 'oldest blue jeans in the world'. They have a timeless style that could be on sale in any shabby chic clothes store, right down to the patch sewed over a rip on the left knee, the result of a battle injury sustained in Sicily in 1860, not long after the flag was planted. These jeans are seen by more than a million visitors every year.

Risorgimento is a vital word in the Italian language and the history of the nation. As mentioned briefly in the last chapter, it translates into English as 'rising again' – and was the name given to the movement for Italian unification inspired by Giuseppe Mazzini's ideas and which above all else succeeded thanks to Garibaldi's victories on the battlefield. There are Risorgimento museums all around Italy, but the one here in

Genoa was exceptional, not least because it is the house where Mazzini, the founder of the Young Italy movement, was born.

Genoa is a city of many treasures, and it was only a short walk from one to another Leaving the street of jeans behind I wandered along a couple of alleyways and into a wide avenue, the most important road in the city, one which has mesmerised visitors for 500 years. Its name is Via Garibaldi, the finest and most celebrated Via Garibaldi of them all, and quite possibly the most beautiful street in all of Italy. Yes, that's a bold claim, but is there another road anywhere in the world where numbers 1, 2, 3, 4, 5, 6, 7, 8, 9, 10, 11, 12 and 18 are all garlanded with UNESCO World Heritage status?

Millions of people visit this avenue each year, captivated by the beauty of the various palazzi. Among those who have been astounded was Charles Dickens, who wrote of their 'voluptuous splendour'. It used to be known as the Golden Street but was re-named in honour of Garibaldi when he died in 1882, a small recompense from the city in which he was once condemned to death as a 'bandit of the first degree'. These palazzi were created in the sixteenth and seventeenth centuries to feed the vanity of various super-rich Genoese families, who competed madly to possess the most magnificent of all. Who won? That seemed to me a fine game to play in Via Garibaldi, and I discovered that only Palazzo Lercari-Parodi at No.3 and Palazzo Doria-Tursi at No.9 had been deemed worthy of hosting kings, emperors, and popes. The rest had to make do with mere princes, ambassadors, and cardinals; oh, and playing host to fabulous art, works by Caravaggio, Tintoretto, and Rubens among others. My favourite among them was No.5 Via Garibaldi, otherwise known as the Palazzo Angelo

Giovanni Spinola, which featured fortress iron and wood front doors that open onto formidable stone staircases. It was now an everyday working branch of Deutsche Bank, but one that felt like a renaissance Fort Knox.

The official town hall of Genoa was housed in the ornamental wonder of No.9, now that kings, emperors, and popes lodge elsewhere. It was from here that the city's mayor Marco Bucci launched a clean-air crusade in 2016 with a ban on vintage Vespa scooters. It was a good idea – but akin to a declaration of war. The old scooters may have been horribly polluting, but Vespas are one of the iconic symbols of Italy and nowhere are people more attached to them than in Genoa, the city where they were first created by the Piaggio company. Around sixty per cent of people here drive scooters because of road congestion and the sheer impossibility of parking a car. Protests created headlines around the world – 'The Home of The Scooter Bans the Scooter' and so on. The battle lasted four years before the mayor was finally able to force the vintage Vespas into early retirement. Modern, more eco-friendly versions continue to buzz around the streets of course.

Via Garibaldi marks the northern boundary of the unique maze of tiny alleyways that create the largest and most atmospheric *centro storico* of all Italian cities. It is mostly beautiful, but not always. One of the lanes is the Vico dei Garibaldi, named in the plural, not just for Giuseppe, but the Garibaldi clan in general. Here I found dilapidated tattoo parlours, dog mess all over the cracked pavements, but also a bewitching violin maker's shop – the contrasts of modern Italy in miniature. The alley led onto Piazza Dei Garibaldi, a small square of brutal architecture, its buildings constructed with ugly concrete slabs. It was barely 100 metres from the 'voluptuous splendour'.

These alleyways tumbling down towards the port were the scene of Garibaldi's first political adventure, a deeply flawed attempt at insurrection in Genoa as part of a planned revolution by the Young Italy movement he had joined the previous year. His role had been to sign up to the Sardinian navy in December 1833 and try to stir unrest among its sailors drinking in the bars of the city. The conspirators would sometimes meet in the Caffe di Londra in the tiny Piazza San Marcello (it's still there, but the caffe isn't) and there is a painting of Garibaldi making a speech with a glass of beer in hand, rather too conspicuous for a secret agent. The rebellion was crushed within a few weeks by the authorities and Garibaldi was forced into hiding.

Various stories are told about how many women helped him as he was chased by police. One is that a fruit-seller friend called Teresina gave him refuge. Another is that he was assisted by a woman called Caterina who ran an osteria close to the port. A third tale is that Garibaldi hid in the back of a fruit and vegetable shop in Piazza Sarzano. This building was destroyed by a bombing raid in World War Two, but I found an official plaque in the nearby Museo di San Agostino which testified he was given help at that address by another fruit seller, Natalina Pozzo, who apparently dressed him up in farmer's clothes as a disguise. Some accounts suggest he made love to all three women, which would fit in with the influence of the Saint-Simonians on Garibaldi's attitude to sexual affairs and is a story that has appealed to generations of Italian males. The truth is likely to be rather more prosaic.

Garibaldi escaped the city on 3 February 1834 through a gate close to its famous lighthouse, La Lanterna, and headed on foot for Nice, about 100 miles away. It is very likely he would have tramped past the small town of Pra, a few miles west of Genoa, perhaps even through its celebrated basil-growing fields. Did he stop to smell the famous green leaves? It is certainly possible, because the Sacco family, for one, have been growing basil continuously on the slopes here since 1831. Pra is said to be the spiritual home of pesto; where the basil leaves are reputed to be smaller and more fragrant than anywhere on earth, and which aficionados claim make the finest pesto of all. The word comes from the Italian *pestare*, which means 'to pound or to grind', the process used to turn the basil leaves along with pine nuts, garlic and parmesan cheese into the delicious sauce of pesto.

You will find few disbelievers across Italy that Genoese pesto is the best; the only other serious contender for that title is the town of Trapani in western Sicily where their wondrous pesto is made with almonds rather than pine nuts and with added dried tomatoes. Pesto is one of so many food obsessions across Italy, a land in which authenticity at the dining table is non-negotiable. For most people the equation is simple: Genoa = pesto. And there is another equally precise equation: Genoa = focaccia, the local soft, oily flat bread, which I swiftly discovered is served every day at breakfast, lunch, and dinner. No, it's not the same anywhere else, but whisper it quietly to the Genoese – you can have too much of a good thing.

Garibaldi walked for 10 days to reach Nice, sleeping under bushes in the day, making progress at night. His home town was too dangerous though for him to linger with his family.

It would be the last time he saw his father as he departed for France, swimming across the nearby River Var that served then as the border. He was arrested by the French authorities but escaped the police station at Dragiugnan by jumping through a window and outrunning the officer who chased him. Next stop was Marseille, where Garibaldi discovered in a newspaper report that a trial had been held in Genoa in his absence and declared him guilty of insurrection. He had been sentenced to 'ignominious death' as a bandit of 'the first degree'.

The fugitive Garibaldi avoided detection by purchasing the identity papers of an English sailor called Joseph Pane, one of many pseudonyms he adopted in these early years. As a member of Young Italy he had been Giuseppe Borel, and he used the name 'Cleombroto' in the navy, taken from an old Spartan king who died in battle. Guiseppe Pane, Cipriano Alves, and Jose Garibaldi were other versions. One day in Marseille he saved a fourteen-year-old boy from drowning in the harbour, diving into the water even though he was wearing an evening suit ready for dinner. The watching crowd cheered the heroism of Joseph Pane. First and last, Garibaldi was a man of the sea.

When I asked people in Genoa what makes the city special for them, the invariable and almost instantaneous answer was the sea. It is visible from every angle, from every house perched on the steep hills that ascend from the harbour and frame the city along many miles of exquisite coastline. You can reach water within ten minutes wherever you live, and the long vistas are daily inspiration for the eyes and the soul. The wealth that created the palaces of Via Garibaldi was made at sea. For many centuries Genoese ships ruled the waves, dominating the Mediterranean and trading east to Turkey and on to India. It was a merchant city with the most respected and the most feared navy. The symbol of this can be seen in almost every street and alleyway of the twenty-first century city – and it was the answer to a question that had been nagging me almost from the moment I arrived in Genoa. Why was the flag of England flying on every street?

The flag of Saint George belonged first to Genoa, a fact I discovered, curiously enough, while walking around the museum of the Genoa Cricket and Football club (known by the English name for the city rather than the Italian Genova). The story is told with some brio of how in 1190, when Richard the Lionheart was King of England and focused on the Crusades, his fleet was often attacked by pirates lurking around the Mediterranean. He knew that pirates dared not attack the ships of the powerful Genoese navy that flew the flag with the red cross on the white background. So, the King of England paid the Doge of Genoa to be allowed to fly the emblem. It was a deceit, and the rest, as they say, is history.

Genoa, Genova, whichever you prefer, is the port for all Italy. It was the birthplace of Christopher Columbus, whose family home is today a museum in the city. It was also the place of embarkation for most of the thirteen million Italians who left their homeland between 1880 and 1914 to sail across the Atlantic searching for a new and better life in the Americas, away from the poverty which cursed much of southern Italy in those years.

The city has been known for centuries as *La Superba* (no need for a translation), and when I reached the harbourfront of Genoa it was easy to understand why the nickname still holds good. A wonderful glass dome created by the Genoa-born architect Renzo Piano dominates the scene and is the largest aquarium in Europe, while alongside are a legion of fine restaurants and bars. At the end of the nineteenth century, however, this was a scene of cruelty and despair, laced with desperate hope. Many people slept in the streets waiting for a place on board, prey to criminals and rogue travel agents as they waited to cross the ocean to a new life.

Such a journey was taken by Garibaldi himself in 1835 when he decided that exile in South America was preferable to the dangerous existence of living on false papers in Marseille, or the alternative of working as a merchant seaman. It was a huge turning point, a period of thirteen years away from Italy in which he became a renowned guerrilla fighter and revolutionary, and in which he met his wife Anita, the greatest love of his life. It is essential to recount this time to understand how and why Garibaldi had such an impact on his homeland when he returned in 1848.

His ship landed in Rio de Janeiro, and the taste for rebellion and conflict he had enjoyed in Genoa now inspired him to join the revolutionaries of the southern region of Rio Grande do Sul, who craved independence from Brazil. It meant instant danger to Garibaldi when, in a gun battle on the River Plate, a bullet struck him just below the left ear and lodged in his neck. Had it been an inch higher it would certainly have killed him. It would be the first of many miraculous escapes throughout his life amid the ferocity of battle. Six months of recovery followed in the town of Gualeguay, just across the border on the Argentine side of the river, where locals kept him safe from arrest. It was during this time that Garibaldi learned to ride a horse, a vital skill in the nineteenth century for any commander of troops.

Eventually, he was captured, and then tortured, tied to a beam with his arms above his head, and left hanging in agony for hours. The Argentines wanted details of who had assisted the renegade Garibaldi; he gave no names and spat in the face of his interrogator. After two months in jail he was freed, but the effects of the torture probably accounted for the severe arthritis that afflicted him in later years.

Garibaldi's skill at sea earned him a new role when he returned to the Rio Grande rebels. They gave him the luminous title of Lieutenant-Captain, Commander of the Naval Forces of the Republic. In reality he was a buccaneer in charge of only two ships, one of which soon sank in a hurricane, the commander swimming to shore to survive.

One of the many raids on Brazilian shipping brought the most important day of his private life, the moment he set eyes on Ana Maria de Jesus Ribeiro da Silva and instantly determined to marry her. He was lonely, in search of company, and looking through his telescope he saw on the shore the woman all Italy now knows simply as Anita. He was entranced, and in his memoirs Garibaldi recalled the moment he found her: 'We both remained enraptured and silent, gazing on each other like two people who had met before. At last, I greeted her and said: "You must be mine." I had come upon a forbidden treasure, but yet a treasure of great price.' Anita was aged just fifteen, and already married to another local man, Manoel Duarte, an inconvenience they ignored. She sailed away with Garibaldi and so began one of the great love stories of Italian history.

They shared a passion for combat. Anita adored the buccaneering life and would stay in the heart of battles, firing her musket during fierce fighting on land and sea. She was captured in one showdown when her horse was shot away from beneath her and told by her captors that Garibaldi had been killed. Anita was allowed to inspect the corpses on the battlefield at Curitibanos – a scene recreated on the side of the statue dedicated to her in Rome – but she couldn't find him. When her guards were drunk, she escaped into the forest, living for days on wild berries and nuts before being reunited with Garibaldi. Throughout this ordeal she was pregnant with their first child, who was born in September 1840 and named Menotti after an executed Italian patriot, Ciro Menotti. When he was a few days old their house was attacked while Garibaldi was away and Anita fled on horseback, baby on the saddle.

It was time to retreat from the front line, and they moved in the summer of 1841 to a modest house in the Uruguayan capital of Montevideo, where Garibaldi initially earned a living as a teacher of mathematics and history. It would be their home for seven years and is today a museum. Even when Garibaldi became commander in chief of the Uruguayan navy and a national hero, he continued to live frugally, refusing offers of money, and even extra candles to provide more light in the house. The humility and self-sacrifice was not a gesture. It was essential to his character and his idealism; he would resist gifts and luxury all his life.

Garibaldi and Anita were married in March 1842 in Montevideo. The question, a mystery most likely never to be solved, is whether the union was bigamous. The fate of her first husband, Duarte, is unknown. There was no official death certificate, but the substantial belief is that he had already died in battle fighting for the Brazilian army before the Garibaldi wedding ceremony took place. The life of teaching and domestic quiet ended when war broke out between Uruguay and Argentina, and the reputation he had established with his buccaneering in Brazil saw him appointed as an officer in the Uruguayan navy. The first escapade was a battle on the river Parana against a superior Argentine fleet, and an honourable defeat. Garibaldi retreated overland and stayed two months in Santa Lucia de los Antos where he had a relationship with a local woman, Lucia Esteche. She later gave birth to a girl who called herself Margarita Garibaldi and was acknowledged by Italy's great hero as his daughter. Once again, the influence of the Saint-Simonians on his sexual conduct is apparent, and surely also the rough-and-ready perilous nature of life amid the conflict that consumed South America at the time.

Montevideo, for instance, was a city under siege for eight years, resisting the threat of Argentine invasion with the help of outsiders like Garibaldi, who formed an Italian legion among his countrymen in the city, and was soon enough appointed as commander in chief of the Uruguayan navy. When he won a few minor battles, they were used by his old comrade Mazzini for propaganda back in Europe. He wrote of 'the heroism of those Italians who have taken up arms in the name of liberty and their great leader Giuseppe Garibaldi'. The legion adopted a black flag, to symbolise the sadness and mourning of Italy, with a picture of Vesuvius in the centre to suggest the power of hidden volcanic fire burning within the land. And they adopted a famous uniform – the red shirts.

These were, to begin with, long and loose red robes that hung to knee height, worn outside trousers, with holes only for head and arms. There were no buttons, just a belt around the waist. They had been fashioned as an overall for butchers to camouflage the blood in the slaughterhouses, and because of the war they were lying unused in a Montevideo warehouse. It was a cheap and cheerful way to provide a uniform for an Italian Legion that possessed almost no funds, and they became a symbol of Garibaldi's troops. He instantly understood its power, and his men, wherever he fought battles for the rest of his life, were dressed in red shirts. Although the colour made them more visible on a battlefield, it also had a strong psychological effect on the minds of enemy troops. It is doubtful that Garibaldi knew they were inspiration for the colour used by so many football teams around the world, starting with Nottingham Forest and then Arsenal among grand old English clubs, but he would surely have been delighted.

Garibaldi's image forever remained the red-shirted gaucho with cowboy jeans and heavy wool poncho – that of the South American rebel. He had thrived amid the harsh rigours of life in the pampas and forests; he had discovered what the human spirit can endure, what could be expected of soldiers. He had also developed the guerrilla tactics that would help liberate Italy, sometimes using small groups of irregular troops to mount ambushes on opponents and using hit-and-run raids. One important victory was the capture of the town of Salto, but his most notable battle was in February 1846 at San Antonio, where the Italian Legion were outnumbered six to one by Argentine forces. Garibaldi sang the Uruguayan anthem in his tenor voice to help inspire his men to immense courage and was himself wounded amid fierce fighting. Eventually, he organised a retreat back to Salto in what is regarded as one of his moral victories in defeat because 500 enemy were killed against only 35 of his Italian Legion. It brought a promotion to General, and reports sent to Italy burnished the growing legend of Garibaldi the invincible hero. It was a triumph of propaganda, with all the value that possessed.

At first, he refused the title, but was persuaded to accept it, and happily and defiantly called himself General Garibaldi for the rest of his life. As his fame grew, there were several offers of money and land by the Uruguayan government. He refused it all, as he did a huge offer of gold from Argentina to switch his fighting skills to the other side. Garibaldi chose to live day-by-day in strict austerity, to the dismay of Anita. They had four children together – Menotti, Rosita, Teresina and Ricciotti – although Rosita died aged four.

By 1847 Garibaldi had grown increasingly disillusioned with the internal politics of Uruguay and craved a return to Italy. He was nominated into the Uruguayan parliament, his first purely political appointment, but he never once attended. When a ship brought Italian revolutionary newspapers to Montevideo, full of accounts of rebellious fervour and even the accession of a supposedly liberal Pope, he knew it was time to sail for home. Anita left in January 1848 for Nice and he soon followed, correctly assuming that the death sentence passed some fourteen years earlier in Genoa would have been forgotten. The grateful Uruguayan authorities bought him a ship, which he named Speranza (hope in Italian), and he departed with sixty men of his Italian Legion and the coffin of little Rosita.

He left behind a huge reputation in South America, of the fearless warrior ready to sacrifice all for freedom and justice, and became an inspiration to so many who followed, including Che Guevara. You can still find his name today around and about in Montevideo; a pharmacy, a pizzeria, a garage, a veterinary surgery, an optician, and a taxi firm. There is a splendid statue and a separate Garibaldi monument, along with the museum at his old house. There are others across the region, too: an equestrian statue of Garibaldi in the city of Buenos Aires, and three statues of Anita in Brazil, at Laguna, Belo Horizonte and Porto Alegre. In the latter she is depicted alongside her husband Giuseppe, the Hero of Two Worlds.

That was a description which stuck and is the nickname by which by everybody in modern Italy knows him. Having made his name in one world, the emergent hero was bound for another. Revolutions were breaking out all over Europe in 1848, and they began in the Italian peninsula with a five-day revolution in Milan that drove out the Austrian army and delivered a brief period of independence for the surrounding region of Lombardy. The old free republic was restored in Venice under the radical leadership of Daniele Manin, and these events prompted the start of what has become known as the First War of Italian Independence, led by Carlo Alberto di Savoia, the King of the Piedmont/Sardinia state. It was into this maelstrom that Garibaldi arrived in Genoa with his Italian Legion at the beginning of July 1848.

One of the great mistakes that politicians, monarchs and enemies made about Garibaldi was to underestimate the nature of his character and the extent of his popularity with ordinary people. One who made this error was Carlo Alberto, who had declared his war aim of liberating Italy, but who now scorned the returning Hero of Two Worlds, a proven warrior with a giant reputation. When the pair met, the King was dismissive of General Garibaldi's desire for high command and told him to help the radicals in Venice instead. 'They will give you some small ship and you can ply your trade as a buccaneer. That's where you belong – there's no place for you here.'

Garibaldi chose to join the rebels in Lombardy rather than go to Venice, and they welcomed him to the cause. There would be only one contribution on the battlefield in this opening war of Italian independence, a guerrilla campaign on the shores of Lake Maggiore, where Garibaldi won his first battle on Italian soil on 15 August 1848 against Austrian forces at the town of Luino, on the eastern shores of the lake.

Soon after, Carlo Alberto lost heavily against the Austrians in another battle and the First War of Italian Independence ended. But Luino was not forgotten. The first ever statue of Garibaldi was erected there in 1867, the only one put up when he was still alive and which still stands on the lakeside. He returned to Genoa and another crucial crossroads in his life. In the wake of defeat to Austria, a new parliament had been created in Turin for the state of Piedmont/Sardinia, and Garibaldi was persuaded to stand as a candidate at Cicagna, a small town about thirty miles east of Genoa, where the main square today is, of course, Piazza Garibaldi. It was his first election, and he won with twenty votes against one for the man standing against him. He told the voters he had no intention of turning up to talk in the assembly chamber, that war must be resumed.

The question was where to go. Garibaldi at first decided to head for Venice, which was still independent, but when he reached Ravenna he heard the news of a major uprising of the people in Rome that had forced the Pope to flee from the Eternal City and whose authority had been replaced by a new democratic *Repubblica Romana*. In January 1849, on the way to Rome, Garibaldi won another election, gaining 2,069 votes at the town of Macerata to serve in the constituent assembly of this newly declared independent republic. The Hero of Two Worlds was now officially a member of three different parliaments at the same time: in Montevideo, Turin and Rome. His heart was never in any of them. His place was on the battlefield.

4

ROME/GIANICOLO

'One hour of life here in Rome is worth a century of normal existence.'

Giuseppe Garibaldi

Via Garibaldi rises steeply up from the river in Rome. It is a road of dramatic curves, the switchbacks too sharp for normal buses, so when the No. 115 eventually came along I hopped onto a rackety red minibus, a fact which did nothing to dissuade its driver from believing he was at the wheel of a Ferrari as we raced up to the great square at the top of the hill. Nobody seemed to mind, even though the little bus was full to bursting and we were hanging onto the grab handles for dear life. The No. 115 emptied at the summit and everybody surged across the square to find a good place on a long viewing ledge. People had come to witness a daily ritual, when exactly at noon a single cannon shot is fired to synchronise all the church bells around Rome. Most people then lingered for the view – the sublime view from the top of the Gianicolo hill, across the

Eternal City to snow-covered peaks beyond. Here, as historian G.M. Trevelyan declared, you see 'the heart of Europe, the living chronicle of man's long march to civilisation'.

So much history, so much culture and so many places of worship crowded into the panorama below. So many colours, too: yellows, reds and oranges, pale greys, pinks and browns, white marble, travertine limestone and fifty shades of ochre. At first glance it seemed impossible to pick out individual buildings amid the ocean of stone, as if the pageant of time had been blended into one organic structure. Concentrating hard, though, individual glories came into focus: the Pantheon, the Colosseum, the baths of Caracalla. There were more church domes than you could shake a stick at; a vivid symbol of the grip held on the city for so long by the Papacy, a grip Garibaldi fought to release all his life with obsessive fervour.

There was another reason why I caught the No. 115 up the hill, and the clue lay in the name of the square: Piazzale Garibaldi. In its centre stood a bronze statue of the warrior general on his mighty horse. There was nowhere else in Rome it could be. It's almost impossible to imagine strolling around the Gianicolo today, but in the summer of 1849 this area was a bloody battleground amid the epic defence of a briefly liberated city. Many thousands died, and buildings, streets and parks were left devastated in two months of fighting to determine who would rule Rome – the people or the Pope.

Why here? That's simple enough – it is the magnificent view from what locals like to call the Eighth Hill. It is higher than the seven hills of legend, and although the Gianicolo stands on the other side of the river Tiber from the ancient centre, it has a commanding position over the Eternal City. It is crucial for military and political control, a symbol and a guarantee of power. Why in 1849? That's straightforward, too. Conflict came in the aftermath of modest reforms introduced by Pope Pius IX which had encouraged the population to believe they could gain democratic control over their own lives. Street protests led to the assassination of the most senior Papal politician, Pellegrino Rossi, who was stabbed to death in the middle of a large crowd. The Pope fled the city and the *Repubblica Romana*, with a secular constitution, was created, all of which sent shockwaves through Europe. A powerful army of French soldiers was dispatched to restore Papal rule, while Garibaldi galloped to Rome to join the resistance of the people.

Although the fledgling republic was eventually crushed, the gallantry shown by the citizen fighters and Garibaldi's personal courage at the heart of the combat were vital to his life and legend. This was the moment which convinced common people of his glory, the moment which transformed him into the charismatic leader of the march towards Italian unity, the moment also when Rome as a city regained its pride and self-respect.

The defence of the *Repubblica Romana* still stirs strong emotions today. The Gianicolo is filled with many other statues and memorials alongside the hero on his horse, some of them twenty-first century additions. It is a place of celebration, a place of beauty, a theatre of freedom. Follow the trail of Garibaldi up here on the hill and I believe you will view Rome through a more authentic lens than traipsing around the ancient Forum. When the movie director Paolo Sorrentino made his Oscar-winning film *The Great Beauty* (*La grande bellezza*, 2013) as an homage to Rome, the opening sequences were filmed here on the Gianicolo, featuring the cannon shot and the statue of Garibaldi.

There was no other place I could start on his trail in the Eternal City than this statue, the most famous and important of all the many dedicated to him. The first thing I saw was a pigeon perched on his Turkish style cap, which was bleached stark white with the residue of bird droppings. Such is the peril for all statues, but the painter-decorator pigeons of Rome appear to work round the clock. The same can't be said for the municipal cleaners. Underneath the horse, on a giant plinth, I found dramatic sculptures on all four sides designed to tell visitors the epic tales of his life. The one facing east, towards the city, commemorated the momentous battle to defend the Roman Republic. There was a stone wreath at its foot. The scene depicted three men with swords and muskets. Another soldier, wounded, was perched on sandbags, a fifth lay dead.

Facing to the north the carving was of a mother with son and daughter. She was holding a thorny rose stem aloft. This scene was dedicated to America, a nod to Garibaldi's legend as the Hero of Two Worlds. On the opposite side an inscription read *ROMA O MORTE* (Rome or Death), a famous battle cry used by Garibaldi to inspire his irregular troops. The sculpture depicted a princess wearing a crown. A youth was beside her with a book, and a young naked boy held a torch. This one was dedicated to Europe.

Finally, facing west, the stonework depicted the battle of Calatafimi in western Sicily in 1860, which many believe was Garibaldi's single most important victory. One soldier had the green, white and red tricolour flag of Italy wrapped around a stick. Another was blowing a bugle. A third was slumped, wounded, and a fourth lay dead on top of a ruined cannon. There was a large cactus, too, typical of the Sicilian countryside, a clever detail.

This is the finest statue dedicated to Garibaldi, but that day I found it in a state of neglect, surrounded by metal barricades which had apparently been there for some years. The monument had been damaged on the western side during a fierce storm – a stone lion carved below the battle scene was cut in half by a direct hit from a thunderbolt of lightning which also gouged a deep hole. Repairs were promised, but nothing had happened. Protests were loud and long, featured on the local and national TV news. Nothing happened. More protests followed, a giant cushion of flowers was left by demonstrators that blew away in the wind.

It made me understand how Piazzale Garibaldi really matters to the people of Rome. When I asked them about the place, many talked about a puppet show, the *Teatrino di Pulcinella* that has been ever-present since 1959, prompting a cascade of memories and delight. The daily cannon shot is just as popular; there is always a sudden swarm to the square to see the ritual performed by three uniformed soldiers at the precise stroke of noon. It was genuinely ear-splitting standing close by. The custom was begun in 1847 by Pope Pius IX, who wanted to set a standard time for the bells of all the churches in Rome. Now it is fired each day from under the nose of Garibaldi, the fiercest warrior opponent of the very same Pope. You have to believe Italy's hero would appreciate the irony, not least because we know the Vatican was deeply uncomfortable with his presence.

In 1929 an 'unofficial' request was made to the Mussolini regime that Garibaldi's statue be removed from its strategic position on top of the Gianicolo. If not, could the statue at least be turned round? When it was erected in 1895, Garibaldi had been placed looking straight towards St Peter's, as if ever watchful for new signs of trouble. The response was emphatic. The statue would remain, and a new monument would also be added nearby to honour Anita, situated as close as possible to her husband high on the hill. The single compromise was an agreement for a 180-degree turn for the Hero of Two Worlds, so that he would gaze across the perfect view of Rome. As people in the city drily noted, this positioned the rear of the horse to face the Vatican.

The statue of Anita, one of the most dramatic and best-loved in all of Italy, was 100 metres away. She was displayed on a galloping horse, a pistol held aloft in her right hand and newborn son cradled in her left arm. This also had stirring images carved below the main sculpture, including the one which featured Anita searching for her husband amid the carnage of battle in Brazil. The remains of Anita were interred here at the opening ceremony in 1932, and the monument has become a place of pilgrimage for Italian women in particular. It has its own stop on the No. 115 bus route.

Many other combatants from the summer of 1849 are also remembered up here on the Gianicolo. Walking along from the main square I found a statue dedicated to Ciceruacchio, a figure of popular legend in Rome. It was the nickname of Angelo Brunetti, a tavern manager who fought alongside

Garibaldi and was part of an eventual retreat from the city. Ciceruacchio was captured by the Austrian army, who had also arrived to help the Pope, and summarily executed. His statue could hardly have been more powerful: shirt torn open, he was defiantly staring at the firing squad, telling them to shoot straight for the heart. His thirteen-year-old son Lorenzo, kneeling and blindfolded, was at his feet. Ciceruacchio pleaded with the soldiers to spare him. They shot the boy first.

A few steps further down the Passeggiata del Gianicolo I discovered Porta San Pancrazio (St Pancras), one of the old gates into the city of Rome, a place at the heart of the battles of 1849 when it was bombed to rubble. This fine arch was re-built and today houses the museum of the *Repubblica Romana* and several rooms of Garibaldi memorabilia. It was also a traffic island; to reach the museum I had to dodge cars and scooters racing past on either side. There were supposed to be zebra crossings, but these faded long ago and nobody had bothered to re-paint them, hardly a surprise in this town.

One road leading away from Porta San Pancrazio west out of the city was the scene of the most intense fighting. I walked a few hundred metres to the entrance of what is now Rome's biggest park, the Villa Pamphili. From there, a wide path swept up to a mighty arch built on the highest spot of the Gianicolo. Another road headed east towards the centre of Rome. This was Via Garibaldi, where it begins a spectacular descent into the heart of Trastevere, and if you are foolish enough to walk without stopping you can be down by the riverside in fifteen minutes. It took me many hours as I discovered a treasure at every turn.

The first of these was Villa Aurelia, an elegant *palazzo* that was Garibaldi's headquarters and where, oblivious to the dangers of the French bombardment, he would walk out onto the watchtower every morning at dawn to light a cigar, deliberately poking fun at the enemy. The reconstructed building now houses the American Academy in Rome, from where the view remains sublime, as it does from the next building down, No.29 Via Garibaldi.

It is the official address of one of the great fountains of Rome, the Fontana dell'Acqua Paola, commissioned by Pope Paul V and completed in 1614. Strolling down the hill there was no inkling of its existence. From the back it seemed just an ordinary grey stone building, which you barely notice given the magnificent vista of Rome that lay ahead. Even from ten yards away there was no clue. Then, suddenly, I turned round to face a blinding-white marble facade with six columns, three arches, and torrents of water cascading into an azure pool. With a strong sun shining, the glare made it almost too dazzling to look at close up. It was built with stone plundered from the Temple of Minerva, which had survived for 1,500 years in the heart of ancient Rome. The culprit was the Pope, who wanted the finest building material for his fountain, as well as for the altar of the new St Peter's Basilica he had commissioned. In any other city this fountain would be a top ten attraction, a symbol of *la dolce vita*. Here it's one of a thousand minor glories. Romans cherish it as *Il Fontanone* (the big fountain), yet few know it was the inspiration for the more celebrated Trevi Fountain down in the centre below.

The treasures kept on coming. Around the next sweeping turn I saw a striking if austere open marble structure. This was

Il Mausoleo Ossario Garibaldini (official address No. 30 Via Garibaldi), a memorial to those who died fighting for Rome to become the capital of a united Italy. The crypt holds the remains of all those who perished. They were listed on the marble, from generals down to eleven-year-old drummer boys. At the back of the crypt was the tomb of Goffredo Mameli, who was wounded in one of the 1849 battles and died a few weeks later at the age of just twenty-one. Mameli is known by every Italian as the author of the words of their national anthem. He was a soldier-poet who sent lyrics for battle songs to Verdi to put to music and was also an adjutant to Garibaldi.

Say the name Goffredo Mameli and it brings a smile of recognition to young and old in Italy. They know that the anthem, *Fratelli D'Italia*, is by Mameli, but almost none of the people I asked knew that Mameli died so young as a fervent Garibaldino. They are surprised by this information. I was surprised about their surprise.

The mausoleum was the idea of Garibaldi's grandson Ezio. It was financed by the Mussolini government and completed in 1941. Inscribed on the front is *Ai Caduti per Roma 1849-70* – to those who fell for Rome. Various battles are cited, including one that is barely remembered now, the struggle for Casa Giacometti. We need a brief diversion back up the hill to tell this story. It was a house in the thick of the fighting to defend the *Repubblica Romana*, the closest to the advancing French soldiers, a place on the edge of the Villa Pamphili that today is the popular Ristorante Scarpone. Among those firing from the windows was Garibaldi himself, who would tie up his white horse on a tree which, it is claimed, still stands in the outdoor dining courtyard. It is certainly true that the restaurant's name,

Scarpone (Big Shoe), came from Garibaldi. It was the nickname he gave to the owner of the inn, Antonio Arducci, a man who tramped through fields to bring wine to the soldiers, leaving his shoes caked with mud and looking ten sizes too big.

The restaurant has been there ever since, still owned by the Arducci family. During the Second World War it was a favourite haunt of Mussolini, who regularly dined there with an SS colonel, the No.2 German officer in Rome. They never suspected that the family who ran Ristorante Scarpone were hiding several Jewish families in the cellars beneath. Who can doubt that Casa Giacometti deserves its place of honour on the Mausoleo? The food they serve is still excellent.

Further down Via Garibaldi the next swooping curve delivered me to the church of San Pietro in Montorio, built on the spot where it was thought St Peter had been crucified and buried. It was once considered the most sacred place in Rome, which is saying something in this town. It was also the final headquarters for Garibaldi when the French army advanced. The church was badly damaged in the bombardment, but miraculously the cannon fire did not strike the Tempietto in the middle courtyard. This was a small but perfectly formed circular commemorative tomb designed by Bramante and built in 1502 as a shrine to mark the supposed exact spot of St Peter's martyrdom. The consensus now is that this was not the location of the crucifixion of St Peter, but gaze at the exquisite perfection of the Tempietto and you may prefer to believe so. On the outside of the church wall I found a plaque marking the time the church was attacked on behalf of the Pope, and embedded into it was a cannonball discovered during restorations.

What else lay on Via Garibaldi? Across the road from the church I wandered past the curse of modern life in Rome, a massed rank of ugly, over-loaded rubbish bins on the edge of the road; battered old skips for paper, plastic, glass, organic and general waste. There is usually more garbage reeking and rotting in the gutters outside them because collection is so haphazard. These public bins are on every street, and their hopeless upkeep is a symbol to locals of how the city is embarrassingly grubby and incompetently governed. Visitors revel in the glories of this place; Romans rarely stop moaning about it. Another endless gripe is that leaves are never cleared from the streets in late autumn and early winter, clogging up the drains to leave roads and underpasses flooded. And don't forget the parks, they always tell me, how branches and trees come crashing down because the authorities can't be bothered with routine maintenance. Oh, and did we mention the decrepit municipal buses that suddenly catch fire when they are driving along?

Yes, that's all true. I have seen a burnt-out bus on the side of the road, and cars smashed by fallen trees, and the shameful mountains of rubbish on the streets. Perhaps it's little wonder that monuments can be neglected. Perhaps this is a city where treasures have to lie in ruins for 2,000 years before their value is appreciated.

Round the corner from the cannonball-in-the-wall were steep steps leading straight down to the river as an alternative to the winding road. This was the path Garibaldi would climb on his horse when moving between the city and Gianicolo. The alternative, taking the road, was noisy cobbles all the way to the bottom of the hill. Tyres crunching on uneven cobblestones are one of the soundtracks of Rome, along with ambulance sirens, church bells, car horns and the singsong chatter of crowds sitting outside bars for aperitivo.

It was just about time, and I found a bar right at the bottom of Via Garibaldi among the tourist crowds in Trastevere and ordered a glass of wine that came with a small plate of food thrown in, containing mini pizzas, parmesan cheese and slices of salami. The ritual of aperitivo is a daily delight of living in Rome, meeting friends for a drink and a snack after work, whether at the trendiest new enoteca (wine bar) or the scruffiest workaday cafe. Much of the city pauses for this hour or two of carefree conviviality. It is a timeless rhythm of life; even Garibaldi and his men would relax by drinking wine together during lulls in the fighting. It is a rhythm as essential as the siesta used to be, the mark of a civilised everyday culture. I realised I had properly arrived in Rome when the lady in charge of my favourite enoteca called me 'amore' while refusing to serve the glass of red I'd ordered from the ever-changing list on the chalk board behind the bar. She volubly insisted that she knew I wouldn't like it, and maybe she was right. The one I was allowed to drink was fabulous. There was also a popular aperitivo cocktail on the menu, a mix of Campari and orange juice. This was the Garibaldi cocktail, and it's available everywhere.

Trastevere, with its atmospheric lanes, beautiful basilicas and a galaxy of bars and restaurants, is a magnet for millions of visitors each year. In 1849 it was where Garibaldi lodged during the conflict on the Gianicolo hill above. The story had begun there with the stabbing to death of Rossi, the Pope's minister, and the creation of the *Repubblica Romana*, to whose assembly Garibaldi had been elected in January 1849. The first impression he gave on his arrival in the Eternal City was hardly the one he desired; he had to be carried into the debating chamber because the arthritis which long plagued him had been exacerbated by marching on the frozen slopes of the Appenines that winter. The second impression was electrifying. He spoke for action to create a united Italy – for the immediate implementation of the new constitution rather than endless days of discussion and process. Garibaldi roared:

> The question today is a vital one of principle. To delay one minute would be a crime so long as one third of the Italian nation lies in slavery. Can you not hear the groan of despair which comes from a million Italian throats? And, meanwhile, we are asked to go on discussing mere forms! I believe profoundly that what we need in Rome is a republic. Can it be that the descendants of the ancient Romans are not fit to constitute a Republic?

Much has changed in Italy since that day, but not the propensity to 'discuss mere forms'. It's a burden of life from the moment you are born, or the moment you arrive as a *straniero*, a foreigner. Bureaucracy is a torture until you happen to chance on the right person in authority to help you stumble along. They are gold dust. My application for residency in Rome required a blizzard of forms and documents, and then one last twist of buying the correct Marca da Bollo (revenue stamp) for final processing. I bought these at the Tabacchi shops identified by capital T, which are on every street in the land. A mere four 16 Euro stamps and four 0.52 Euro stamps was the end game for me. Marca da Bollo are ubiquitous. I even needed to buy the two Euro variety when I paid a dental bill to make the receipt official.

Garibaldi had better luck. It took only four days after his speech for the constitution to be officially proclaimed. The fundamental principle was that religious faith was irrelevant to civic and political rights. There were promises of universal suffrage, freedom of worship, agrarian reform, and the abolition of the death penalty. Import duties were abolished, along with the most hated taxes and special courts. Rome had changed from one of the most backward states of Europe into the one of the most modern and most purely democratic – at least in political terms.

The 1849 constitution was so ahead of its time that it was the main reference a century later when the current constitution of Italy was written in 1947. A decade ago, the full text was inscribed onto a wall fifty metres wide, up on the Gianicolo close to the statue of Garibaldi.

Democracy and the city of Rome have the longest history, yet also of course a chequered one. The initials SPQR are everywhere in the city; on buildings and monuments, on the iron railings around trees, on the back of buses, on every manhole cover, on the four corners of Ponte Garibaldi. It is from the democracy of ancient Rome, the acronym for Senatus Populus Que Romanus – 'the Roman Senate and People'. Many of today's SPQR signs were created in the time of Mussolini, who wanted to hark back to a supposed golden age of the city, but who was a dictator as hostile to democracy as many of the emperors of ancient Rome and a legion of Popes. For much of the city's history the people have been cowed, exploited and ignored.

These days, the joke goes that SPQR stands for Sono Pazzi Questi Romani – 'They're crazy these Romans' – and it's easy for the outsider to believe so amid the chaos of the traffic, where stopping for a red light seems quirky and where scooters dart dangerously between the cars while trying to avoid giant holes in the road surface. The biggest bugbear of all is the sheer impossibility of finding a space to park and the absolute need to resort to double parking. It was my rite of passage to living in Rome, one which demanded the learning of fundamental lessons and unwritten rules. The first was to take the giant leap of faith and understand that 'doppia fila' (double parking) is acceptable. The second was learning how to do it, an art form involving endless ingenuity, an intimate knowledge of the precise angles required, an instinct for which street corners are possible and which aren't, when and when not to put on hazard lights, and how close I could nudge to other cars already parked (answer, within millimetres). It's almost impossible to find a car in Rome without dents or scratches on its bumpers.

I learned, eventually, to cast aside anxiety. I learned to tolerate double parking by others. I learned why even the richest Romans drive around in tiny Smart cars (the happy option of perpendicular parking). I learned how and where to pay the parking fines you will inevitably acquire (at the tobacconist's shop, of course). I learned, most importantly of all, what is beyond the pale. When (not if) you hear an orchestra of car horns, it will almost certainly be fury at someone who has double parked but left their vehicle unattended to go shopping and blocked others in with no chance of escape. There is no greater social crime in this town.

None. Back in 1849, difficulties in finding a place to tether a horse did not exist.

Back then, the democratic politics of the new republic was led by Giuseppe Mazzini, the intellectual revolutionary who had long agitated for a united nation, and whose Young Italy movement had first inspired Garibaldi to action. For a few months Mazzini lived the dream of a free Eternal City. He was elected by the assembly as one of the triumvirs (a nod to the democracy of ancient Rome and its policy of three leaders). The others were Aurelio Saffi and Carlo Armellini, but Mazzini was the real power and the prime author of the radical new constitution.

Garibaldi wanted overall charge of military operations, not just control of his irregular army. he told the governors of the city:

> Let me be immodest, In a hundred engagements I have never been defeated. In my long life as a soldier have you ever heard a single accusation against me of cowardice or lack of skill? Sometimes I have been called a pirate, smuggler, or guerrilla, because such epithets are deliberately used to defame a feared rival. The fact is that again and again I have had to fight against hundreds, against thousands, and beat them.

His wish was denied; he had to be content with the rank of General.

The French army expected an easy march into Rome. Recent history of conflict on the peninsula had given the impression the Italian people were reluctant soldiers. It proved otherwise with Garibaldi to inspire them. He knew the crucial vantage point was the Casino Dei Quattro Venti, otherwise known as Villa Corsini, the highest point of the Gianicolo, and on a fierce day of fighting on 30 April the French attack was repulsed. Garibaldi rode everywhere on horseback amid the conflict to inspire his men. One young Roman who left his job to join the battle described the effect:

> I shall never forget that first day I saw him on his beautiful white horse. He reminded us of nothing so much as Our Saviour's head in the art galleries – everyone said the same. I could not resist him. I went after him; thousands did likewise. He only had to show himself. We all worshipped him. We could not help it.

One of his contemporary biographers, Jesse Mario White, put it this way: 'Always at the front was Garibaldi – handsome, masculine, face bronzed, a long copper beard, wearing a Calabrian style hat with a wonderful black ostrich feather, a red shirt under a white poncho. He seemed to have been born on a horse; he looked so natural.' Garibaldi understood the power of his appearance and his presence. When he was wounded in the side by cannon-shot, blood seeping into his saddle, he refused to see a surgeon until after dark to keep the injury secret.

The successful defence of Villa Corsini was celebrated with wild enthusiasm and pride in the streets of Rome below. It was the first time in centuries of invasions that outsiders had been sent packing. A precious measure of self-respect had been earned. 'We are again Romans' was the chant among the crowds. Even though they would succumb to eventual defeat, the importance of this day of triumph to the ordinary people of the city cannot be exaggerated.

Garibaldi wanted to chase the defeated opposition back to the coast and out of Italy. His strategy was always to seize the moment, push forward. Mazzini rejected the plan. Naively, he hoped France could be persuaded into neutrality. It was a grievous error. A ceasefire was negotiated with the French representative, a young Ferdinand De Lesseps, who years later won worldwide fame for building the Suez Canal, and the fate of the republic was settled. There was a brief lull in the fighting as the French re-grouped and all the other Catholic armies of Europe started to gather: the Austrians to the north-east, the Spanish landing at Gaeta where the Pope was skulking, the Bourbons heading up south from Naples. Then came two battles outside Rome, victories against the Bourbons at Palestrina and Velletri. Once again, Garibaldi wanted to press home the advantage with further attacks, but Mazzini rejected the idea and called him back to focus on the defence of Rome against the French. Orders were followed, but the pair were never close again.

The inspirational charisma and spirit of Garibaldi was vital to a month of monumental resistance by the people of Rome in a doomed attempt to save their fledgling republic. It began on 3 June, when French commander General Oudinot attacked at dead of night, two days before the negotiated end of the ceasefire. Garibaldi, recovering from wounds suffered at Velletri, was sleeping in Trastevere. Woken at 3am, he scrambled up the hill on his horse knowing it was the moment of truth. Everything depended on control of Villa Corsini. It was lost to the first French advance, won back by Garibaldi's men, lost again, reclaimed a second time, and eventually lost for good. The relentless fighting, the surges up and down the hill, perhaps contained more valour and sorrow than any other day in the history of Rome.

Today, these few hundred metres of land are a wide and peaceful path in the great park of the Villa Pamphili; it is called *Viale del Battaglione della Speranza* (avenue of the battalion of hope). It is where people take their dogs for a walk, others hold impromptu exercise classes under the shade of the trees. Further over the brow of the hill, if you walk along Viale de Maglio, is where I saw the Bangladeshi immigrants who run the flower stalls and 7-11 corner shops of modern Rome playing cricket. There was a concrete 22-yard strip with crease markings planted incongruously in the middle of an open grassy space surrounded by umbrella pine trees that are such a symbol of the city. Maglio is described on the sign as a *storico gioco*, an old game, whose full title is *Pallamaglio* – the inspiration for Pall Mall (see page 13).

The battle for Villa Corsini was, in Garibaldi's words: 'one of the most glorious episodes in Italy's military history, lasting from dawn until night'. The General certainly made mistakes in his tactics; the head-on frontal attacks on Villa Corsini saw too many men killed unnecessarily. Yet it was also true that unless they secured the villa that day, the eventual outcome would be the ruin of the *Repubblica Romana*. It can be argued that there was no other option; that an attack on the flanks was not a viable alternative and would only have meant even more men slaughtered. Garibaldi never lost the loyalty of his soldiers amid the carnage; this is also a truth of that day. They wanted and needed a warrior leader to inspire them, and in Garibaldi they had not only that but a leader of personal humility, dignity, and calm amid the tumult. They saw genuine courage rather than showman bravado from their leader. He was lucky to survive; musket balls and flying metal shredding his poncho. It was a day when the legend of Garibaldi was lifted another notch.

A month-long siege of Rome followed. On 21 June, Garibaldi wrote a letter to his pregnant wife Anita, almost exultant amid the desperation of impending defeat: 'We are fighting here on the Gianicolo, and these citizens of Rome are now proving worthy of their past greatness. One hour of life here in Rome is worth a century of normal existence. How happy my mother should be for giving me life in this wonderful period of Italian history.' Anita never received the letter; she had already left Nice to join her husband. It was the third time she had attempted to do so that year, twice before sent back. She could and would not stay away this time, not amid the battle for Rome. By the time she arrived on 26 June, the headquarters at Villa Aurelia had been vacated, bombed to rubble. For a few days Garibaldi was lodged further down the hill at Villa Spada, which is now the embassy of Ireland to the Vatican. Next and final stop was San Pietro in Montorio, but the end was near.

On the morning of 30 June Garibaldi was summoned to the assembly chamber to report on the situation. His sword was bent so badly it could not fit into its sheath. His shirt was soaked in blood and pocked with holes from bullets and swords. His words spoke the truth, that no more defence was possible. Only at this moment was he given full authority over the troops which remained, promoted to commander-in-chief of the Roman army, with orders to keep the revolution alive wherever possible. It was a title Garibaldi cherished to his grave, though he never fought within the city again. He believed it forever entitled him to try to re-establish the Republic, and to remove the Pope.

That evening the surviving 4,000 Red Shirt soldiers gathered outside St Peter's Basilica to await further instructions. Garibaldi was now a hero far beyond the walls of Rome and the hill of the Gianicolo as accounts of the battle were telegraphed daily to newspapers around the world. He was offered passage out of Italy on an American ship by the US envoy in the city. He declined, although accepted an American passport. Instead, he made a famous speech as they prepared to depart, telling his men: 'All you can expect is heat and thirst by day, cold and hunger by night. You can hope for no wages, but hard work and danger, without roof, without rest, just death and poverty, long night watches, long marches, and fighting at every step.' The thousands were not deterred. If you hear an echo of this in Winston Churchill's 'blood, toil, tears and sweat' speech during the Second World War, you are not alone.

The exact number of people who died in the battles to save the *Repubblica Romana*, and in the bombardment during the month-long siege of the city is unknown. It is reckoned that as many as 3,000 Italians and 2,000 French troops were killed fighting for control of Villa Corsini. The defenders did not die in vain. Although the immediate battle to maintain the republic was lost, this was the crucial turning point for the future of Rome and the nation. Heroism in defeat was also a moral victory. The immense gallantry on the

Gianicolo showed the watching world the Eternal City was also indisputably an Italian city, and that the Pope's political power was doomed.

Garibaldi's legend in Rome has never dimmed – for one profound reason. The defence of the *Repubblica Romana* is the piece of history, in the city with more history than any other, that most fills its people with pride. Rome was the capital of the ancient world. It has long been a capital of civilisation. It remains a capital of religion. Nowhere else could truly be the capital of Italy, and Garibaldi understood this. '*O Roma O Morte*' (Rome or Death) his motto, is still visible today on so many monuments, nowhere more than high up on the hill.

Among all the commemorations I found on the Gianicolo, though, there was an outlier – a giant red arch standing on the exact spot of the Villa Corsini where so much blood was shed on 3 June 1849. It was a few hundred metres inside the Villa Pamphili and in a state of complete neglect when I went to take a look. There were rusty padlocks on the gates, the plaster was crumbling, and weeds were growing high by the walls. There was no information board for the curious, no plaque of description, which was quite incredible in Italy where they do love a plaque.

On Google maps I discovered that it stands in the *Piazzale Ragazzi del 1849*, a piece of land clearly named in honour of the boys of Rome who fought that year with Garibaldi. Its official title is the *Arco Dei Quattro Venti* (arch of the four winds), and it is situated directly in line with the smaller arch of the *Porta San Pancrazio*, some 800 metres distant. It looked as though it should be important, but it stood unloved. The only information I could find was that it was designed by Andrea Busiri Vici, an architect who worked on many projects for the Catholic Church, and that it was built between 1856-9 when Papal rule had returned with repressive force to Rome.

The only credible explanation was that it had been commissioned as a triumphal arch to celebrate the defeat of Garibaldi and the *Repubblica Romana*. It was the most cheerless chunk of stone in the Eternal City.

5

CESENATICO/RAVENNA

'Anita was a formidable woman, free from any conditioning, revolutionary and very modern. She is a genuine heroine that we should all look up to.'

Costanza Ravizza Garibaldi

Sunday morning. Ten o'clock. Halfway along the main canal next to the bridge. Uniform optional, but highly recommended. Those were the orders for the marching band, for the police, for the red shirts – and for the whole town it seemed as thousands of people gathered for the annual carnival parade in the little port of Cesenatico on the Adriatic coast of Italy. This was the centrepiece of a Garibaldi Festival which takes place each summer on the first weekend of August to commemorate a dramatic episode during his retreat from the battlefields of Rome in 1849 – the night he escaped a chasing army by commandeering all the fishing boats of the town and sailing away during a fierce storm.

The parade didn't start at ten, of course it didn't. I had learned that timings are elastic in Italy, merely a basis for negotiation, whether it's shop opening hours, dentist appointments or dining arrangements. There was simply no hope that a carnival parade would run like clockwork. So, when I arrived just after ten, although still with a touch of Anglo-Saxon anxiety about being late, the scene on canal-side at Cesenatico was relaxed. The red shirts, men dressed up in the old costume of Garibaldini fighters, were chatting among themselves, posing for photos or sitting in the coffee bars having breakfast. Huge Italian flags hung from the windows above, and then the watching crowd stirred from its slumber a little as a Garibaldi lookalike arrived to take centre stage alongside a woman dressed as Anita. He doffed his feathered hat for more photos. The band practised a few notes, and the Red Cross volunteers fell in at the back of the parade in case of casualties. Nobody I could see was checking their watches with a tut of frustration.

Then it started, without fuss, and without apparent command. Suddenly, everyone was moving across the bridge as the band played their tunes and the crowd kept chatting. There were maybe 100 men in red shirts on parade, strolling rather than marching it has to be said, but full of pride. This was their big day, the highlight of the year for these enthusiasts and obsessives who help to keep the spirit of Garibaldi alive in modern Italy.

Within two minutes they had reached the first stop, a little square with a rather weathered and scratched stone statue of Garibaldi in the centre. His face looked traumatised as he stood resting on his sword. Underneath there was an inscription: 'We placed the effigy here, and it is enough that Italy is a truly unsurpassable monument to him.' The band played the national anthem, a wreath was laid, a few words were spoken, and they went strolling off again. I realised that some of the crowd were now joining the parade as thousands of others watched it pass by. I couldn't miss this chance to march with Garibaldi's irregular troops, even if I hadn't come dressed in red. I confess this was a moment of unexpected delight. We headed along the other side of the canal, along the Corso Garibaldi, out towards the harbour of Cesenatico. There were several more stops to lay wreaths; on the wall outside a house where Garibaldi and Anita had rested, by a stone bust of Anita, and a rosebush which has a new variety of the flower, Anita, dedicated to her.

The band kept playing, the red shirts kept strolling, the crowds kept applauding, and another wreath was placed outside the town hall, which was decorated by a huge plaque that contained the names of all the Garibaldi troops who were ferried out to sea by the fishermen of Cesenatico on a stormy night in August 1849. Were they finished? Not likely. This was no half-hearted nod to history. The parade set off again and we marched out to the end of the canal. This time a wreath was thrown into the water and floated slowly out towards the sea. I knew by now this wasn't the end of the matter, even though we'd been going for more than an hour. There were still the official speeches to be made, and at least one more rendition of the national anthem. We headed back to the centre, walking along Viale Anita Garibaldi to Piazza Ciceruacchio, the roads still lined with people. The mayor of Cesenatico spoke, the chief of police had his say, the mayor of nearby Ravenna said more than a few words, but the final speech came from the Garibaldi lookalike, a university professor from the north of Italy, a man named Fabio Facchinetti, who surprised the crowd by announcing that he was hanging up his poncho after twenty-two years acting the role of the great general at this festival. He spoke with rare emotion, saying he how had been inspired by the story of Garibaldi since he was a small boy, and the applause of the audience suggested he was far from alone in that sentiment.

Marching with the red shirts in the morning sun had been a treat, yet the most engaging feature of the Garibaldi celebrations had taken place in the blazing heat of the afternoon before. This was the sight of forty traditional fishing boats with colourful sails moored on the canal ready to go out to sea. These are known as *bragozzi*, and were the vessels which enabled Garibaldi, his wife Anita, and the remnants of his troops to escape the fast-approaching Austrian army.

It is a crucial moment of Italian history re-enacted each summer in Cesenatico, but only when the participants decide they are ready for action. Posters for the Garibaldi Festival declared it would start at 2.30. At which time, naturally, the place was completely deserted except for the boats. The temperature was 35°C and people were hibernating behind shuttered windows. A few sailors eventually sauntered towards their boats and I asked them when it would begin. They shrugged their shoulders. Who knows? It seemed also a case of who cares. But they did. The town did. By 3.30 the *bragozzi* were teeming with life, weathered boatmen and their happy families pushing off down the canal. No cannon had been fired to signal the start, not even a whistle. When a boat was ready, it went. And, as if by magic, there were suddenly crowds of onlookers watching and waving. The boats were magnificent as they slipped along the canal. They had come for the event from all round the region of Emilia Romagna, and each one had individual decorations and markings, mostly in reds, yellows and greens. I particularly liked the one with a horse dancing on a snake, the *Bragozza d'Altura*, a deep-sea fishing boat, now part of the town's floating museum.

Before I went, many friends in Rome had asked with incredulity why I was heading off to Cesenatico. Nobody goes there, they told me. All I can say is, more fool them. The town is one of Italy's secret treasures, and not just for this festival. The canal which runs through the heart of the place was designed by Leonardo Da Vinci, and its elegance is most obvious in the evenings when the *Passeggiata* is in full swing and the bars and restaurants that line each side are teeming with people. It was a fabulous spot, and celebrating the exploits of Garibaldi was just a happy bonus.

Perhaps that's just as well because the festival is built on a myth. The flotilla is supposed to be recreating the story of 1849, painting the fishermen of Cesenatico as heroes, saving Garibaldi and his men in a desperate hour of need. What actually happened is that they were distinctly unwilling to help, fearful of reprisals by the Austrian army who had issued proclamations warning of the death penalty for anyone giving assistance to Garibaldi. The fishermen were forced into action at the point of a sword by the Red Shirts amid a storm that night. Thirteen bragozzi were commandeered and sailed off at dawn. The Austrians arrived an hour later. Needless to say, none of this was mentioned in the speeches by the mayors of Cesenatico and Ravenna at the close of the Sunday morning grand parade.

Cesenatico, some twenty miles south of the historic city of Ravenna on the Adriatic coast, was the end point of a long march by Garibaldi and the Red Shirts who had so valiantly tried to defend the *Repubblica Romana*. The retreat from Rome, with Garibaldi accompanied by Anita who was five months pregnant and increasingly unwell, is among the most vivid stories of Italian history. It began in the square in front of St Peter's Basilica and ended at the Leonardo canal.

Garibaldi's aim leaving Rome with his 4,000 men was to head for Venice to help the city state still independent there under the leadership of Daniele Manin, another important figure of the Risorgimento. The journey took them through the heart of what is modern Italy, across the regions of Lazio, Tuscany, Umbria and Emilia Romagna, climbing over the Appenines along the way. These areas were controlled in July 1849 by various foreign states, which meant the Red Shirts were being hunted by a combination of French, Spanish and Austrian soldiers. The eventual final escape of Garibaldi to freedom was little short of a miracle, marching at night, resting by day.

The route twisted this way and that, both to confuse the enemy chasers and to navigate the terrain of rivers, valleys, hills and mountains. Garibaldi and Anita rode on horseback at the front, she dressed in a green male uniform with a plumed Calabrian hat. They camped one night at Hadrian's Villa on the outskirts of Rome, and at the next stop Anita browbeat monks to give them food and wine. In these early days, the column of men was three miles long, and they often had to march in silence not to attract attention. A plaque on a wall in Terni, the home town of St Valentine, records a place where Garibaldi stopped to eat lunch. All along the route there are similar markers. Every town, small or large, has captured and displayed its morsel of history.

My favourite among these was the statue of Garibaldi in the main square of the small Umbrian hilltop city of Todi, where the Red Shirts rested for forty-eight hours. It was erected in a commanding position overlooking the valley below. Garibaldi was standing, wearing his famous cape, leaning on his sword, and the white stone was framed by a perfect azure sky behind. Close to the statue was a giant cypress tree, now 36 metres tall, which was planted in 1849 during his short stay to honour him.

He was welcomed in some towns, such as Todi, but received very little help from people in the countryside who were usually loyal to the church and the Pope, the bitter enemies of Garibaldi, who demonised the Red Shirts as bandits and brigands. This propaganda wasn't true, and Garibaldi showed it in his reaction to an incident when one of his men stole a hen from a peasant woman's house near Orvieto. He would not tolerate looting and ordered the man to be shot as an example to the others. The marchers skilfully evaded the Austrian army to reach the edge of Arezzo on 22 July, where in the modern town a monument now stands to those who fell fighting for free Italy. There is also a separate statue of Garibaldi himself, his arm outstretched, perhaps pointing the way forward for Italy. It does not depict an actual event of the time. The locals refused to help him and demanded the Red Shirts remain outside the town.

The 4,000 men who left Rome were down to fewer than 2,000, with many now deserting. They reached San Marino on 31 July, a safe haven because the independence of the small hilltop republic was accepted by all nations. It was the end of any hope of leading thousands of men to a new battlefield. Garibaldi discharged his remaining Red Shirts, but declined to accept terms for a formal surrender from the Austrians that would have allowed Anita and him free passage across the Atlantic on a ship to the United States. Even in this impossible position, 200 men stayed with Garibaldi, who had decided to try to escape and reach Venice. Anita insisted on coming as well, even though she was severely ill with a fever.

In the dead of night, shown the way by a local guide, they walked in single file out of San Marino and headed for the sea, hoping to sail up the coast to freedom. And so Garibaldi arrived in Cesenatico on the evening of 1 August and forced the reluctant fishermen out of their beds to get ready before the Austrian soldiers arrived. They departed at dawn in thirteen boats and sailed past Ravenna before being spotted by an Austrian naval patrol. It was an almost hopeless situation, and ten *bragozzi* were quickly captured, with no resistance from the locals of Cesenatico and not much from the Red Shirts. Only three boats made it ashore, among them the one carrying Garibaldi and the stricken Anita, and they landed at Magnavacca amid the marshes of Lake Comacchio.

The landscape here has barely changed in the 175 years since. It is still off the beaten track, although Magnavacca has since been re-named Porto Garibaldi, and is now a fairly sleepy fishing village. Garibaldi carried Anita in his arms off the boat and they waded ashore through the reeds. The scene has been re-created with a fabulous copper sculpture on a traffic island close to the harbour that was erected in 2011. Many statues are dull. This one was alive with the anxiety and anguish of the hunted couple. There was a jungle of reeds taller than the life-size figures of Garibaldi and Anita, who were standing in a small rowing boat. She was clearly in pain;

he was pointing the way ahead to an uncertain fate. A wreath, of course, was placed in front of the statue, forever renewed as each one faded. I have seen many of the memorials to the epic adventures of Garibaldi, and this was one of the most evocative of all, a reminder of the bleakest moment in his life.

His wife was dying, and he faced certain death if captured. Posters placed in every town on the order of Austrian general Karl von Gorzowski, declared: 'Warning is given that Summary Military Justice will be inflicted upon anyone who knowingly shelters or shows favour to the fugitive Garibaldi.' It was little wonder the fisherman of Cesenatico declined to be heroes, and that the few remaining Red Shirts were ordered to scatter by Garibaldi. These included Ciceruacchio and his two sons, but they were soon captured by the Austrian troops and executed by firing squad, as commemorated in the statue high on the Gianicolo hill in Rome.

The one Red Shirt who stayed with Garibaldi and Anita was a long-time friend and comrade they first met in Montevideo in 1839, Giovanni Battista Culiolo, otherwise known to the world as Leggero (or Major Light), for his nimble physique. Leggero had been badly wounded during the battle to defend the *Repubblica Romana*, and only escaped from a hospital in Rome some weeks after Garibaldi left the city. He had travelled alone to catch up and they were reunited on the stormy night in Cesenatico. This was another remarkable slice of luck, because Leggero now played a crucial role. While Garibaldi tended to the stricken Anita in the marshes, Leggero scouted the area for shelter and by fortune came across Giacomo Bonnet, another friend of Garibaldi, who had fought in the battle for Villa Corsini where his younger brother was killed and then gone home to the Comacchio region.

Bonnet took them to a nearby hut with a thatched roof, where Garibaldi, Anita and Leggero put on peasant clothes to disguise their identities. The hut, capanno in Italian, is still there, now a tiny museum, and I found it among modern houses on a main road out of Porto Garibaldi. It has been maintained as a commemoration, with a plaque which said it was a place of refuge on the run from the Austrians. A wreath with ribbons in the colours of the Italian national flag always lies in front of what is called the Capanno di Garibaldi.

They stayed just a night. Bonnet knew the best hope was to reach a group of radicals in Ravenna who could help with their escape. Garibaldi, however, refused to leave Anita, who was suffering badly from fever, and after another journey in a rowing boat across the lake they headed to a farm at Mandriole where a doctor was waiting to see her. Shortly after arriving here Anita died on 4 August 1849. She was twenty seven years old. Garibaldi wrote in his memoirs:

> I wept bitterly over her loss, she who had been my inseparable companion in the greatest adventures of my life was gone. I asked the good people of the house to bury her and, at their urgings, left straight away since I would put them at risk if I stayed any longer.

The farmhouse, Fattoria Guiccioli, is still there on a quiet main road halfway between Porto Garibaldi and the marvels of Ravenna. It is now a small museum, although the door was locked and the place silent and deserted when I arrived. Sure, it was a blazing hot morning in August, the kind of day most Italians head to the beach, but all the guidebooks and tourist websites insisted it was open to visitors. There was another door further along the farmhouse, and when I rang the bell it was eventually opened by a man with a generous beer belly who hadn't had time to put a shirt on. 'Yes, you can see the museum,' he said. 'Just give me a couple of minutes.'

Having found something to wear, he emerged into the sunlight and sat down on a white bench in front of the building, his dog lying comatose by his side. By this time six people had turned up to visit, but the museum door remained firmly closed. Nobody could enter before the introductory talk. And so Paride Danesi, the inimitable farmhouse custodian, launched into a long and wonderful account of the life of Anita and the dramatic events of her final few days. He took questions, he went off on tangents, and he showed no inclination whatsoever to move from his chair. Give me a couple of minutes, he'd said. By the end he had given us forty minutes of magic. You will rarely come across a more knowledgeable speaker, and never a more enthusiastic one. It was with great reluctance, it seemed to me, that he finally lifted his hefty frame from the chair and unlocked the door to the museum.

Inside, there was a famous painting of the scene when Anita died, with Garibaldi weeping over her. There was some red shirt memorabilia and maps of the journey taken through the marshes of Comacchio. The prize exhibit was the tiny bed on which Anita died, but this was in fact a copy, because the original was destroyed by a fire during the Nazi occupation of the area during World War Two. Out in the courtyard there was a bronze bust of Anita, and above the museum entrance a plaque which read: 'More than marble monuments, the memory of Anita Garibaldi lives in the hearts of Italians.'

This is not an exaggeration. Anita, one name, is known by everybody across Italy. She is the ultimate heroine of the nation, even though she was Brazilian, and her story is taught to every child in every school. Partly, this is the legacy of the use of Anita's life as propaganda for the nation-building of Italy through many decades. The mythology and symbolism of her life were used by governments of all political persuasions from left to right. More and more, though, teaching the story of Anita has become about her as a female role model, a woman of independence, intelligence and warrior spirit. This narrative is actively encouraged by her great great granddaughter, Costanza Ravizza Garibaldi: who says: 'Anita was a formidable woman, free from any conditioning, revolutionary and very modern. She is a genuine heroine that we should all look up to.'

Costanza spreads the word wherever she can in speeches, events, and visits to schools. The importance of this cannot be doubted in a country which still has a widespread problem with hypermasculine attitudes, and in which there are hundreds of femicides each year. The red shoe protest movement to stop violence towards women is a worldwide campaign, but its strongest manifestation is in Italy where piazzas all over the country are filled with countless pairs of red shoes as a powerful emblem of the struggle. The story of Anita is another symbol, a link from the red shirts to the red shoes.

We should not overlook the truth that her unwavering support for Garibaldi was central to his life from the moment they first met. In another passage in his memoirs, Garibaldi wrote:

Anita, my treasure, was just as fervent as me for the sacred cause of the people, she looked on battles as entertainment and the discomforts of camp life as a pastime. She consoled me in the hard times, and she encouraged the men in battle with serenity, with her voice, with her gestures, while she brandished the scimitar in a threatening manner.

He admired and relished her independent character, and it was no coincidence that he was among the few men of influence in Italy of that time who argued for women to have the vote.

Other women played stirring roles in the Risorgimento, equally brave in battle and as fiercely dedicated to the cause. Colomba Antonietti died amid the rubble of Porta San Pancrazio fighting to save the *Repubblica Romana* in the summer of 1849, having impressed Garibaldi himself in an earlier battle at Velletri. She was just twenty-three. Antonietta De Pace played a key part in organising the takeover of the city of Salerno in 1860 as Garibaldi advanced on nearby Naples to complete his annexation of the whole of southern Italy. She was often called 'Mrs Garibaldi'.

Anita, however, was the one chosen by history, the one honoured with a magnificent statue on the Gianicolo hill in Rome. Her remains were taken there in 1932 amid much pomp and ceremony as the myth of Anita was burnished. The burial on her death nearly 90 years earlier had been conducted in secret, the location marked today by another monument about one kilometre from the farmhouse where she died. Garibaldi and Leggero departed even before the grave was dug; it was too dangerous to remain with Austrian soldiers hunting them down. And so began the escape from these obscure marshes to freedom and future glory.

They hid in a pine forest north of Ravenna, and then in a remote thatched barn by a lagoon. This hut was declared a sacred monument by the new nation of Italy in 1867, just a few years after unification, and later meticulously restored when destroyed by fire in 1911. It was also called Capanno di Garibaldi, and although the barn was hard to find, it was worth the effort. The official car park lay on a main road more than a kilometre away, opposite a giant steel works. I walked past a long parade of traditional fishing nets on the edge of the lagoon and eventually the thunder of industrial lorries faded to an ancient, natural silence. The path became narrow and tangled as I crossed small bridges, and it was easy to understand why this was a fine place to evade detection, and why Google maps places it in the middle of the water. Eventually, the hut came into view, along with the gorgeous vista of the lagoon, which is today a nature reserve. Locals have dubbed this place the European Capital of Birdwatching, and the flamboyance of pink flamingos was easy enough to spot. Experts say you can also find purple herons, plovers, mute swans, snipes, cormorants and sandpipers here.

Inevitably, the front of the barn was covered in plaques, while the museum inside housed a selection of paintings and maps and memorabilia. It has been lovingly maintained by a conservation society dedicated just to this place, and their highlight is an annual celebration of the time Garibaldi spent here – dressed up in red shirts, obviously. On every other day you can just sit on the bench outside in solitude and contemplation. That was the most blissful half hour of my journey, feeling the warmth of the sun on my face, enjoying the almost perfect stillness, in no hurry to jump back into the maelstrom of everyday life.

Garibaldi had to move on as swiftly as he could, and his next stop was the city of Ravenna, a place steeped in history and the base for an underground republican organisation which provided protection in several safe houses. On one of them today was a plaque which read: 'When I find myself among the people of Ravenna, I feel like I am in the bosom of my family. Here I not only have good friends, but also I have my saviours.' This was absolutely correct. Without their assistance he would have been arrested, and possibly executed, by the Austrian soldiers searching the area.

Garibaldi and Leggero moved between many buildings, inside and outside the city. The most famous story from these days is when the pair were eating at a tavern and were joined at their table by soldiers who spoke of how they would soon capture the 'infamous Garibaldi'. The troops did not even look at the man across the table, however, apparently besotted by the pretty waitress serving the tables. This is probably an apocryphal tale, but it has become an accepted part of the Garibaldi legend.

Ravenna is one of the most beautiful and important places in Italy. In the fifth century it was the capital of the Western Roman Empire and the centre of the entire Christian world. The surviving Basilicas and churches from this time are decorated with astonishing mosaics, and I defy anyone seeing them not to have their breath taken away. I read that eight of the buildings here have UNESCO world heritage status. Another destination for the millions of tourists who flock to Ravenna is the tomb of Dante, the greatest literary figure of Italy, who lived and died here after being exiled from his native Florence in the fourteenth century. The square next to his burial spot was, you might have guessed, another Piazza Garibaldi, this one decorated with palm trees and a statue of the Hero of Two Worlds resting on his sword.

Three hundred metres away I found another fine square, this one named Piazza Anita Garibaldi, and with an inscription which read: 'To honour the wife and companion in glory and misfortune of Giuseppe Garibaldi – and to honour the people of Ravenna who died on the scaffold, in prison, in war and in exile for the cause of independence.' It was a further example of Anita's special place, far beyond her marriage. The monument here depicted a female figure in the guise of the goddess Athena as she gave a laurel wreath to a fallen soldier. It said that she represents the city of Ravenna. A small carving below illustrated the death of Anita herself.

The route from Ravenna to freedom took Garibaldi and Leggero back across the Appenines, mostly through Tuscany. They travelled by horse and cart, helped by republicans in many small towns that recall the time with the usual blizzard of plaques. One unique memorial is an obelisk to Garibaldi in the small, fortified hilltop town of Volterra, dedicated by the citizens of his home town Nice/Nizza. On the top is a revolutionary star, Garibaldi's face is carved into the rock at the bottom.

After 14 days they reached the coastal village of San Dalmazio, and sailed away from the Austrian pursuers to reach Chiavari, where one of Garibaldi's relatives lived. The incredible escape was complete – but the initial prize was another spell in jail. Chiavari was in the independent state of Piedmont/Sardinia, where Garibaldi had been elected to parliament only the previous year. Now he was treated as a hostile threat, a danger to the new political order following the failure of the 1848/9 revolutions across the peninsula. The Hero of Two Worlds was arrested and put into jail in the Ducal

Palace in the heart of Genoa. The prison cells here are not in the dungeon but almost at the top of its imposing tower. I took the guided tour, which showed where Garibaldi was locked up. Another prisoner of that time was the violinist and composer Niccolo Paganini, charged with 'the abduction and seduction of a minor'. It felt claustrophobic. The cells were small, enclosed by metal bars, with only the narrowest of slits for light.

Garibaldi was a curious kind of prisoner, though. He was visited by friends, supporters and generals. He was allowed to hold press conferences for journalists. His standing with the public, which had only increased following his courage in the battle for Rome and his escape from the hated Austrians, prompted strong protests outside the Ducal Palace against his arrest. He was too popular to keep locked up but perceived by the authorities as too much of a threat to be set free inside Piedmont.

A compromise was agreed that Garibaldi could have his freedom if he left the country, and he travelled first to Nice to visit his three children who were living with his ageing mother, before sailing on to Sardinia. He was refused permission to land at the capital Cagliari and stopped instead on a small island off the north-eastern coast called La Maddalena, where Leggero had been born. It is an enchanting place, surrounded on all sides by hills, the sea and other islands such as Caprera. Its rugged beauty and tranquillity captivated Garibaldi and it became his long-term home and refuge.

6

SARDINIA/CAPRERA

'We make very fine candles. I spend my time threading wicks and kneading tallow.'

Giuseppe Garibaldi

A fierce sun shone in my face and a strong breeze ruffled what's left of my hair as I stood on the top deck of the small ferry boat sailing across from the port of Palau to the rocky island of La Maddalena. It is a scene of spectacular beauty, the stark granite hills a sublime contrast to the turquoise blue waters. There are rocks on the shorelines that resemble Henry Moore sculptures, and islands which have fingers of land at their extremities like giant green crocodile feet. Hundreds of isolated golden sandy beaches with a Caribbean feel are hidden among the inlets. I was looking at this glory, and all the time a man next to me was talking earnestly to his family, seemingly oblivious to the paradise landscape. He said to his children: 'And this is where Garibaldi would have passed.'

La Maddalena is the mother island of an archipelago off the north-east coast of Sardinia, the only one that's inhabited, and linked by a rudimentary bridge to the second biggest island, Caprera. This lay further ahead, but even from long distance a white house was visible on a hillside covered in low green bushes. It is called Casa Bianca, the house that Garibaldi built, and where he lived for the last twenty-five years of his life. It was where he plotted and schemed, where he farmed, planted olive groves, where he was twice effectively imprisoned by the Italian government, and where he died. Garibaldi first saw this magical place in 1849 soon after his escape from Rome and Ravenna, and he bought half of Caprera in 1855 to make it his home and quiet refuge from the madding crowd.

These days it's different. This whole area of Sardinia's north-east coastline has become a playground for the richest people in Italy and Europe, the so-called Costa Smeralda, filled with luxury hotels, infamous nightclubs and extravagant restaurants. One example is a beachside place to eat at a divine setting on La Maddalena, visible across the water from Garibaldi's old house. It charges 250 euros for a bottle of white wine you can buy in an enoteca for twenty-five euros. The cheapest pizza margherita will set you back eighty euros. Its website says the harbour is perfect for luxury yachts and boasts about the jet-set clientele who dine there, such as footballer Cristiano Ronaldo. The absurd prices succeed in their aim of excluding the rest of us, happily so.

I stopped for lunch instead at a wooden shack on the roadside in the centre of Caprera called *Chiosco Mille*. It nestled in a clearing under pine trees and had long queues thanks to high-class food at ridiculously low prices, and probably thanks above all to its burgers. They came adorned with mushrooms, aubergines and Sardinian pecorino cheese, and were beyond magnificent, easily the finest I've tasted.

The shack feeds the day-trippers to Caprera, those going to the beaches, those coming to see the fauna and flora of its official nature reserve, and others like me heading for the historical monuments dedicated to Giuseppe Garibaldi, not only the Casa Bianca where he lived but also a second museum in an old fort built on the highest point of this granite island. Nobody lives permanently on Caprera anymore, but thousands of people visit each week to get a glimpse into the life of Italy's hero. It was a long haul even from Rome – a flight to the city of Olbia in northern Sardinia, a drive through the wine hills of Gallura, the ferry from Palau, and then another short drive from the port of La Maddalena – but few journeys can be more worthwhile than this.

Garibaldi's white house had a South American feel, with a central courtyard garden dominated by three large umbrella pine trees he planted himself to celebrate the birth of his last daughter Clelia. They provided a welcome natural canopy. The inspiration came from the farmhouses that Garibaldi admired during his years in Brazil and Uruguay, and it had a similar mellow mood to the house in Cuba where the writer Ernest Hemingway lived. To the side of the courtyard was a huge barn, which housed the grave of Garibaldi's most famous horse, Marsala, a white stallion on which he rode during some of the fiercest battles in the charge towards Italian unification. There were also frayed leather saddles from his South American gaucho days, and a bathtub where Garibaldi would wash because it was the warmest place to do so.

The place was now a museum, full of memorabilia, the walls decorated with paintings, photos, banners and flags. There were swords, muskets, sextants, the field stamps Garibaldi used during battles, and an early multi-use pocket knife complete with corkscrew. One of the binoculars was made of gold and ivory, presented to him during his visit to London in 1864; a pair of crutches had silver handles. Three wheelchairs were a reminder of how he was severely afflicted by arthritis for many decades. Best of all, maybe, there was Garibaldi's own red shirt and his famous poncho.

Museums all across Italy have a strict unwritten rule that you must follow the *Percorso*, the prescribed route, indicated by a blizzard of arrows. Plenty of officious staff are there to make sure you do, and they pass stern words and a withering look when you don't. The route here took in bedrooms, the kitchen, the antiques room, and a final one called 'The Room Where Garibaldi Died'. Time has been suspended ever since. All the clocks were stopped at the exact moment, six o'clock in the afternoon, and the calendar left on the date, 2 June 1882.

The burning sentiment Garibaldi kept in his heart for Nizza was revealed by the lay-out of the room. His bed was positioned so he could look out of the window in the direction of the city where he was born. It was now covered in a glass case for protection, encircled by bronze railings donated by the Veteran's Society of Livorno. In the corner of the room was a large wooden medicine chest with glass doors, and inside more than a hundred bottles of potions and lotions. All were made from herbs grown in the garden and from plants found on the hills of Caprera. The room had white walls and a white ceiling, wooden doors, and tiled red floors. There was a desk, a wheelchair, a piano in another corner. Three paintings of Garibaldi hung on the walls. It was clearly maintained with tender loving care, but there was a robust enthusiasm in the firm closing of the big door to the garden by museum staff as we visitors wandered out. No lingering another twenty minutes for small talk here, which is usually the gregarious Italian way of things.

From the terrace there was a panoramic view across the islands of the archipelago, and next to it a large stone statue of Garibaldi, just the head and body, arms crossed, an old man depicted deep in thought – or just plain exhausted after a lifetime of adventures. Next to the statue I saw an abandoned shell of a windmill, built by Garibaldi, and once in use like the oil press when the house was also a working farm. Beside this was a flagpole with an Italian tricolour waving in the breeze. All around were olive trees, cacti and mirto bushes. Geckos and lizards darted across the ground as I walked 200 metres in burning sunshine down a wavy stone path to a little gate. Through this I found the tomb of Giuseppe Garibaldi, lying alongside a few others of his family under the shade of ubiquitous pine trees. In the gentle breeze, the silence was broken only by birdsong.

As I was leaving a party of schoolchildren arrived, tumbling out of their bus in a burst of delight, no doubt after many lessons about the importance and courage of Garibaldi. The white house remains a vital place to visit now, as it was back in the 1860s and 1870s when politicians, thinkers and generals flocked to visit him at home on Caprera. Among them were the Russian revolutionary anarchist Mikhail Bakunin and the writer Alexandre Dumas, author of *The Three Musketeers*.

The house was three kilometres from the rough and ready road bridge which now links Caprera to La Maddalena. There were concrete slabs planted at odd angles on the side of the road, the only barrier between vehicles, cyclists, walkers and the water. There was no bridge in Garibaldi's time, back then you arrived by boat, moored at the bottom of the hill from the Casa Bianca. Now, there was one dusty, stony track down to the sea, but the area was mostly fenced off as a military zone.

Far more rewarding was a journey the other way, along the track to the top of the hill where an old fort had been transformed into a Garibaldi museum. Well, actually, I should rephrase that. This was *the* Garibaldi Museum, the only one entirely dedicated to his life and times. The story was told in vivid detail, celebrating above all his relentless bravery in battle through almost five decades of fighting, as well as his endless thirst for adventure evident in his sailing to every corner of the globe, from Australia to Peru to Russia. This courage can't be faked; this sense of adventure can't be invented as myth. Garibaldi revelled in them.

This was a wonderful museum located in a hopeless place, inaccessible to all but the most dedicated visitor. It's impossible for buses to take tours up the narrow stony track that leads there. On the road I passed a few cars, but they were mostly parked for access to paths down to the glorious beaches nearby. The fort was built to be impregnable. It feels as if it still is. But I don't want to deter anyone. This was a jewel, not least the 360 degree-view across the archipelago. From here I could truly understand the scale of these islands, their beauty, and their maritime advantage. Lord Nelson based his Royal Navy fleet in the waters of La Maddalena from 1803 to monitor the activity of Napoleon's ships and described it as 'the most beautiful port in the world'. It was from here that he sailed to the Battle of Trafalgar. A pair of silver candelabra given by Nelson to the parish are still on display in the town's main church.

The fort was only converted into a museum in 2012, and the modern displays made it livelier than most. The isolation meant I was never in danger of being crowded out as I wandered around. On the walls were observations about Garibaldi from writers and historians. Dumas said: 'He has blond hair, blue eyes, a Greek forehead nose and chin, and comes as close as possible to resembling the authentic type of beauty of Jesus in the painting of The Last Supper by Leonardo Da Vinci.' It was completely over the top, of course, but accurately reflected the idolisation of Garibaldi during his life.

Another exhibit was a delight for anyone like me who used to collect Panini football stickers as a child. It was a stickers album dedicated to the history of Italy, with Garibaldi the main figure on the front cover, flanked by Da Vinci and Christopher Columbus. These albums were on sale from 1978 to 1980 and are rare collectors' items now.

After two museums on a hot day, it was time for a rest. I did what the vast majority of Italians do when a fierce sun shines – I went to the beach. After parking on the way down the hill I had to clamber like a goat along narrow undulating paths and shrug past barricades of spikey shrubs and bushes to reach an almost deserted beach and dash into the water to cool down. This was one of hundreds of little beaches on the archipelago, and so isolated that the look on the face of the few other people there was: 'Oh wow, you made it, too.' There was a Garibaldi beach on Caprera, but only a handful of people bothered to sunbathe there. The sand and the waters are more enticing elsewhere on these islands, particularly on La Maddalena itself. These can become crowded, however, as people trek to see the incredible stones and rocks which have been sculpted by wind and rain and sea to resemble all kinds of animal shapes. Among them you can find the Rabbit Rock, the Eagle's Beak Rock, the Dinosaur Rock, the Poodle Rock and the Cobra Rock. Best of all is the stunning cove of *Spiaggia La Testa Del Polpo* – the Octopus Head beach.

There was no seaside infrastructure here, these were what Italians call *Spiaggia Libera* (free beaches) where you just find a space, put your towel down, and eat and drink what you bring. They are known as free beaches because so many across this country are not. Vast swathes of wide sands on every stretch of coastline can only be accessed if you pay for them, hiring a sunbed and an umbrella. In the smartest spots this can cost 100 euros for a couple. These are called *stabilimento* and will have at least one rudimentary shower and, far more importantly, very often an excellent bar or restaurant. Foreigners often find them daunting, if not intimidating, but they are beloved in Italy by people of all social status. Families and friends will go to the same *stabilimento* year in year out for their summer holidays or weekend trips.

Beach culture is a window into Italian society like no other. There is no inhibition and no reserve about swimwear of the kind you see in Britain, where newspaper articles ask: 'Can you wear a bikini over the age of thirty?' When I tell people in Italy about this it prompts incredulity and then dismay. It's a nonsense question. Women of all ages, all body shapes and all social backgrounds put on bikinis without a second thought. Men don their shorts or trunks without a trace of anxiety, too. What else would you do on the beach when you want to swim and tan? It is the uniform of the beach rather than a fashion statement, and this is true whether you're rich or poor. There is an engaging and boisterous equality of life at the seaside across Italy, whether it's a *stabilimento*, a free beach, or a wooden platform by the water in a town.

I've seen Francesco Totti, an idolised World Cup winning footballer, kicking a ball around with his kids on the nature reserve beach at Sabaudia south of Rome without being pestered, just another dad at play. On the wild beach of Feniglia in Tuscany people build giant wigwams with driftwood to make shelters. I've been to the remote beach of Tindari in northern Sicily, a mile-long strip of sand jutting out into the sea with no natural shelter and no services, where suddenly everyone is running to the water's edge because the ice cream boat has arrived with supplies. And the two ice cream sellers on the boat are wearing the smallest pair of budgie-smuggler swimming trunks you have ever seen.

There is a delightful *stabilimento* in Calabria where a bottle of beer costs just one euro and a huge pizza only three euros and the sea was clean and just the right side of cool, and life seemed perfect for a few hours at least. I've seen a middle-aged couple walking along the beach in Puglia conducting the noisiest and most ferocious public argument you are ever likely to hear, stopping every few seconds to berate each other, then stomping on, hands and arms waving like windmills in a hurricane, unaware or uncaring that hundreds of people were watching transfixed by the spectacle. An hour later everybody noticed as the pair, some yards apart, marched back the other way in sullen silence.

I've seen the glory, too, of the Octopus Head cove on La Maddalena, and I won't argue with those who believe Sardinia has the finest beaches in all of Italy. Certainly, it's easy to understand why Garibaldi fell in love with the area when he first visited in 1849 after the fall of the *Repubblica Romana* and his escape from Ravenna. He had been sent to Tunisia, but the local authorities there refused to allow him to land and the ship was turned away. It was captained by Francesco Mille, who came from La Maddalena. So, too, did Leggero, the trusty lieutenant who had remained with Garibaldi after the death of Anita, and to La Maddalena they sailed while the future destination of the Hero of Two Worlds was decided. This would be a second period of exile on the other side of the Atlantic.

Garibaldi stayed for a month on La Maddalena, working in the fields with the local farmers, and one day diving into the sea to save three men and a boy from drowning when their boat turned over, which is commemorated by a plaque on the wall of a house in the Barabo district. When he left, Garibaldi wrote to the people of the town to thank them for their hospitality, and in the town hall there is another plaque displaying a copy of the letter.

Statues? Of course there were statues. In the largest square there was a monument dedicated to Anita, and in one corner a statue of Leggero, the local legend. In another area of the port stood a Garibaldi Column, while you could not miss the essential Via Garibaldi which ran into Piazza Garibaldi. This was an intimate square in the heart of the town close to where the ferry docks, full of busy bars and a church where children constantly played football outside. On the northern side there was a curved stone bench for people to sit on, but with one permanent occupant. It was a bronze statue of Garibaldi at rest, created in 2011 to celebrate 150 years of Italian unity. He sat with a hat in his lap and an arm leant on a walking stick and, in contrast to so many other statues of him, Garibaldi was depicted here as an ordinary man of the town rather than a hero. A small scarf was round his neck, which is very modern Italian. A seemingly never-ending line of people queued up to have their photo taken sitting alongside him, and I took my turn. The scene was far busier than the church, even on the Sunday morning I was there, and Garibaldi would have liked that. According to local superstition, it's a good luck charm to touch the statue on the bench. Across the square an old tramp was sitting in a doorway, sporting a long white beard and bearing a passable if tatty resemblance to Garibaldi. It was not a coincidence; he told me he makes more money that way.

The people have always loved Garibaldi. The authorities were seldom so keen. In 1849 they insisted he leave La Maddalena, and for seven months he lived in Tangier in northern Morocco – walking, shooting, riding and fishing, but mostly grieving for Anita. He was a dejected man, the dream of liberating Italy crushed and so many friends and colleagues killed in battle. He considered other places to stay in exile, but he was refused permission to live in Spain and decided against a return to Montevideo or joining Mazzini and other Italian political refugees living in London. Instead, after a four-day stop at Liverpool, he took a transatlantic steamship to New York. The few quiet days lodged at the Waterloo Hotel in Liverpool was the first time he set foot in England. The building is still there today, re-named the Royal Hotel. Garibaldi had wanted to remain anonymous but went shopping in the city and the *Liverpool Mail* newspaper was alerted. 'His manners are pleasing and lively, but in general his demeanour is staid and grave,' was their description.

He arrived at Staten Island in July 1850 and had to be carried off the ship 'like a bale of goods' because his rheumatism had flared up badly crossing the ocean. Garibaldi's fame had gone before him, and the New York mayor and the city's large Italian community wanted to honour him with a civic reception and big banquet. Garibaldi resisted the idea, partly due to his natural humility, but mostly because he felt he had arrived as a failure rather than a champion.

Slowly, his spirits revived, in large part thanks to his friendship with Antonio Meucci, an Italian inventor, a strong supporter of Italian unification, and a small-time entrepreneur then running a candle factory. Garibaldi lived with the Meucci family in their home on Staten Island, and worked for many months as a candlemaker as well as doing the heavy lifting duties of carrying barrels of tallow from dockside to the factory. In a letter to his children back in Nice, he wrote: 'We make very fine candles. I spend my time threading wicks and kneading tallow.' On display in the white house in Caprera there is a box of red, white and green candles, the colours of the Italian flag, made by Garibaldi. Nobody is minded to doubt their authenticity.

The house on Staten Island is now the Garibaldi-Meucci Museum, and more interesting for the story of its owner. Everyone in Italy will tell you that Meucci was the true inventor of the telephone, the man who first created a working 'voice communication apparatus' in 1849 – when Alexander Graham Bell was just two years old. Meucci, though, did not have the finances to make his telephone a commercial product, and when he finally lodged a patent in 1871 it was worded poorly. Five years later, Bell was granted a patent for the 'telephone'. Historians have debated ever since as to who invented the machine that so changed the world.

Garibaldi spent his spare time in New York playing bowls and dominoes, but he was thoroughly bored. Work as a candlemaker was dreary, and he longed to go back to sea; the life he knew best. He sailed on trips first to Panama and Cuba, and then with an old friend, Francesco Carpaneto, on a business trip to Callao, which is the port for Lima, the capital of Peru, and where today there is a Plaza Garibaldi close to the docks. Garibaldi, back in his old haven of South America, now took command of a boat called *Carmen* and spent two years on the oceans as a merchant seaman. Peru had a monopoly on guano, used as fertilizer, and back in the early 1850s there was a huge trade in the product. Garibaldi took guano to China on a 93-day voyage across the Pacific Ocean, sailing close to Hawaii. Following that he went on to the Philippines and then took the southern route back, sailing around Australia, close to Melbourne and Tasmania, and through the central straits of New Zealand.

In these years Garibaldi visited every continent in the world – Europe, Africa, North and South America, Asia and Australasia– except Antarctica. It is one of the least known elements of his life story in his native Italy, but to my mind one of the most fascinating. This is Garibaldi in the rich tradition of Italian travellers from Christopher Columbus and Marco Polo to Amerigo Vespucci and Giovanni Caboto, better known in the English-speaking world as John Cabot.

Garibaldi was at sea for more than two years. He sailed round Cape Horn with a cargo of copper picked up in Chile and delivered to Boston. This took him back to the Meucci home in New York, where in early 1854 news came of change in the Piedmont/Sardinia government in Turin that would allow Garibaldi to return from exile. He was more than ready. In a letter to a friend, Augusto Vecchi, he revealed that despite the thrill of ocean life he craved more than ever the fight for Italy. He wrote: 'I thought distance could diminish the bitterness of my soul, but unfortunately it is not true. I have led an unhappy life, restless and embittered by memory. I am thirsty for the emancipation of our country.'

England was the first staging post on another cargo boat, and the initial port of call was London, where he stayed for a month talking with the many Italian radicals and patriots who had been forced to flee their country. These included Mazzini and Sir Anthony Panizzi, an Italian exile who became head of the British Museum library, and the conversations allowed Garibaldi to gain a greater appreciation of the situation at home, and to understand the time was not yet ripe for another attempt at unifying Italy.

This was when Garibaldi proposed marriage to a wealthy and erudite English widow, Mrs Emma Roberts, who lived in Arlington Street, just off Piccadilly. She accepted, and they were officially engaged. Mrs Roberts was well connected, her home was the venue for many meetings of exiled Europeans, so it was natural that Garibaldi gravitated there during his stay. It seems an unlikely romance in retrospect, but throughout his life Garibaldi was strongly attractive to women, and they to him. Emma Roberts was the first of many rich women to fall for him during the following decade, and although their relationship was strong, a wedding never materialised. One reason, which seems too simplistic, is that Garibaldi disliked the long dinners and being fussed over by her servants. Much more likely is the fierce opposition to their romance from her eldest son.

Nevertheless, she went on trips with Garibaldi to Nice and Sardinia, and she took his son Ricciotti back to London to see specialist doctors for a leg ailment and paid for him to go to boarding school in Liverpool. Mrs Roberts made these trips with a young companion Jesse White, who later married an Italian activist Alberto Mario and became deeply engaged in the Risorgimento. As Jesse White Mario she worked as a nurse tending Garibaldi's soldiers in four separate battles, and she also wrote extensively, including a biography of Garibaldi.

Next stop on the trip was Newcastle, on the north-east coast of England, where the boat would pick up coal bound for Genoa. His fame was still very much alive and Garibaldi was offered a public reception to acknowledge his arrival. Once again, he declined, although he did receive a delegation of local coalminers who presented him with a sword and a telescope paid for by donations from more than a thousand working men. The sword cost four pounds, ten shillings. Speaking in reasonably fluent English, acquired during his time in New York, he told them: 'Should England at any time in a just cause need my arm, I am ready to unsheathe in her defence this noble and splendid sword received at your hands.' There is a curious postscript to this. The sword was used in battle nearly half a century later by one of Garibaldi's grandsons, Peppino, during the Boer War – but against the British army rather than in defence of England.

The short visit to Newcastle is remembered by a blue plaque that can be found in a quiet street in Tynemouth on the coast east of the city. He lodged there for some days at a house in Huntingdon Place. The plaque describes Garibaldi as 'a sailor/soldier' and reads: 'He was hailed throughout Europe as a true idealist and an honest politician.'

A few months were then spent in Nice, still Nizza at this juncture, allowing Garibaldi to spend time with his children. When his brother Felice died in the autumn of 1855, Garibaldi inherited a sum of money substantial enough to consider buying a house of his own. He had dreamed of somewhere in northern Sardinia following his stay there six years earlier, and by the end of 1855 he had decided on Caprera. Most of the island was owned by an English couple, Richard and Claire Collins, who were often absent, and they agreed to sell the northern half to Garibaldi for £360. It was wild and rugged, populated mostly with wind-bent olive trees and by the goats who give the island its name – goat in Italian is 'capra'. Garibaldi, his eldest son Menotti, and some friends slept in tents at first while they constructed a small wooden house. At this point he still considered himself a sailor, and Mrs Roberts bought him a boat which he named *Emma*, and began trading around the islands.

One night the ship was destroyed in a storm, and Garibaldi decided to instead put his energies into creating a farm on his new land. A windmill was built, and then the Casa Bianca, copying the style of South American farmhouses. He acquired his own goats, a few sheep, some donkeys and five cows. Even in this barren landscape he also had success growing vines, beans, chestnuts, potatoes, figs and sugar cane. The peaceful isolation of farming his land melted away, though, when a boat appeared on the waters around La Maddalena and Caprera in late 1858. It had been sent by the government of Piedmont/Sardinia to bring Garibaldi back to the mainland and join the preparations for battle against the formidable Austrian army in what became known as the Second War of Italian Independence.

7

COMO/MILAN

'Garibaldi allowed himself to be swayed by every vanity: the old partisan found it quite normal that a young girl of seventeen should be madly in love with him.'

Horace de Viel-Castel

Market day in the small village high in the verdant hills above Lake Como was typical of so many across Italy. There were stalls selling the local produce of autumn, chestnuts, mushrooms and pumpkins along with the staples of salami, ham, honey and taleggio cheese. There was a hum of conversation in the air, recipes and storage hints offered with every transaction. I was told that soaking chestnuts in water overnight keeps them fresh if you can't eat them immediately, and it was fine advice. Everything was conducted at an unhurried pace – a weekly ritual that epitomises the conservative nature of rural Italy. The produce is always seasonal, brought in from nearby fields. There is no need for a zero kilometre food revolution here. And you never eat strawberries in autumn or winter. Even to suggest the notion will prompt a withering look of disdain.

The market stalls were set out in the main square of the village, surrounding and almost obscuring a memorial obelisk. A sanctuary with an impressive bell tower stood silent and closed on one edge, while the local bar was packed full on the other side. This was San Fermo di Battaglia, the name of the village indicating its importance in the story of Giuseppe Garibaldi. It may be a tranquil spot now in one of the richest areas of Italy, but in May 1859 it was a battleground where he won an important victory against the Austrian army during the Second War of Italian Independence. It is a place, like so many up and down the country, which proudly celebrates its role in the creation of modern Italy. The memorial is dedicated to those who died in the battle, and directly to Garibaldi himself – 'To the brave, and the leader of the brave.'

San Fermo di Battaglia invites you to take *Il Percorso Garibaldi* the Garibaldi path – following the key locations of the fighting and then the march of his volunteer army down into the city of Como below. But where was it? I stopped for a coffee to ask at the bar, but the waitress had no idea. I wandered around the market, probably looking more than a little lost, and an old man approached, asking if I needed some help. There was sheer delight on his face when I said was looking for the *Percorso*, and he talked for half an hour with great knowledge before pointing to one of seven sign boards of the path. It was just twenty metres away.

Starting the *Percorso* at No. 1 seemed logical, but to reach it I had to walk along a busy main road and round a sharp uphill bend with no pavement as cars whizzed by, hooting at the stupid pedestrian who dared to be on the tarmac. Eventually, there was the sanctuary of a bus stop, and here was the start of the Garibaldi trail. Why? Well, that's because this where people get off the bus when they arrive in San Fermo di Battaglia, and this was also the route of Garibaldi's men into the fighting.

The No. 2 spot was just as risky, placed on the side of the road on the bend, with barely space to stand and read about two of the heroes of the battle of San Fermo. No. 3 was also in a tricky spot, but worth the effort. This is the resting place of two Garibaldini who died in the battle, including General Carlo De Cristoforis, a soldier from Milan who led the assault against the Austrian defensive position in the Bell Tower of the main square. He had been involved in the Five-Day revolution of Milan in 1848 and also fought alongside Garibaldi in defence of the *Repubblica Romana* in 1849 on the Gianicolo hill in Rome.

Maybe No. 4 had been deemed too dangerous, because it had vanished. No. 5 honoured another victim, and No. 6 was in the main square, the epicentre of the battle where the Austrians were driven out of the Sanctuary and the Bell Tower, and thus out of the strategic stronghold of Como itself. The old man I met in the square told me the village staged a re-enactment every few years, with muskets and cannons firing up and down the main road, flanked by soldiers and horsemen in costume. I watched TV clips of the most recent event, staged on the 165th anniversary of the battle. Just as at Cesenatico, there was a Garibaldi lookalike, riding a horse along the road with his volunteer army. He was by the No. 3 signpost in the TV pictures. A crowd of thousands were watching from the main square. My visit was a few months too late.

Finally, there was the No. 7 signpost: 'The triumphal entry of Garibaldi into Como.' This was where he left the village and headed down the hill into the city vacated by the Austrians. This road was their Via Garibaldi, a winding lane that was the last and long stretch of the *Percorso*. It was an incredibly beautiful walk that took the best part of an hour, especially with stops to take in the spectacular views across Lake Como. Even on a cloudy day it was fabulous, a moody scene with the hills on other side of the lake shrouded in mist. The shores of Lake Como are studded with grand houses, some owned by celebrities such as George Clooney and Richard Branson. It also entices the most famous visitors, from Taylor Swift to Brad Pitt and Mick Jagger and has become one of the most exclusive and expensive places in the world.

Garibaldi's arrival was celebrated by the people of Como as they shouted '*Viva Italia*' when his men marched in. He stayed for just one night before moving on to chase the Austrians across the plains of Lombardy. The place was marked by a plaque on the front of what is now a restaurant in a fine square in central Como, one dominated by a statue of the city's favourite son, Alessandro Volta, the scientist who invented the electric battery and discovered methane. '*In questa casa*' the plaque began – 'in this house' – and sometimes it can seem as if Garibaldi slept in every house in the land.

Como also has a particular place in the life of Garibaldi because it is where he was married for the second time, but then walked out on his bride less than an hour after the wedding service. This unedifying episode was mostly neglected at the time, and it still is. Many people I have spoken to knew nothing of this story, nor about Garibaldi's endless amorous escapades.

His attitude to women and sexual affairs was moulded as a young man by the influence of Saint-Simonian philosophy, and especially its espousal of free love, that he had encountered as a young man sailing to Constantinople a quarter of a century earlier. He was never shackled by convention, and the year of 1859 illustrated this in startling fashion. Although he was still loosely engaged to Emma Roberts, the English widow, this relationship was never heading to marriage and the idea was quietly abandoned. Ten years on from the death of Anita, the only true love of his life, Garibaldi was desperate for a second wife while having a string of lovers.

In May 1859, the same month as the battle of San Fermo, his maidservant Battistina Ravello give birth at Caprera to a daughter they named Anita, a name clearly chosen by the father. Garibaldi did not want to marry her, though in his memoirs he wrote that he wondered if he should have done so out of duty. Instead, aged fifty-two, he proposed marriage to three other women in quick succession, starting in August 1859 with Maria Esperanza, Baroness Von Schwartz, who had visited him at Caprera, ostensibly to procure the German translation rights for his first memoir. She was twenty-six-years old, a wealthy travel-writer and romantic novelist, already divorced from a second husband after the first had committed suicide. The Baroness and Garibaldi swiftly became lovers, but she stalled on commitment to another marriage.

Two months later, in Bologna, there was a liaison with Marchesa Paulina Zucchini, a young widow who was the granddaughter of King Joachim Murat of Naples. She gently refused the prospect of engagement to the old general. Through this period Garibaldi was also writing love letters to Teresa

Araldi Trecchi, the sister of one of his volunteer soldiers, and to Sofia Bettini, whom he had encountered during his time in New York. There was an enduring close friendship with Maria della Torre, a Piedmontese countess he first met in London in 1854 and corresponded with throughout his life.

That was at least seven different women in his life in 1859, and none of them was the girl he did persuade to the altar. She was Guiseppina Raimondi, a seventeen-year-old marchioness, whom he first encountered just outside Como in June 1859 during the campaign against the Austrian army. She had been sent as a courier with a message for Garibaldi about the movements of enemy soldiers and the possibility that Como might be recaptured by the Austrians; the idea being that nobody would suspect a young girl as a messenger. Garibaldi was impressed by her courage and good looks and, once again, was immediately infatuated. He went back to the city, established a headquarters in a hotel on the lakeside (now the Villa Olmo exhibition palace), and there began to woo Giuseppina, writing a stream of love letters, even while proposing marriage to others.

Confusion and loneliness would be a kind way of assessing Garibaldi's motivations. Desperation and cynicism might be more accurate. He went to the town of Fino Mornasco, eight kilometres south of Como, where Giuseppina's father, the Marquis Raimondi, owned a villa. The Marquis was an ardent supporter of Garibaldi, and positive about the prospect of the General marrying his daughter. This time the proposal was accepted. She was now eighteen years old and, unknown to Garibaldi, having affairs with two other soldiers much closer to her own age. News of the engagement was mostly hidden from the public at the time, but gossip was rife, as shown by a diary entry recorded by Horace de Viel-Castel, an author and a director of the Louvre. He wrote: 'Garibaldi, although a republican hero, allowed himself to be swayed by every vanity: the old partisan found it quite normal that a young girl of seventeen should be madly in love with him.'

They were married on 24 January 1860 in the private chapel of the Villa Raimondi at Fino. Accounts from the time say that Garibaldi looked serene walking out of the ceremony until he was handed a piece of paper by a young soldier, a spurned lover of Giuseppina. It said she was having an affair with another young soldier and was pregnant. Garibaldi responded with rage, perhaps sensing he was on the brink of humiliation, calling her a whore and threatening her with a chair. She responded by telling him she had thought Garibaldi was a hero, but now realised he was 'just another brutal soldier'.

Until recently you could visit the chapel where all this occurred. But the villa has been converted into a series of exclusive apartments and the place is now strictly private. The gates remained firmly shut when I visited. Garibaldi retreated to Villa Flori, a magnificent house on the shores of Lake Como also owned by the Marquis Raimondi, with whom he surprisingly remained friendly, and he lodged there for a few nights, nursing his wounded pride. The building is now a four-star hotel, trading on this slice of history. You can stay, if you so desire, in the Garibaldi Junior Suite, with a balcony overlooking the lake, although it will cost you around 950 euros a night for the privilege. You can also dine in the Raimondi restaurant, recently refurbished in nineteenth-century style that deliberately evokes the memory of 1860.

This is the elegant glamour of Como nowadays, but I gave it a miss. The views across the lake cost nothing and last a lifetime.

There was, of course, an imposing statue of Garibaldi in the city. He was standing high on a large plinth, dressed in a cape, with a sword in his right hand ready for action. A stone wreath lay underneath, donated by the students of Como on 27 May 1889 – exactly forty years after the battle of San Fermo. The statue was surrounded by students the days I was there, but they were merely waiting at the nearby bus stop, oblivious to the old partisan watching over them.

Garibaldi's reputation survived and soon flourished. Giuseppina was less fortunate. She gave birth to a still-born child seven months later and was spurned by both the young lovers as well as Garibaldi. When she tried to visit him in Caprera he refused to see her. They were eventually divorced in 1879, and she then remarried. Shortly before she died in 1918, she gave the love letters sent to her by Garibaldi to the State Archives in Mantova. It is a sorry tale sharply at odds with the legend of the great national hero, which is probably why most Italians prefer it to remain in the shadows of history.

The battle of San Fermo and the first meeting with Giuseppina occurred during the Second War of Italian Independence in the summer of 1859. Garibaldi's involvement began with the boat sent to Caprera in December 1858 by Camillo Cavour, prime minister of Piedmont/Sardinia, for a meeting in Turin. They discussed plans hatched with Napoleon III for a war against Austria, which then ruled over large swathes of northern Italy, including Milan, Como and Verona. Garibaldi was asked if he would be willing to train a regiment of volunteers to fight in this conflict as a guerrilla force, exactly his forte, and he accepted the task with enthusiasm. They would become known as the *Cacciatore D'Alpi* – the Hunters of the Alps, and Garibaldi immediately travelled to Genoa to begin his planning. He met the composer Luigi Mercantini and asked him to write a war song to inspire his volunteers on the battlefield. Thus came into being the Garibaldi Hymn, sung not only throughout Italy but also in London and New York. The first verse was:

> The tombs are uncovered, the dead come from afar;
> The ghosts of our martyrs are rising to war,
> With swords in their hands and with laurels of fame;
> And dead hearts glowing with Italy's name;
> Come join them, come follow, O youth of our land;
> Come fling out our banner and marshal our band;
> Come all with cold steel, and come all with hot fire;
> Come all with the flame of Italia's desire;
> Be gone from Italia, be gone from our home;
> Go from Italia, go from Italia, O stranger be gone.

Enthusiasm for the war was first stirred by the creation in 1857 of the Italian National Society, with Garibaldi installed as its vice-president. Another strong supporter was an even more famous composer, Giuseppe Verdi, although the organisation was mostly orchestrated by Cavour, the prince of machinations. If Garibaldi was the warrior architect of modern Italy, and Giuseppe Mazzini its intellectual inspiration, then Cavour was the political genius. The three of them were poles apart in personal relationships, but each played a vital role in the unification of Italy. Garibaldi was wary of Cavour and his scheming methods, but he also felt these were of more practical use than Mazzini's intransigent republican idealism. Cavour and Mazzini in turn were worried about Garibaldi's emotional and instinctive nature, but knew he was too popular to ignore. Napoleon III of France shared this dilemma; he didn't want Garibaldi at the centre of the action but also agreed it would be dangerously counter-productive to exclude him completely.

So, in May 1859, Garibaldi's force of 3,000 men, his Hunters of the Alps, attacked the Austrians on the northern flank near the lakes and the Swiss border. The hilly terrain was suited to their guerrilla tactics, and they won a first battle at the town of Varese, with Garibaldi's old sidekick Nino Bixio and his eighteen-year-old son Menotti among the volunteers. This was a morale-boosting victory for the people of the area, and a rapturous moment for Garibaldi, whose last action in Italy ten years earlier had been fleeing from the Austrian soldiers at Cesenatico with a dying Anita. This was swiftly followed up with the glory of San Fermo that allowed the capture of Como, and the successes served to increase his popularity, including with Napoleon III. When the French troops defeated the Austrian army at Magenta, he allowed Garibaldi's men to march east through Bergamo and Brescia. It was a spectacular personal triumph for Garibaldi, and he was awarded the gold medal for valour.

The war ended soon afterwards, following the carnage of the Battle of Solferino just south of Lake Garda. It was won by the combination of Piedmont/Sardinian and French forces, but the casualties were catastrophic. The Austrians lost 22,000 men, the French nearly 12,000 and Piedmont/Sardinia 5,500. Many of the wounded lay untended on the battlefield under a fierce sun for three days because of the almost non-existent medical services. The horror led directly to the foundation a few years later of the International Red Cross – and it persuaded both sides to sign a peace treaty.

Garibaldi agreed with this decision, but it stalled the momentum which had been growing for independence. His prestige was now unrivalled, and he became president of the Italian National Society, touring many cities to speak for the cause of unifying Italy and driving out the foreigners. There were large crowds in Milan, Bologna, Florence and Ravenna desperate to get a glimpse of the charismatic hero and listen to his fiery words. He also made a return trip to the farmhouse at Mandriole where Anita died, and to visit her grave. Alongside all this was the frantic complexity of his private life – the affairs, the marriage proposals, the endless love letters. He was forever attracted to women, and throughout his life they were attracted to him. He was what the Italians call, mostly with admiration, a *sciupafemmine*. There is no direct translation of the word, the nearest in English might be 'ladykiller', but no English word or phrase would prompt the laughter that *sciupafemmine* delivers.

It's clear enough that the fame of Garibaldi is one reason for women being attracted to him. Celebrity has forever been an aphrodisiac. His natural humility as a character when people encountered him is widely acknowledged to be another. There was also the way he dressed. Garibaldi understood the immense value of cutting a compelling figure, of showing a unique, bravura style. This fascinated not only women, but also the vast crowds who heard his speeches. The poncho was his trademark, along with dashing capes and hats, as well as the red shirts of battle and the jeans. It was a deliberate ploy. With his colourful gaucho style he would be recognised instantly, he would never be ignored and never forgotten. The panache was integral to his vast influence on the people of the Italian peninsula and beyond. It is an influence that has continued long after his life, for example in the 1960s spaghetti westerns of the film director Sergio Leone. A book that accompanied an exhibition in the Risorgimento museum of Turin in 2003 makes the connection:

> The classic iconography of Garibaldi has him wearing a poncho, holding a pistol and sometimes smoking a cigar. It seems that Leone studied this deeply Italian, and at the same time stateless look, and applied it to the figure of the gunman without a name played by Clint Eastwood in the film *For a Few Dollars More*.

The similarities in style are apparent, and Leone was an Italian born in 1909 who would have grown up on the legend of Garibaldi – and who in the early 1980s made plans for a major television series on the Hero of Two Worlds which was eventually abandoned as too expensive to produce as he wished. Leone also knew the ultimate importance of 'the look'.

It is a very Italian trait. The people of Italy are not fashion victims, they are fashion makers. Wearing stylish clothes, owning a look, is a fundamental part of the way of life, symbolised by the phrase: *fare la bella figura*. This can be loosely translated as 'to make a good impression,' but there is much more to it than that. It's about always looking good, it's about keeping up appearances, it's about elegance, individuality, respect, confidence and deception. It's about following the unofficial rules, too. I soon discovered that short-sleeved shirts invite ridicule. It must be a polo shirt, and preferably the Lacoste brand with the crocodile logo, or a long-sleeved shirt with the cuffs rolled up twice, and only twice – and absolutely never rolled up over the elbow. Its's amazing how many Italian men follow this style whatever their status, wherever they live. It's as natural to them as eating spaghetti.

Clothing is only one element in making a good impression. Statistics show that cosmetic surgery is far more popular in Italy than other major Western nations, 400 per cent higher than in the United Kingdom, for example. It seems to me there are also far fewer elderly ladies with grey or white hair in Italy than anywhere else on earth, and this in a country with one of the longest life expectancies. They may not be so young, but they can still show off, still show style, still give old father time a run for his money. Perhaps there is a wider cultural aspect too. John Hooper, a distinguished British foreign correspondent based in Italy for many years, wrote that: 'The *bella figura* mentality also points to a deep-seated insecurity that echoes the historic vulnerability and fragile sense of national identity.' According to this view, showing off is perhaps about hiding problems; or it could be seen more sympathetically as an expression of the spirit of the Risorgimento.

Whatever inspires *la bella figura*, I couldn't miss it walking round the streets of Como, and certainly not when I made the short journey from there to Milan some thirty miles south in search of perhaps the most famous of all Garibaldi's ponchos. A carnival of fashion brands are based in Milan – Prada, Gucci, Dolce & Gabbana, Armani, Versace, Valentino, Zegna, Moschino and Missoni all have their headquarters in the city. The fashion hub is Via Montenapoleone, an unremarkable looking road at first sight, but which in 2024 had overtaken New York's Fifth Avenue as the most expensive shopping street in the world. I had to take a look, and strolling along it was like being in the middle of a catwalk. This was not merely about razor-sharp suits. Every other person, it seemed, was wearing outlandish or cutting-edge designs, the kind you see at a glitzy fashion show but never actually worn on the streets. Here they were. At the end of Via Montenapoleone I crossed over to Via Borgonuovo and the catwalk continued its astonishing parade. On this road there were also giant Italian flags hanging from several buildings, the largest of them outside my destination, the Museo Del Risorgimento of Milan.

Naturally, some of the prize exhibits on display were Italian fashion icons, particularly the poncho Garibaldi wore when fighting his way into Palermo during the Expedition of The Thousand in May 1860 – a 'double face' poncho, grey on one side and red on the other. There was his grey bowler hat and his red shirt uniform. Pride of place was given to the first ever Italian tricolour flag, tatty but priceless, and an English language Bible, a present to Garibaldi from a group of English women on his famous visit to London in 1864. And then, spookily, planted below the Bible and the poncho, was a plaster cast of Garibaldi's right hand, painted red – with no explanation of how, when or why.

This museum was notable, too, for the quality of the paintings which tell the story of the Risorgimento. Many were by the Milanese artist Gerolamo Induno, who was a soldier as well as a painter. He took part in the Five-Day revolution in Milan in 1848 and fought alongside Garibaldi in the 1849 defence of Rome, where he was severely injured, suffering twenty bayonet wounds leading a charge. He was also one of the volunteers at the 1859 battle of San Fermo.

It was Induno's painting of Garibaldi planting the Italian flag at Marsala which was copied in the jeans painting I had seen in the Genoa museum, and which is the most well-known. The finest piece here in the Milan museum was his painting of Garibaldi on a horse at Gianicolo looking over the devastation caused in Rome by the battles against the French. Another historic painting, this one not by Induno, captured the scene in Taganrog in Russia where a youthful Garibaldi first encountered the Young Italy movement, the inspiration for all his subsequent fighting to unify the country. Most moving of all was a depiction of Garibaldi carrying a dying Anita through the reeds of Lake Comacchio.

After the museum I took a stroll along Corso Garibaldi, a trendy avenue full of bars, restaurants and designer stores. Amid the bright lights and classy window displays I noticed a slightly decrepit arch that was the entrance to the old Teatro Fossati, and above it the life-size stone figure of Giuseppe Garibaldi waving to the crowds of the city. There was no nametag, no inscription, but it was unmistakably him. This is the forgotten statue of Garibaldi in Milan – and above him the statue of a woman, again with no dedication. A little research told me this was supposed to be Anita, carved in red granite, not that anyone passing by would know. The one and only website I found with any information said these statues were put up in the 70s, but whether that was the 1870s or the 1970s they didn't specify. Corso Garibaldi leads up to Porta Garibaldi, one of the gateways into the city, this one on the road in from Como. It was built in the 1820s (definitely) to honour the city's then ruler Francis I of Austria, but was re-named for Garibaldi to celebrate victory at the battle of San Fermo. The whole district is known as Garibaldi, and close by is Milan's second largest railway station, called Porta Garibaldi. It's overkill.

A few stops on the metro took me to Largo Cairoli, next to the mighty Sforza Castle where Leonardo Da Vinci worked, and where many of the rooms and ceilings are decorated by his frescoes. In the square outside the castle was my target, Milan's main statue of Garibaldi. The sculptor here placed him on horseback, with a heavy poncho and a Turkish-style cap. Nowadays, he is hemmed in on a tiny traffic island with trams clanging past on each side. The names of eight battles are inscribed on the plinth below – Montevideo, Roma, Calatafimi, Palermo, Varese, Bezzecca, Mentana and San Fermo.

I walked on from here along Via Brisa, a quiet and delightful part of central Milan where the ancient Roman imperial palace once stood, and where some of the ruins are still evident. The street took me to an elegant square, Piazza Mentana, the final stop of the Garibaldi trail here in Italy's second biggest city. Standing in the centre was a memorial to those who perished at the battle of Mentana in 1867, the last one fought by Garibaldi on the Italian mainland, when he was vainly trying for a third time to capture Rome. Sculptures on the side illustrated the sadness and agony of that episode – one of them showed a soldier with his arms crossed and head bowed as he stood over the corpse of a colleague. The inscription talked of 'a dark defeat' and 'the trail of blood'. This was an unusual memorial for Italy, which prefers triumph on its monuments, and it was unique because this is the only one of so many commemorating his life to be inaugurated by Garibaldi himself. On the wall of a nearby house I spotted a plaque. Under a stone carving of his head, it read: 'Here, Giuseppe Garibaldi, on 3 November 1880, by inaugurating this monument to the immortal vanquished of Mentana, preached to the people the peace of the free and the strong.'

By then he was an old man, mostly confined to a wheelchair, close to the end of his life. Twenty years earlier, in the first months of 1860, there was no peace, no freedom, no Italy, and the most crucial battles of his life still lay ahead. It was a period of political intrigue as France, Austria and Piedmont/Sardinia negotiated how to divide up various cities and regions following the carnage of the Battle of Solferino. For a few months, in an attempt to mollify and neutralise him, Garibaldi was made deputy commander-in-chief of Tuscan forces in central Italy. There was no action, just endless stalling, and it left him deeply frustrated. He felt this was the moment to unite Italy, and in a speech at Cremona he took matters into his own hands by making a public appeal for 'a million rifles and a million men' to drive foreigners out of Italy. It was the start of the Million Rifles Fund, which became the Garibaldi Rifle Fund in England. It was also the day he met the novelist Alexandre Dumas for the first time.

Garibaldi returned to Caprera but did not stay long. A secret deal hatched between Cavour and Napoleon III to carve up areas of northern Italy between them was now enacted. It included giving away Nice/Nizza to France, which prompted a final angry split between Garibaldi and Cavour. The move enraged Garibaldi. Nizza was his home town, where he had been born, and which he considered an Italian city. Before the switch could be confirmed there had to be a plebiscite of the people of Nizza, and prior to this there was a general election in Piedmont/Sardinia, of which Cavour was prime minister. Garibaldi was elected as one of two representatives for Nizza, and he spoke in the Turin parliament in April 1860 against the decision. It was to no avail; the plebiscite was carefully managed to ensure the desired outcome for Cavour and France.

This was a bitter blow. Garibaldi was a superb warrior but a naïve politician, easily outmanoeuvred away from the battlefield. Now his life was in turmoil, with the loss of Nizza, the torment and shame of his failed wedding, and a turbulent private life which offered no lasting comfort. He yearned for a new conflict, to fight and to risk all for Italy. In a letter to relative in April 1860, he wrote:

Everything crushes and humiliates me, my heart is full of mourning. What should I do? For me it is enough to be in an Italian expedition. I have only one remaining desire: To die for Italy, and this destiny and these dangers I will risk earlier than I expected.

Where would that be? His first idea was an armed raid on Nizza to capture and burn the ballot boxes of the plebiscite, thus invalidating the vote. It would have been folly, and Garibaldi probably knew it. He was persuaded to abandon the plan by Francesco Crispi, a Sicilian lawyer, who told Garibaldi he should turn his attention to helping a revolution which had broken out in Sicily. Events were moving very fast now. Italian independence felt as if it was moving closer, but the outcome was by no means certain. Within a few weeks, the next phase of Garibaldi's life began, a stirring adventure that did more than anything else to create the unified Italy we know today.

Right: The bust in Lancaster House of Giuseppe Garibaldi, the only one in Britain. (This picture kindly supplied to the author by His Majesty's Government)

Below: A drawing of Garibaldi's carriage crossing Trafalgar Square amid the multitudes on his famous visit to England in 1864. (Courtesy World History Archive/Alamy)

Above left: The statue of Giuseppe Garibaldi in Nice, with an infant Garibaldi on the plinth below. (Nicoletta Zacchetti)

Above right: A portrait of Giuseppe Garibaldi on his return to Nice in 1848, wearing red shirt and jeans, The painting by Carlo Garacci hangs in the *Musee Massena* in Nice. (*Musee Massena*)

Below: 1888 image of the house where Garibaldi was born in Nice in 1805, long since demolished. (Howard Blackett's *Life of Giuseppe Garibaldi, Italian hero and patriot*, 1888)

Above left: The 'voluptuous splendour' of Via Garibaldi in Genoa, adorned with the city's flag. (Cristina Zacchetti)

Above right: A portrait of Giuseppe Garibaldi during his time in South America by Gaetano Gallino, which hangs today in the *Palazzo Tursi* in Via Garibaldi, Genoa. (Palazzo Tursi)

Right: A portrait of Anita Garibaldi in 1845 in Montevideo, also by Gaetano Gallino, which hangs today in the *Museo del Risorgimento* in Milan. (*Museo del Risorgimento*)

Above left: The blue jeans of Giuseppe Garibaldi on display at the *Museo Centrale del Risorgimento* in Rome, reputedly the oldest jeans in the world. (Nicoletta Zacchetti)

Above right: The magnificent statue of Anita Garibaldi on the Gianicolo hill in Rome, a pistol in one hand and a baby in the other. (Author)

Left: The statue of Giuseppe Garibaldi on the Gianicolo, sitting on his horse looking out over the Eternal City. (Author)

Above: One of the colourful bragozzi boats on the canal at Cesenatico for the annual festival celebrating Garibaldi's narrow 1849 escape from the Austrian army. (Nicoletta Zacchetti)

Right: The statue in Porto Garibaldi erected in 2011 of Anita and Garibaldi in the reeds close to Ravenna, fleeing from pursuing soldiers. (Nicoletta Zacchetti)

Above left: The evocative Capanno Garibaldi hut on the shores of Lake Comacchio where Giuseppe Garibaldi hid from the Austrian troops after the death of Anita. (Author)

Left: The author with Garibaldi on a public bench in La Maddelena. Visitors queue to sit with him for a photo. (Nicoletta Zacchetti)

Below: A panoramic view of the island of Caprera off the north-east coast of Sardinia, which Garibaldi made his long-term home. (Author)

The pine tree outside Garibaldi's 'white house' on Caprera that he planted himself in 1867 to mark the birth of his daughter Clelia. (Nicoletta Zacchetti)

The view of Lake Como on a misty day from the Via Garibaldi, which leads from the village of San Fermo down in to the town of Como. (Courtesy Laura Marcalli)

The poncho and red shirt of Giuseppe Garibaldi on display in the *Museo del Risorgimento* in Milan. (Courtesy Stefano Stabile under Creative Commons 3.0)

The monument to The Thousand at Quarto, near Genoa, with a naked Giuseppe Garibaldi at the front. (Courtesy Camillo Ferrari under Creative Commons 4.0)

Right: The statue of Giuseppe Garibaldi in Marsala, daubed with hostile graffiti in 2018. A similar incident also occurred two years earlier. (Courtesy ANSA, the Italian News Agency)

Below right: The plaque at Salemi which records Garibaldi declaring himself to be the Dictator of Sicily, when the town was the capital of Italy for three days. (Author)

Below: The vandalised bust of Garibaldi with his nose knocked off in the otherwise delightful *Giardino Garibaldi* in Palermo. (Nicoletta Zacchetti)

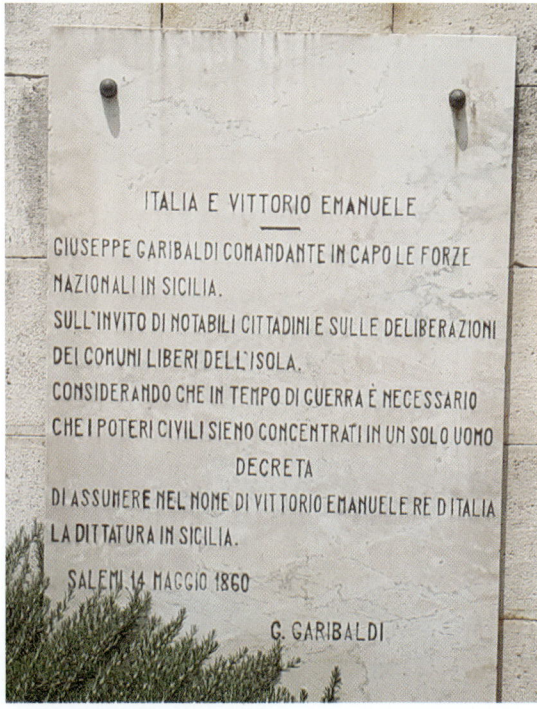

Left: The extravagant plaque above the Palazzo Villafranca in Palermo which celebrates the fact that Garibaldi rested there for just two hours. (Author)

Below: Milazzo Castle in eastern Sicily, where the Bourbon army surrendered in July 1860 after being besieged by Garibaldi's red shirt troops of The Thousand. (Courtesy Effems under Creative Commons 4.0)

Above: A painting by Wenzel Franz Jager of Giuseppe Garibaldi's tumultuous arrival in Naples in September 1860, which hangs in the *Castel Nuovo Museo Civico* in the city. (Courtesy of the Museum under Creative Commons 3.0)

Right: The colourful street sign in the small town of Vairano, which few people know is where Garibaldi actually met Vittorio Emmanuele II to hand over the south of Italy and create the new nation. (Author)

Above left: An albumen silver print of Giuseppe Garibaldi made by Gustave Le Gray during the 1860 conquest of Sicily. (Courtesy of the Getty Museum Collection)

Above right: The statue of Giuseppe Garibaldi in Turin, of historic importance because it was the first statue used as nation-building propaganda by the new Italian state. (Author)

Below: A 'Forza Garibaldi' banner waved by Nottingham Forest supporters in the crowd at the 2025 FA Cup semi-final at Wembley. (Courtesy Ben Radford)

Above left: The tree on the Aspromonte mountain where Giuseppe Garibaldi was famously wounded by Italian government soldiers. (Nicoletta Zacchetti)

Above right: Garibaldi's boot from Aspromonte, including bullet hole, on display at the *Museo Centrale del Risorgimento* in Rome. (Nicoletta Zacchetti)

Below: Giuseppe Garibaldi meeting Poet Laureate Alfred Lord Tennyson at his home on the Isle of Wight in 1864. (The Print Collector/Alamy)

Above: The official reception at Stafford House for Giuseppe Garibaldi on his acclaimed 1864 visit to London. (The Print Collector/Alamy)

Below left: The monument at Bezzecca, north of Lake Garda, where Garibaldi won a famous battle during the Third War of Italian Independence, but then obeyed an order from the King to stop fighting. (Nicoletta Zacchetti)

Below right: The statue of Giuseppe Garibaldi in Venice, adorned by the obligatory seagull and guarded by one of his soldiers who had been a ghost. (Author)

The 1867 Battle of Mentana, as depicted in an 1893 edition of *La Tribuna*. (Public domain)

The bones of soldiers who died at the Battle of Mentana, kept to this day on display inside the monument in the town 25 kilometres north-east of Rome. (Nicoletta Zacchetti)

The granite tomb of Garibaldi on Caprera. (Courtesy Gianni Careddu under Creative Commons 4.0)

A portrait of Giuseppe Garibaldi sitting in lonely isolation below his house by Giacomo Mantegazza, which hangs in the *Museo del Risorgimento* in Milan. The landscape is barely any different in Caprera now. (Courtesy Cuboimages)

8

MARSALA

'Who is this Garibaldi? He is a man, nothing more, but a man in the most sublime meaning of the term. A man of liberty. A man of humanity.'

Victor Hugo

As the fierce glare of day faded into a sepia glow and the heat of the sun eased, so the shops and bars and enotecas opened their shutters and the people of Marsala ventured out to play. Half an hour earlier it had seemed like a ghost town. Now the streets were humming with conversation and life, nowhere more so than on Via Garibaldi. I encountered old men and women chatting and arguing merrily as they sat on sofas and armchairs parked on the pavement outside their houses – the street transformed into an open-air living room. I found a seat on a café terrace, ordered a glass of chilled Grillo, the local white wine, and admired the parade of people strolling by. Everyone was watching everyone else – to see who was who and what was what, who was happy or sad or angry, who was joking around or sulking, who was missing, and perhaps most importantly of all, who was dressed to kill. I was part of the *struscio*, pronounced 'stru-show', a daily ritual which occurs on the main street of smaller towns all across Italy in the early evening. Whether you're young or old, whether you're walking or drinking, whether you're a local or a visitor, whether you like it or not – if you're there, you're in the *struscio*.

To be precise, which the Italians prefer with language, the full term is actually *fare lo struscio* – to do the *struscio*. And if you do happen to find yourself in Via Garibaldi in the town of Marsala on the west coast of Sicily in the early evening, then you are a participant, not merely an observer. You are doing the *struscio*. For teenagers it's a chance to flirt. For the elderly it's the time of gossip and laughter. For people of all ages it's obligatory to put on your best clothes and sunglasses and just show off. For the outsider it's a bewitchingly intimate natural theatre, the finest free entertainment. And it happens, quite specifically, only on the main street of small towns. There is no *struscio*, for example, in Rome or Milan or Florence, even though it began as an eighteenth-century religious tradition in another major city, Naples.

The Italian verb *strusciare* translates into English as 'to rub', and the word *struscio* is 'the rub'. The ritual derives from the practice of people in Naples to visit seven churches on Maundy Thursday, always dressed in their finest outfits, whatever their background. It became known as the *struscio* because of the noise of shoes rubbing on the ground and people's clothing rubbing against passers-by. Some say this was a kind of music, the rustling sound of soft-shoe feet and silk skirts.

I'd experienced the *struscio* in other places, but it seemed to me there was a certain extra magic in Marsala because here the streets of the *centro storico* were paved in pure marble and the town was enveloped by a warm, joyful, life-affirming glow as the sun went down. It was as if the old white stone had absorbed the harsh nature of the day and physically enabled the relaxed pace of the nightly fiesta. The only similar place I know is the jewel of Ortygia on the other side of Sicily. An identical mood and colour exists there, and the *struscio* feels like the art of living more slowly, and living well.

After a couple of glasses of Grillo, I joined the people strolling by and wandered up to the end of Via Garibaldi and into the main square of Piazza della Repubblica dominated by an ornate cathedral dedicated to San Tommaso di Canterbury, Thomas Becket. It is the mother church of Marsala, and it was astonishing to see a marriage ceremony spill out into the streets and cafes all around, and into the *struscio* itself. Apparently, this was quite normal for Italian weddings, the whole town invited to celebrate, the whole town expected to take notice.

Marsala sits on the west coast of Sicily, just about the furthest outpost from the centre of power in Rome as it is possible to find. It is also the town where modern Italy began to become a reality; here, and in the dusty hills just outside. The next morning I walked to the other end of Via Garibaldi and found, you've guessed it, Porta Garibaldi, the oldest gateway into the town. From there a road of ordinary tarmac tumbled down to the harbour where in 1860 two ships full of men led by Giuseppe Garibaldi landed to begin the fight for Italian unification. They are glorified in Italian history as *I Mille* (The Thousand), a tiny band of soldiers who won a series of incredible victories in battles against armies numbering 25,000 or more.

I found the exact spot where they came ashore, marked by a monument in the shape of a ship. It was designed to honour the exploits of the Expedition of the Thousand, but the place was a sad and sorry mess when I visited. The absence of the tricolour flag was one ominous clue. It flies everywhere on official buildings in Italy, but here it was missing. The entry gates were locked, plastic bottles littered the floor, and a giant bank of seaweed had formed by the water's edge. The scene resembled nothing so much as a shipwreck. It had taken thirty years to complete, hardly a good sign for a relatively small exhibition space, and far less time to fall into neglect. Perhaps this was a legacy of the pandemic, or maybe the local council was just spending its money elsewhere.

One very effective and evocative impression remained intact, though – the names of all The Thousand cut in capital letters into the steel panels of the 'ship'. This is a monument which celebrates one of the most fabled episodes in Italian history. The name Marsala may mean sweet wine for the British, but in Italy the name is taught to every schoolchild; it is as significant as the Battle of Hastings in England and the Boston Tea Party in the US.

Marsala was where The Thousand landed, but the journey had begun back in Genoa as Garibaldi had gathered together a small and relatively motel crew of soldiers and dreamers to fight for freedom. Having abandoned the idea of saving Nice, the best hope now for rebels with a cause was to join the stirrings of revolt in Sicily. This was part of the Kingdom of the Two Sicilies, effectively the whole southern part of Italy, which was under the repressive control of the Bourbons, with Naples as its capital. Mazzini had long been trying to stir up rebellion on the island, but there were other factions, too. Some idealistic local revolutionaries wanted Sicily to be an independent state, and there were early mafia criminal gangs feeding on the instability. Added to the mix was the fact that *Bomba*, the harsh old King Ferdinando II, had died in 1859 and been replaced by Francesco II, his ineffectual 23-year-old son. It was the Sicilian lawyer, Francesco Crispi, rather than Mazzini, who eventually cajoled Garibaldi into the most significant adventure of his life.

Crispi was the organiser, and they set up headquarters in a house overlooking the sea at Quarto, four miles southeast along the coastline from the *centro storico* of Genoa. A quarter of a century earlier Garibaldi had fled for his life from this city after his secret plotting against the authorities had been exposed. This time there was nothing covert about the plans being hatched to change Italy forever. The house was surrounded by journalists, police agents and foreign spies, while Garibaldi conspicuously decided to wear the famous red shirt again for the first time since the battles of 1849 in Rome. Volunteers from around Italy came to join, more than 1,000 by the time they left. Money flowed in from all over the world, including donations from Lady Byron and the Duke of Wellington. One hundred revolvers were sent by Colonel Colt across the waters from America, and a few rifles were delivered by the Royal Ordnance Factory in England.

There was less help closer to home amid the feverish Italian politics of the time. The two most influential men were King Vittorio Emanuele II of Piedmont/Sardinia and his scheming Primer Minister Camillo Cavour. They declined open support for Garibaldi but also turned a blind eye to the obvious preparations for a hostile attack on a neighbouring state launched from their territory. Garibaldi was too popular to oppose publicly, and they reasoned that if he were successful, they could make use of any triumph and disown any failure.

Garibaldi himself was cautious, unsure of the strength of the rebellion in Sicily. Several previous rebel ventures to the south during the 1850s had been disasters. Accurate news was hard to obtain, and accounts could be contradictory. One telegram from Palermo said the insurrection in the city was weak and hopeless. Another claimed it was thriving. Truth, as ever in this world, could be what you wanted to hear. Most historians agree it is likely Crispi that deliberately falsified the most encouraging message that arrived at the house in Quarto towards the end of April 1860, the one which finally convinced Garibaldi to embark on the mission. Fake news has been effective through the ages.

Two paddle steamers were seized, and on the night of 5 May the legend of The Thousand began. They actually numbered 1,089 men and one woman, who was Crispi's wife. Most of them came from the wealthier towns and cities of northern Italy – 160 from Bergamo, 156 from Genoa, 72 from Milan, 59 from Brescia, 58 from Pavia and just seven from Cavour's city of Turin. There were 50 exiled Sicilians, 11 men of Rome, and 17 non-Italians. The oldest rebel was aged 60, a soldier who had fought with Napoleon Bonaparte. Half were aged under 20 and the youngest just twelve years old. By this time Garibaldi was aged 52, but still a leader blessed with irrepressible energy and optimism. The backgrounds of The Thousand were mixed, with 500 from the urban working class, 150 lawyers, 100 doctors, 100 businessmen and 50 engineers.

Then there were a few artists, authors, journalists, students, barbers and cobblers. Among them, also, were two men who would in future years become Prime Ministers of a united Italy – Crispi and Benedetto Cairoli.

They sailed from Quarto, which is now a wealthy suburb of Genoa, filled with fine houses, manicured parks and exclusive beach clubs. The Thousand are commemorated here. I wandered down to a small stone obelisk, with a star on top, which marks the exact spot on the water's edge where the ships departed. It is called the *Scoglio dei Mille* (Rock of The Thousand), and waves crashed relentlessly against the rocky shore below. A few hundred yards away, on the opposite side of the bay, I found another tribute, the *Monumento Dei Mille*. This one is less conventional, more imposing, more visited, more thought-provoking. On a small square at the side of the busy harbour road there is a large sculpture which symbolises the struggle to unify Italy. It was placed there in 1915 and is not to everyone's taste, featuring people bonded together with their faces full of pain. At the front, like the figurehead on a ship, is the carving of a man who is unmistakably Garibaldi. It is the only public depiction of him in the nude. Figureheads were said to represent the spirit of a ship, and there is no doubt that Garibaldi was the spirit of Italian unification. The sculpture was commissioned fifty years later in 1910, and was finished during World War One, when its inauguration was used for political ends to build popular support for joining the conflict.

This was only part of the display here. Down below, built into the rocks, was a modern monument in the form of a ship's bow. The names of each one of The Thousand, as at the monument in Marsala, were cut into a metal barrier by the sea where the waves crashed in. There were a number of plaques, too, where the letters of the text had been cut into the metal in capital letters, symbolising the strength of the words. One was a tribute to Garibaldi from the French novelist Victor Hugo, who wrote *Les Miserables* and *The Hunchback of Notre Dame*. It read:

GARIBALDI.
WHO IS THIS GARIBALDI?
HE IS A MAN, NOTHING MORE.
BUT A MAN IN THE MOST SUBLIME MEANING OF THE TERM.
A MAN OF LIBERTY.
A MAN OF HUMANITY.
DOES HE HAVE AN ARMY?
NO.
A HANDFUL OF VOLUNTEERS.
DOES HE HAVE THE GUNS FOR WAR?
NOT AT ALL.
SO WHERE DOES HIS STRENGTH COME FROM?
WHAT DOES HE BRING WITH HIM?
THE SOUL OF THE PEOPLE.

I felt there was a power in this modern tribute. The words are effective, complimenting the roar of the heavy waves, and the place is clearly well cared for. It was a contrast not only to its ship monument cousin in Marsala, but also to the old house on the hill above Quarto which had been the headquarters of The Thousand before they sailed. For many years it was a museum known as 'Casa Garibaldi', with memorabilia from the time, but when I visited the place was silent, a sign on a frayed door declaring it was 'closed indefinitely'. The back half of the building had been converted into a police station.

It was a speculative mission when Garibaldi and his irregular army sailed off from Quarto. They had few guns and almost no ammunition, so the first stop at the coastal village of Talamone in southern Tuscany was to try to acquire coal, supplies and munitions. The place is dominated by an old stone fortress on top of a hill, and to reach it I had to walk up a particularly steep Via Garibaldi. Close by was Piazza Garibaldi, where I discovered a bust of the general on a plinth. On one side of the small square was a plaque that said he had lodged there for two nights while acquiring as many guns, bullets and shells as he could, both in Talamone and in nearby Orbetello. The house was now a small bed and breakfast hotel.

Orbetello is a smart, alluring, unique town in the middle of a lagoon that separates the Italian mainland from the promontory of Monte Argentario, and boasts one of Italy's finest wild beaches, *Spiaggia Feniglia*. The main square was dedicated to the 'Hero of Two Worlds', with a bust of Garibaldi sitting on top of the town hall building. This was another classic small town where I encountered the *struscio*, sitting in a bar amid a vibrant mix of locals and holidaymakers. I asked the waiter why this main square was not simply called Piazza Garibaldi like so many others. He had clearly been asked this question before and launched into a happy tirade about the bureaucracy that bedevils life in modern Italy. 'The rules don't allow it,' he told me. 'Two towns that exist in the same district are now not allowed by law to have the same street name. And because they let Talamone keep their Piazza Garibaldi we had to change ours to *Piazza Eroe dei Due Mondi* (Hero of Two Worlds Square). It's crazy, just crazy.'

From Orbetello the two ships journeyed south towards Sicily, sailing between the remote Egadi islands as Garibaldi pondered where best to land. The local rebellion was in the island's capital Palermo, but that city was certain to be heavily defended. The fishing town of Sciacca on the south coast was one obvious possibility, and Marsala on the west coast another. On the morning of 11 May, the Bourbons decided Garibaldi was heading for Sciacca and sailed towards it from their base in Marsala. A few hours later Garibaldi chose to go for Marsala. It was one of many pieces of good fortune he enjoyed. Another was that the Bourbons decided to change generals in Marsala. The first withdrew his troops on 10 May, but the replacements did not arrive immediately, and the town was left undefended for one day, 11 May, the very day Garibaldi's ships sailed in.

Marsala has a long history, and a particular one in the story of warfare. It was besieged in 279 BC by the Greek king Pyrrhus, who eventually won the battle but lost too many soldiers in doing so, thereby coining the term pyrrhic victory. The town was then known as Lilybaeum, but the modern name comes from the period when Arabs ruled the island – *Marsa Alla* is Arabic for God's Harbour.

On the night of 11 May 1860, its harbour was home only to two British warships. One was commanded by a Captain Winnington-Ingram, who had known Garibaldi in Montevideo some fifteen years earlier. It was one more element of good luck. The Royal Navy ships were there to protect the interests of the British trade in Marsala wine, and when one Bourbon vessel did sail back from Sciacca, the presence of British boats probably deterred them firing at Garibaldi's men as they went ashore. It's a jolly thought that the English dessert wine trade played a part in the creation of Italy, and Garibaldi definitely thought so, writing in his autobiography: 'The noble flag of England once more on this occasion helped to prevent bloodshed, and I for the hundredth time received their protection.'

The fortified wine of Marsala was first popularised by an English trader John Woodhouse, who landed at the town in 1773 and discovered the local wine similar in style to sherry and port. It was such a roaring success that Lord Nelson arrived in Marsala in 1800 to acquire it for his sailors and immediately dubbed it 'Victory Wine'. It was the favourite tipple, too, of Garibaldi, who drank it throughout the battles of Sicily and beyond. Today you can buy a Marsala Garibaldi Dolce, a sweet variety, which the makers claim is the type he preferred. A rival company produces the 'Anita Garibaldi Marsala', and in a shop in the town I acquired a book entitled, *Il Vino di Garibaldi Che Piaceva Agli Inglese*, or 'The Wine of Garibaldi loved by the English'. It tells the story of the Whitaker family from Yorkshire who created another brand of Marsala wine and bought the nearby island of Mozia. This was a treasure to visit and where Garibaldi himself slept for a night two years later in 1862 as a guest of the Whitakers in a house next to the excellent modern museum on the island.

Another factor which helped the Expedition of The Thousand on the night of 11 May 1860 was some quick thinking by Garibaldi when the town's telegraph office was seized. He saw that the last message sent to the authorities in nearby Trapani said two ships had landed at Marsala with Sardinian troops. There was a reply from Trapani asking for confirmation. Garibaldi sent back a message saying this was wrong, that they were just merchant ships. 'Idiots' came the next reply from Trapani – and then Garibaldi had the wires cut. It gave him valuable extra time to consolidate the landing, and by morning they had control of the town. Crispi took charge, persuading the local council to draft a declaration that Bourbon rule was over and that Garibaldi was now the Dictator of Sicily. They did so, although without much enthusiasm. The people of Marsala were cautious about these dramatic events, and mixed feelings are still evident to this day.

There were plenty of plaques in honour of Garibaldi. One identified the house where 'he stayed on the first night in Marsala and meditated.' Another read 'This house in 1862 was the first place that Garibaldi declared *O Roma O Morte*' (Rome or Death). Across the same square, however, I saw a bust of Garibaldi that had been vandalised three times in as many years. The official inscription talked about the 'miracle of unifying Italy after the first landing at Marsala'. The unofficial graffiti included '*Pirata*' and '*Assassino*' daubed with paint spray. There was also a capital A inside a circle below, the symbol for anarchists, and certainly not A for affection. It was the first overtly negative sign I had found on my travels about Garibaldi, the first indication that many people across the south of Italy have mixed or hostile feelings about him and his legend. It would not be the last.

Garibaldi and his men stayed just one day in Marsala before heading north-west in the direction of Palermo and monumental battles ahead. The first stop was a small mountain town called Salemi, which would be the most defensible place against a Bourbon attack, and also a good spot to rest. Unlike the caution in Marsala, there was an enthusiastic welcome for Garibaldi when he reached Salemi on 13 May. He declared himself 'Dictator of Sicily' in a ceremony at the town hall and then climbed to the top of the cylindrical tower of the town's Norman castle, hoisted a tricolour flag, and told the cheering crowds that Salemi was officially the capital of all Italy.

And for three days it was. And, ever since, this obscure little town, population 9,600, has revelled in being the first capital of the nation. Almost nobody in modern Italy knows about this. When I tell people, very few are willing to believe it. But when you do come across an Italian who knows about Salemi, you are greeted with a huge smile and joy that you, too, have discovered one of the most secret true facts about the country. The declaration of Salemi has authenticity, apparently, because Garibaldi enacted new laws while he was there. One of these was a decree against looting, which was aimed also at his own soldiers. There are no doubts in the town itself about its capital status, where the local museum has a sign above the entrance reading:

MUSEO DEL RISORGIMENTO
PRIMA CAPITALE D'ITALIA

When I was in Salemi it happened to be a day of 44°C heat. I was alone with the mad dogs in the midday sun having decided that was a good moment to look at memories of

Garibaldi, especially as it meant a winding walk up the long hill from the modern town centre to the Norman castle and the town's museums. This road was (how could you doubt it?) Via Garibaldi. I found relics of 1860, guns, pamphlets and the ubiquitous red shirt. It was actually five museums in one, with an excellent section dedicated to the history of the mafia. The first items here also dated back to the 1860s.

Outside the museum in the cathedral square was a stone inscription – the declaration of dictatorship by Garibaldi in Salemi. On another stone plaque outside the castle was a similar Garibaldi proclamation that he had assumed the role of Dictator of Sicily on 14 May in the name of King Vittorio Emanuele II. Back down the hill I stopped for a glass of water in a bar, where they proudly displayed a bottle of Syrah red wine with the label Salemi 1860, made to celebrate the 150th anniversary of Italian unification. It was in the window, roasting in the heat, long since undrinkable.

Garibaldi and his men did not rest long. One day later, on an afternoon of scorching heat, the first and the most vital battle fought by the Expedition of The Thousand took place on the hills close to Calatafimi, another small town in the region. They needed the morale boost of a victory against the Bourbons to persuade Sicilians to the cause. Only around 100 locals had joined the 1,089 men from the boats as they prepared to face a rival force numbering about 2,000 soldiers, who were better trained and had far superior weapons – cannon, modern guns and a large supply of bullets. Garibaldi rode among his troops on a white horse he named Marsala, singing to himself as he did so. Legend has it that he heard a lone bugler playing among his men, the same reveille sounded in battle at Como the year before, and he demanded it be played again as fighting started and the Garibaldini flooded towards the Bourbon forces, advancing with bayonets because they had so few bullets. One of his closest comrades-in-arms, Nino Bixio, tried to persuade Garibaldi to stay out of the fighting, but there was no chance of that. The General attacked with his men, sword unsheathed, in the thick of the action. The initial exchange lasted for two hours, and during the lull that followed Bixio thought their position hopeless, stuck on a hillside below an enemy of greater numbers in a far stronger position. Bixio made the commonsense suggestion that they retreat, but he was met with a rare flash of anger in response from Garibaldi, who shouted: 'Here we make Italy, or we die.'

As he spoke, Garibaldi was a mere stone's throw away from the enemy – a mathematical as well as metaphorical truth. He was hit on the back by a stone thrown from the Bourbon position above, and Garibaldi's instant thought was that the opposing army had run out of bullets. Instead of retreat, he ordered an immediate assault up the hill, a bayonet charge he led from the front. It was a crucial moment. In fact, the Bourbons did have bullets, but they had stopped firing because the shots were going over the heads of the Garibaldini, who were hidden from view on the terraces of the hill where vines grew. They stormed over the top of the hill and overwhelmed their astounded opponents, who fled back to the safety of the town of Calatafimi.

They had made Italy.

Victory came with casualties. Forty-one Red Shirts died in this battle and 126 were wounded. The numbers were slightly lower for the Bourbons, but their defeat was profound in its consequences. Victory gave Garibaldi and his men an unstoppable momentum and spread panic among the soldiers of the Kingdom of the Two Sicilies. It inspired thousands of Sicilians to join the red shirts of the Garibaldini. It opened the door to Italian unification. And it was the day of which Garibaldi would later say: 'Calatafimi – if at my last breath my friends see me smile with pride, it will be remembering you, because I do not recall a more glorious battle.'

Today these hills are peaceful, almost desolate in the dusty heat of a Sicilian summer. They were deserted when I drove through to see the monuments which recall the battle. There is a small one on the road out of Salemi, in honour of twenty-five-year-old Simone Schiaffino, who was killed holding the tricolour flag during the charge. An Italian flag was flying above the memorial, even in this baking wilderness, a rebuke to the ship monument in Marsala.

The main monument was just outside Calatafimi on the western slope of the Pianto Romana hill where the battle took place – a striking square mausoleum, with a bulky limestone obelisk rising above, created to house the remains of all the Garibaldi volunteers and the Bourbon soldiers who died in the conflict on 15 May 1860. It was decorated on the sides by two bronze groups, one depicting the landing of The Thousand at Marsala, and the other the brutality of the battle of Calatafimi. This was a striking place, and a solemn one. An avenue of cypress trees lined the *Viale della Rimembranza*, which had a stone by each tree inscribed with a town in Italy and the names of The Thousand who came from there. A century later, in 1960, another reminder was added. This was a stone structure of four robust legs and a curved stone beam lying across the top. Inscribed on the beam were the words, '*QUI SI FA L'ITALIA O SI MUORE.*' Here we make Italy or we die.

The day after their victory, many of Garibaldi's men went to see the nearby ancient Greek temple at Segesta, one of the marvels of antiquity. It was a Doric temple built in the fifth century BC, almost entirely preserved, and which is the main tourist attraction of the area. Indeed, the town is now known as Calatafimi-Segesta. As the Garibaldini wandered around the mighty temple, so the defeated Bourbon troops made a decision to withdraw that same night back to Palermo. They had been thoroughly spooked by the Garibaldi legend made real in front of their eyes, and so the strategic stronghold of Calatafimi was captured without a shot fired, a stone thrown, or a bayonet drawn.

The outside world did not know this for a while. Even as their army retreated, Bourbon diplomats were telling journalists that Garibaldi and his men had been routed at the battle of Calatafimi. This was duly reported as fact in *The Times* of London, which had been writing opinion articles in support of the Expedition of The Thousand.

From the monument on the Piano Romano I drove on to Calatafimi itself, a quiet town with few visitors, although essential on a journey to follow the trail of Garibaldi. The main street was the Corso Garibaldi, with a small Risorgimento museum in a building called Casa Garibaldi. There were two statues, one showing the General with a sword in his hand and dedicated to *ai caduti* – the fallen soldiers. Thirty metres away was another bust. Two billboard-style notices also caught my eye in the centre of the town. One was filled with a colourful drawing of Garibaldi in a red shirt, holding the Italian flag in one hand and a gun with a long bayonet on the other. The end of the bayonet stabbed into at what at first glance looked like an upside-down bucket but was actually the blue hat of a vanquished Bourbon officer. This billboard read: Calatafimi-Segesta '*Citta Libera dell' Italia Unita*' – free city of united Italy. The second billboard proudly recounted the words of Garibaldi about the battle and its place in his heart, and how he would be thinking and smiling about it on his deathbed.

The museum was closed the day I visited. Above the door of the building was a big plaque dedicated to Garibaldi. *In questa casa* it began, as they do all over Italy. In this house on 16 May 1860 he planted the Italian flag of unity in the ground, and in the garden he planted a tree. And then he sprang back on his white horse and headed towards another mighty battle at Palermo.

9

PALERMO

'The name of Garibaldi disturbed him a little. That adventurer, all hair and beard, had caused a lot of trouble already.'

The Leopard

The little park was a haven of shade and calm on another ferociously hot Sicilian day. The temperature had again risen above 40°C, and pounding the chaotic streets of Palermo in search of Risorgimento treasures on the next stage of my journey was not an option on this stifling, airless August mid-afternoon. Here, though, was the perfect resting place – the Garibaldi Gardens – where I sat in front of an enormous and extraordinary tree, its giant branches dropping aerial roots which became rock-solid columns after reaching the ground. It was a Ficus macrophylla, otherwise known as the Moreton Bay Fig from its Australian origins, and a sign planted in the earth said it had been dedicated to the memory of the courage of the heroes who created a united Italy. These giant grey roots look like elephant trunks, only four times the size, and

I discovered that this is the largest living tree in Europe, with a trunk diameter of 21 metres, standing 30 metres high, and with a crown 53 metres wide. It was planted when the gardens were created in 1863 by Giovanni Basile, a follower of Garibaldi. This was just three years after the battle of Palermo, when bloody victory for the Red Shirts captured the capital of Sicily from the Bourbons.

There are three of these macrophylla trees in the park, along with many other botanical gems, and also a bust of Garibaldi, with his nose broken off. This is almost certainly not the weathering of time, but a deliberate act of desecration on an island where his legacy is complicated and his memory often reviled rather than revered. I had already seen evidence of this with the graffiti scrawled across his statue in Marsala. It is another aspect of the Garibaldi story, evident in many classics of Sicilian literature such as *The Leopard*, written by Giuseppe Tomasi Di Lampedusa, and also in the lack of care given to his main statue in Palermo. This stood in neglected isolation on the wide Via del Libertà which runs through the city. In the rest of Italy there is always a fresh wreath by these statues, but here the small bunch of flowers left in front had wilted in the sun. I was the only visitor taking a look. Garibaldi was depicted on horseback, pointing towards the city centre, and that was the way to go.

I headed for Via Vittorio Emanuele, which lies in the heart of Palermo and is the main road sweeping up the hill from the port past the Garibaldi Gardens and the glory of Palermo Cathedral to the Palazzo Dei Normanni with its fabulous Capella Palatina. It is the heart of the city and in 1860, when it was known as Via Toledo, this was the battleground between the Red Shirts and the Bourbon army. The area is dotted with plaques that commemorate crucial and not-so-crucial episodes of the drama, and I discovered my own particular favourite in Piazza Bologni, mentioned in the prologue. The plaque above the entrance to the Palazzo Villafranca, which is now an art gallery, reads 'In this illustrious house, for only two hours, I lay down my weary limbs – Giuseppe Garibaldi.' It was not that Garibaldi lived here for several years, or this was briefly his headquarters, or where crucial battle plans were decided, or where he made a mighty speech, or where he was injured in fierce fighting. No, just where he had a quick lie down. It was clearly ridiculous, but also rather magnificent. What the plaque didn't mention, although far more interesting, is that this was nearly Garibaldi's last act. When dismounting his horse and unsaddling it himself, which he always insisted on doing, a pistol in his pocket fired by accident. Luckily, it only blew a hole in his trousers.

The facade of the Palazzo Villafranca was rather decayed, although it remains one of the most important art galleries in Palermo, housing a masterpiece by Van Dyck. It was symbolic of the city, a crumbling glory in a place with more history than anywhere in Italy except for Rome itself, the architecture, food and atmosphere influenced by centuries of invasion by Greeks, Normans, Arabs and the Spanish. This cultural complexity is especially strong in the exquisite Capella Palatina, where Christian and Muslim art are entwined in the twelfth-century chapel.

All that glory was located up the hill, but I walked round the corner to another fine square, the Piazza Pretoria. This one had a building with not one but two plaques dedicated to Garibaldi. The first was also dated 27 May 1860, and the inscription recorded: 'The liberation of Sicily by The Thousand from the tyranny of the Bourbons, a prodigious triumph towards the freedom of Italy.' The second, dated 30 May 1860, declared that here was the place Garibaldi rested after battle. He stayed a little longer than two hours in this spot, for a few days in fact, because it became his first headquarters in Palermo. The building is now the town hall.

In centre of the piazza was a vast fountain surrounded by elaborate marble sculptures of naked men and women, which explained its nickname – the 'Fountain of Shame'. Garibaldi would sit on its steps each morning, smelling the flowers and eating the fruit brought to him by admiring women. By exuding an image of unruffled calm as enemy shells flew through the air, he was giving a message to his soldiers and to the locals of the city.

The battle for Palermo was among the bloodiest and most intense of Garibaldi's life. Driving the Bourbons out of the heavily defended capital of Sicily should have been impossible. The head of their army, General Lanza, had 20,000 soldiers at his disposal. By contrast, Garibaldi had less than 2,000 men – and some historians say this vast disparity in numbers made this his greatest single military triumph. The strategy he pursued was to get his volunteer troops inside the city without detection and then rouse the locals to insurrection. To achieve this, he first organised a series of decoy runs by the Red Shirts to try to fox Lanza and divert as many Bourbon troops away from his own as possible. Garibaldi's men were arriving from the west after his victory at Calatafimi, but he decided the best way to attack Palermo was from the south-east. Another vital factor for Garibaldi was making contact with officers from British naval ships who were moored in the harbour. He gained their neutrality, and thus their tacit support for his manoeuvres. The British knew the Red Shirts were about to storm the capital of Sicily, but General Lanza did not believe it.

The attack began just after midnight on 27 May and Palermo, where the first revolutionary uprisings across Europe in 1848 had taken place, was ablaze once more. An initial breakthrough was made at Porta Termini, where they dismantled the Bourbon barricades by hand. When they had been cleared, Garibaldi rode through on his white horse and eight hours of fighting followed along the straight road into the city towards a fountain in the square at Fierra Vecchia. In the middle of the fountain is a statuette of the Genius of Palermo, which features an old man feeding a snake at his breast. It is supposed to represent Sicily feeding all its foreign conquerors, and is the exact spot where the revolution of 1848 began. The route taken by the Red Shirts is now called Corso Dei Mille, which eventually turns into Via Garibaldi and concludes at the square now known as the Piazza Rivoluzione.

Via Garibaldi was a modest road in modern Palermo, far removed from the grandeur of Genoa, Milan, or even Marsala. In fact, it was a crushing disappointment looking for evidence of the dramatic events of 1860. This is where the most serious and intense conflict occurred as the invaders reached their first target of the Fierra Vecchia. There was no fountain when the square was captured. It had been removed by the Bourbons in 1849; one of Garibaldi's first acts was to order its reinstallation.

By midday of 27 May most of Palermo was controlled by Garibaldi, including the city's main jail, and all the prisoners inside were released. The Bourbon army retreated towards the Royal Palace and cathedral at the top of Via Toledo, a strong position on high ground. Halfway up the hill, just beyond Piazza Bologni where Garibaldi had lain down his weary limbs for a couple of hours, the Red Shirts and locals combined to build huge defensive barricades. Garibaldi was impressed, saying: 'The people of Palermo ran to erect those citizens' bulwarks which make the mercenaries of tyrannies turn pale – the barricades!'

Three more days of street fighting ensued, a period of mayhem and destruction. Bombardment by the cannons of General Lanza flattened many buildings and killed hundreds of civilians. If the idea was to destroy the morale of the people of Palermo and the Red Shirts, it failed miserably. The rebellion only grew in strength, inspired by anger and by the example of Garibaldi's individual courage. He sat on the fountain outside his headquarters in Piazza Pretoria even under severe enemy fire. Several people close to him were killed, but the tales of his bravery and apparent invincibility spread.

In truth, after four days of brutal conflict, both sides were in dire straits. Garibaldi's army was running out of ammunition, even though people were working day and night in powder mills to make more. The Bourbons were suffering from lack of medical supplies and food for 18,000 men now suffering badly in cramped conditions. General Lanza broke first. On 30 May, he sent a letter to 'His Excellency General Garibaldi' asking for a ceasefire and a meeting on the Royal Navy ship *Hannibal* commanded by Admiral Mundy.

This was another piece of timely good fortune for Garibaldi, because unknown to Lanza, one of his officers, Colonel

Von Mechel, had just arrived south of Palermo after vainly searching for Garibaldi some thirty miles away from the city, fooled by one of the decoy runs. Some historians believe that if Von Mechel had arrived twenty-four hours earlier the rebellion would have been crushed and Garibaldi and his men obliterated.

Instead, at a meeting hosted by the English admiral, a truce was agreed. It gave valuable breathing space to Garibaldi, who cleverly exploited the moment with a rousing speech from the main balcony of his HQ at Piazza Pretoria. It engendered the desired effect. There were enormous roars of approval from an excited crowd, and the noise sank into the bones of the Bourbons. They understood that if they kept fighting for Palermo it would become the bloodiest of all battles. Several more temporary truces were agreed until 6 June, when, on orders from King Francesco II in Naples, the Bourbon troops capitulated to Garibaldi and were allowed to sail back to the mainland.

This was an incredible triumph against vast odds for Garibaldi, outnumbered ten-to-one by the opposition as well as being desperately short of ordnance. Many explanations have been suggested as to why General Lanza did not attack the Red Shirts in Palermo during those momentous days. It seems very likely that a prime reason for his hesitation was the respect he had seen the British give to Garibaldi. Another likely factor was the reports he had been receiving about significant uprisings elsewhere in Sicily in places like Catania. Maybe he was also impressed by the strength of the barricades in Via Toledo and the powerful effect of Garibaldi's speeches on the people of Palermo.

There are other far-fetched theories about Garibaldi's triumph, which include the intervention of international freemasonry and the hidden hand of the mafia. There is no evidence for any of this. It was a combination of Garibaldi's daring and skill, a mountain of luck, and the fact he found instant support from all levels of Sicilian society. Peasants, landowners and clergy all hated Bourbon rule, and he capitalised on that thanks to his charisma and panache.

His success was celebrated across Europe as the emergent mass media relayed news of the victorious battles. Two of the reporters who followed events in Sicily and sent articles back to their newspapers were Alexandre Dumas and Friedrich Engels. The English papers also admired Garibaldi, and stories of his personal bravery and looks made him a romantic hero to English women. Red blouses became a fashionable item, and among those who donated to the Garibaldi fund set up to help finance the Expedition of The Thousand was Florence Nightingale. She gave ten pounds, Charles Dickens gave five pounds and the Duke of Wellington's son fifty pounds. Popular opinion across England was hugely in favour of Garibaldi's exploits, and few foreign leaders have been so admired and so loved.

Garibaldi took the symbolic step of switching his headquarters in Palermo to the Palazzo dei Normanni, otherwise known as the Royal Palace, clear evidence that he was now in control. It is a magnificent building, the oldest royal residence in Europe, dating back to the eleventh century, the seat of the kings of Sicily for hundreds of years, and today home to the Sicilian parliament as well as millions of tourists. Garibaldi took a modest room amid the grandeur, high in the observatory tower over the Porta Nuova, with fine views across the city. Dumas joined him at the palace, lodged in the far more luxurious rooms of the former Bourbon governor, and wrote of Garibaldi: 'He has the entire staff of the palace at his disposal but all he wants is soup, meat and vegetables.' Garibaldi was that rare combination of a man who is humble but also fearless in action. He was now the effective Dictator of Sicily – but he was not a political leader, by instinct, experience or ambition.

'I came here to fight for the cause of Italy, not Sicily alone,' he wrote, and swiftly left practical governmental matters to Francesco Crispi, who became secretary of state and minister of the interior. Some tariffs were abolished, some land reforms were implemented, and the death penalty was imposed for looting. These were all accepted by the people of Palermo, but military conscription proved hugely unpopular. The mood of euphoria that accompanied the exit of the hated Bourbons soon dissipated with the new reality – and it left Garibaldi's legacy forever tainted on the island. He was the symbol of the destruction of Bourbon rule, and he then became the symbol of the long-term disillusionment felt about the disparity in wealth between the southern part of the new Italy and the north.

Whether or not that is fair has sparked intense debate through the years. The capture of Palermo and its immediate aftermath occurred more than 160 years ago, and a vast number of political leaders have taken charge of Italy since then – the Fascists of Mussolini, the Christian Democrats of the post-Second World War era, and a range of centre-left and right-wing governments in the twenty-first century. They have all contributed with their policies to the fundamental north-south divide in Italy, yet many people still focus their discontent on the figure of Garibaldi.

It seems too simplistic to me, too easy to focus on a symbol rather than complicated history, yet it also reveals the enduring hold on the imagination of Garibaldi among modern Italians. It was also easy to see and hear what people feel about him now on my journey around Sicily – the vandalised statues of Marsala and the missing nose of Palermo, for example. I also discovered this negative mood in the delightful town of Piazza Armerina in the centre of the island. It is home to the most magnificent ancient Roman mosaics in all of Italy, which include the earliest known depiction of a bikini. The town features, in no particular order, a Via Garibaldi, Teatro Garibaldi, Corso Garibaldi, Ristorante Garibaldi, Piazza Garibaldi, Giardino Garibaldi and a B&B Garibaldi. In the middle of Piazza Garibaldi was an enoteca with a rustic interior, serving wine from a tap. It was situated underneath two plaques high on a wall, both dedicated to Garibaldi, who visited the town in August 1862 and 'in this house' repeated his favourite cry of O Roma O Morte.

I took a glass of wine, sat outside on a rickety plastic chair, and as an obvious visitor was immediately engaged in conversation by the locals. One was a schoolteacher who told me how the name of Garibaldi was more and more despised because he had given away Sicily to the King of Piedmont and left the island to ruination. He told me that access to the internet had only accelerated this hostility during the past twenty years, something which other people confirmed to me. Was this because they now had access to more information – or to more disinformation? And perhaps more exposure to online haters and hatred available on the uninhibited social media platforms of our modern age?

As we were chatting, the teacher asked me where I was planning to eat that evening. I told him the name of one possible restaurant where I had arranged a table, but said I was also considering another. Behind us, sitting quietly by himself on a stone wall, there was a man enjoying a glass of white wine. He was talking on his mobile phone, but he had overheard our conversation and immediately put his call on hold.

'Pardon me for interrupting, but I have to tell you that I am the official hygiene inspector of this town. Go to the restaurant you have booked, and do not eat at the other under any circumstances.' He then turned away, took a gulp of his wine, and resumed his call. Laughter all round. This was real information – and it seemed to me it could also have been a scene from a play by Luigi Pirandello, pioneer of the Theatre of the Absurd.

Pirandello is one of many famous Sicilian writers who have been vexed by the Garibaldi legacy. He came from a family of radicals, and both his father Stefano and his uncle Rocco Ricci Gramitto fought with Garibaldi's Red Shirts at Palermo and in other battles to liberate the island. His uncle was at Aspromonte in 1862, and when Garibaldi was famously shot in the leg he recovered the boot that had been pierced by a bullet and covered in blood. He kept it in a glass case at his house in Rome, together with a letter from Garibaldi to 'dear Gramitto'. The boot was still there when a young Luigi Pirandello came as a student to the capital and lived with his uncle. Today, it is one of the prize exhibits on display at the Central Museum of the Risorgimento in Rome.

The boot is mentioned in Pirandello's novel *The Old and the Young*, where a character remarks: 'It is a real remnant – real – of the most precious blood. What vertigo at the touch.' Pirandello was initially captivated by the story of Garibaldi, and placed the character of his father in this novel as one of The Expedition of The Thousand who sailed from Quarto to Marsala. In truth, his father only joined the conflict at Palermo. The book also charts the way many Sicilians lost faith in the Hero of Two Worlds when they realised that defeat of the hated Bourbons had not ushered in a golden age with the unification of Italy. Instead, it felt like subjugation by the north. The novel, written in 1913, reflects this widespread disillusion, the mood of resentment, regret and bewilderment. It ends with the needless death of an old Red Shirt who had marched with Garibaldi, a corpse lying on the ground with four medals on his chest stained with blood after being shot by soldiers of the new nation.

Andrea Camilleri, who penned the intelligent, left-wing and hugely popular Montalbano crime novels, had a more sympathetic view of Garibaldi, writing: 'Looking at today's mythology one could consider Garibaldi a sort of Che Guevara. However, he did not make Che's mistake, that is going where there is no fertile ground. Garibaldi chose a perfect theatre in which to operate, that of Sicily.' Camilleri also wrote about the boot to illustrate the difficulty, if not impossibility, of effecting change in his native island. The novella is called *Garibaldi's Boot*, and chronicles the failure of a Tuscan administrator, Enrico Falconcini, when he arrives as the new prefect of the city of Agrigento in 1862. In this telling, Sicilians have accepted the Garibaldian revolution as a colourful change of façade that in reality has not changed anything. Falconcini, who has the boot in his office, departs after just five months, thoroughly defeated by Sicily. The boot is an obvious metaphor, with mainland Italy as the boot, and Sicily the ball of stone that cannot be kicked around.

A similar fatalistic sentiment is found in *The Leopard*, the most well-known novel set in Sicily, made into a movie starring Burt Lancaster and Claudia Cardinale, which is widely considered to be one of the finest films of all time. It begins at the time of the capture of Palermo when Sicily is ablaze with revolutionary fervour. The main character, the Prince of Salina, whose nephew Tancredi has joined the Red Shirts, is hostile in aristocratically phlegmatic fashion.

'The name of Garibaldi disturbed him a little,' writes the author Giuseppe Tomasi di Lampedusa. 'That adventurer, all hair and beard, had caused a lot of trouble already.' By the end of the book, however, the Prince has a dinner guest, a Colonel Pallavicino, who tells the story of how he shot and wounded Garibaldi at Aspromonte. It is fiction mixed with reality, and the mood is summed up by the most famous line of the book, spoken by the Prince. 'Everything must change so that everything can stay the same.' This points to a curious dichotomy among those who disdain Garibaldi. They blame him for not improving Sicily, but at the same time believe that Sicily never really changes.

Pirandello, Camilleri and di Lampedusa are all reasonably well-known to English readers. Many people in Italy have told me, though, that the finest Sicilian author of all, and certainly the best novelist about the mafia, is Leonardo Sciascia. He also focused on Garibaldi, and described the events of 1860 as a failed revolution, merely delivering to Sicily a change of ownership from one class to another. In his novella called *Il Quarantotto*, he writes of 'the silent, fragile hope of Sicilians, a hope that fears itself, and has death close and familiar.' It is the hope of the peasant who follows Garibaldi, even after his anguished disappointment at seeing Garibaldi arm-in-arm with the landowners.

Finally, in this parade of Sicilian authors, there is Giovanni Verga, who was twenty years old when the Expedition of The Thousand landed at Marsala, and who joined the new National Guard set up by Garibaldi on the island. Verga was a member for three years, although there is no record of him taking part in any conflict. He dramatized the events of that time in a memorable short story, *Libertà*, about the brutality that occurred in the town of Bronte in August 1860. In his desire to recruit local volunteer soldiers Garibaldi had promised farmland would be redistributed to the heads of peasant families, and this prompted a popular uprising against landowners and leaders in the local Bourbon regime in Bronte. It left many people dead, and this revolt was then itself crushed by Garibaldi's right-hand man Nino Bixio in violent fashion to restore order.

Verga appreciated the complexity and tragedy of the episode in a Sicilian manner, telling the story of people stirred by the prospect of real change and thirst for vengeance against old masters, but who then become stoic in their final acceptance that nothing really alters. There is a sense of hopelessness at the end of story. Sicily would not be changed by a soldier like Garibaldi who was just passing through, and maybe never changed at all. Yet a great number of people today still cling to the belief that Garibaldi represented the best chance of improvement, and they are angry that he let them down.

The ubiquity of Garibaldi's presence among writers emphasises the importance of literature in modern Italy. The country has a vigorous intellectual culture, particularly in novels, cinema and theatre. Journalists are widely respected, many of them household names, filling the prime time TV schedules with political debates and history programmes. And barely a week goes by without a mention of the Hero of Two Worlds, just as it's impossible to walk through a town without strolling along a Via Garibaldi.

Wandering around Palermo it was inevitable I would eventually come across the Teatro Politeama Garibaldi, renamed for him on his death in 1882. It was an immense building in the heart of the city, with six giant rearing horses on top and a huge neoclassical arch for its entrance. This was now home to the Sicilian symphony orchestra. Of course, but of course, it was not the only Teatro Garibaldi in the city. There was another more modest wooden structure in the Kalsa district, built in 1861, and still used by local theatre groups. While there is antipathy to Garibaldi on this island, there is also sentiment in his favour, illustrated by the fact that many other theatres still carry his name – in Modica, Ragusa, Enna, Piazza Armerina and Mazara Del Vallo. I visited this last one, a quaint and intimate horseshoe-shaped playhouse constructed entirely of wood, located in the Arab quarter of the town. It lay unused for many years but is a jewel recently restored and operating as a working theatre once more.

During the battles of 1860, there is no doubt the people of Sicily were swayed by Garibaldi's charisma and character.

He may have been a northerner, like most of the fighters of The Thousand, but the simplicity of his nature appealed to everyone. It is an important factor in explaining why he is the key figure in the unification of Italy. His path took him to every corner of the country, and he treated people as equals. He had won two incredible victories at Calatafimi and Palermo, and now one more lay ahead: to fully conquer Sicily. The showdown with the Bourbon forces came just outside the key port town of Milazzo on the north coast of the island. It began on 18 July and was even bloodier than the previous two battles. Garibaldi led from the front, in the thick of the fighting, surging straight at the enemy, sword in hand. A young British volunteer among the Red Shirts, Andrew Patterson, recalled: 'He jumped off his horse and rushed towards the enemy riflemen. He did not once look round to see if his men were following, but he knew that none who saw him would linger.' At one point Garibaldi's horse was shot dead as he was riding (this was not the white horse named Marsala), but as he jumped off, he killed the Bourbon rifleman with his sabre.

Once again, the Red Shirts were far outnumbered by their opponents. But their wild courage amid the inspiration of Garibaldi himself pushed the Bourbons back into Milazzo, past the town's famous tuna factories and into the refuge of its castle sitting high on a granite rock 300 feet above the sea. Garibaldi now also had command of some ships to bombard the enemy and by 23 July the battle was over. The Bourbons capitulated again, and they were allowed to slink away back to Naples.

Victory came at a cost. Around 800 of Garibaldi's volunteer soldiers perished in this conflict, and he was also wounded.

But he had now conquered the whole of Sicily within seventy days and won three of the greatest battles of his life – each one with fewer men, less ammunition and inferior weapons. The battle of Milazzo had included the help of an English volunteer regiment, among whom was Colonel John Peard, who became a lifelong friend of Garibaldi and continued on the march of The Thousand onto the mainland. Most of the rest of the English, however, were disbanded for drunkenness, having taken a liking to the local Sicilian wine. How many times since have people in Italy and Europe lamented the sight of Englishmen drunk abroad?

Milazzo lies on a promontory and today is a busy fishing port, with a typically lively modern waterfront area full of bars and restaurants. It was the natural place for me to spend my evening in the city, and it was no surprise to discover the long curving harbour road I was walking along was called Via Marina Garibaldi. The next morning I went to the castle, which also serves as the city's history museum. It was an imposing old stone fortress, but there was barely a mention of the monumental battle of Milazzo in 1860. They were much more concerned with a siege that occurred in the 1700s, which seemed strange.

The next step for Garibaldi was moving on to the mainland, to the region of Calabria across the narrow straits of Messina, to the big toe of modern Italy (just as it would be for Allied forces in 1943). That has never been easy, not even today with its regular ferry service from Messina to Villa San Giovanni. When I had arrived by car some weeks earlier to cross from Calabria to Sicily, the scene was utter chaos. The road into the port of Villa San Giovanni had twelve lanes of vehicles trying to funnel down into the one-lane entrance to the waiting area for the ferry. Each car had to inch forward, trying to ease into non-existent gaps ahead. There were no marshals, no signs, and the only saving grace was the fellow-feeling that we were all locked into this nightmare together and only snail-pace courtesy could prevail. And this was at 6.30 in the morning.

We could see the other side but could only dream about getting there anytime soon. Which probably put us, for a couple of frustrated, indignant hours, in the shoes of Garibaldi in July 1860 as he reached the east coast of Sicily and wondered how best and where to cross the narrow strip of water over to the shores of Calabria.

10

NAPLES/NAPOLI

Mock anything you like, but don't touch mothers, pizza, pasta and Garibaldi.'

La Gazzetta dello Sport

The best way to reach Naples is by rail. It always has been, and probably always will be. Garibaldi arrived by train as an unchallenged conqueror in September 1860, with no need to brandish his sword in action after the Bourbon king fled the city rather than fight to defend it against the Red Shirts. I came on the high-speed inter-city service, one hour from Rome, with no need to succumb to the road rage that would surely have been provoked by the alternative of a two-hour car drive through the most chaotic streets in Europe. The train delivers you efficiently into the heart of this magnificent city; but come prepared for the madness.

Garibaldi was acclaimed by a vast crowd of people at the station and had to fight his way through the multitudes to reach the carriage that would take him around Naples. There were still heavily armed groups of Bourbon soldiers in several areas and Garibaldi had no physical protection, having travelled ahead of his troops. His advisers were fearful he was a sitting duck, but he trusted that the joy of the people was an impenetrable shield. He read the mood correctly. Not a single rifle or cannon shot was fired.

Many people had told me to take great care when arriving at the central station of Naples – known to the locals as Napoli. They'd said it was a dangerous area, that I'd find an atmosphere of menace. So, of course, I was suitably wary walking through the station into the giant square outside, but I felt no threat and encountered no problems. Maybe the Naples of a decade or two ago was different, maybe it was instantly hostile back then. It didn't seem that way now.

The open space in front of the station is another Piazza Garibaldi, and certainly the largest of its kind across Italy. It measures 360 metres long by 165 metres wide, which is about 70,000 square metres, or 17.3 acres in old money. At one end was the entrance to the station, at the other a statue of the Hero of Two Worlds. He was standing high and proud in this one, resting on his sword, wearing his familiar cape. More interesting was one of the carvings at the foot of the statue, which had Garibaldi on horseback waving his cap to the people of the city. This was a rare depiction of him, and it reflected the absence of conflict on his entry to Naples.

This statue stood in the middle of a busy traffic island, where Corso Garibaldi runs past the end of Piazza Garibaldi. It was hard and risky to reach as the cars and scooters flashed past in a frenzy. This was the cliché of Naples made real, although in my experience the traffic in Rome is equally frenetic. It brought to mind the first question I'm always asked by people at home – what's it like driving in Italy? My instinct is to say that it's just like driving in any other big city, and not to fall for the stereotype view that the roads here are uniquely crazy. Yet, there is madness. Scooters and motorbikes are a particular hazard, darting between cars and going in the wrong direction down one-way streets. Most of the riders in Naples don't bother wearing helmets.

Buses go through red lights, as do old men who don't see them, and young bucks who don't care. I've often seen vehicles jump red lights next to a police car, and the cops never think of intervening. I've been told, in all seriousness, that there are red lights which don't really matter, but others where you must stop. How do you know? 'Oh, you just do,' is the standard reply. Drivers holding a mobile phone in one hand and gesticulating madly is also a common sight. I've seen bus drivers turning round difficult corners in city centres with only one hand on the wheel and a mobile in the other.

Then there is the manic junction alongside the Tiber in Rome where four lanes of cars reach a traffic light on the riverside embankment road. At the same junction, three lanes of cars are held up by red lights (this is one where it's best to stop) on a road arriving at a 45-degree angle. The lights turn green for all seven lanes at the same time. If that's not mad enough, the cars can then head towards three possible roads going forward. There is a single lane on the left, a single lane on the right, and two lanes ducking into an underpass in the middle. The cars coming from the angle often want to cut across to the left-hand exit lane, and those coming along the river want to sweep over to the right-hand exit lane. It's a stupendous free-for-all, rather like the queue for the ferry to Sicily, only at speed. The give-and-take required to navigate this bedlam appears to happen as if by some natural-born instinct. Collisions are incredibly rare.

This is all relatively fine, though, once you get used to it. What the outsider will never fathom is how the vast majority of car drivers in Rome see the dotted white line in the centre of a two-lane road as an instruction to drive along the middle of it. They always do – always, always, always. Your friends do so as well. It's second nature, it's just how it is. Overtake the white-line hoggers? Only if you're truly in a hurry and willing to bully them to one side with several blasts of your hooter. And if you do get past they will more than likely shake an angry finger at you, as if you've just committed a mortal driving sin. That's if they're not otherwise engaged in texting someone on their phone while driving at 50mph.

Needless to say, I took the metro to get around in Naples, heading first for a particular square close to *Spaccanapoli* – the dead straight and two-kilometre-long thin alleyway cutting through heart of the city, down from the Spagnoli district and up the hill at the other end close to the Garibaldi statue. *Spaccanapoli* translates as 'Naples splitter', but in fact it's the opposite; it's a magnet that draws in every visitor to the city with its kaleidoscope of bars, restaurants and churches along with its intense street vibe. My destination was right in the dip of the alley, a building with one side on *Spaccanapoli* and the other on Piazza Sette Settembre, the 'September 7 square'. The name honours the date in 1860 when Garibaldi lodged at the then Palazzo Doria d'Angri and spoke from the balcony to a large crowd declaring Italy 'to be a free and united nation'. A plaque on the wall recorded this fact, although it loses some impact today from being positioned just above the garish sign for a Tacos takeaway.

There was a second plaque close by which read: 'At this house the people of Napoli acclaimed Giuseppe Garibaldi as the liberator who unified Italy.' I found another plaque at the town hall, Palazzo San Giacomo, situated in the Piazza Municipio that leads down to the modern port where the cruise ships dock. This tribute was huge but hidden from public view behind imposing wooden doors. It said simply: 'To Garibaldi, from the people of city' and was dated 1882, the year he died. A policemen on guard kindly let me in to look, accommodating an Englishman writing a book about Garibaldi. He politely declined the opportunity to tell me his opinion of Garibaldi, which surely meant it was negative, influenced by social media or not.

It didn't take long wandering round Naples to discover who is the modern icon here. Everywhere one goes there are photos and paintings and murals of the Argentine footballer Diego Maradona, who joined the local Napoli club in the 1980s and inspired them to win the Italian league title for the first time in their history. In the *Spaccanapoli* alleyway there was a shrine to Maradona, while a giant mural of him in a nearby square was seen by more than six million tourists in 2023. Only the Colosseum had more visitors of any attraction in Italy. Napoli's stadium has also been re-named in honour of Maradona, although you could say that merely puts him on a par with Garibaldi, who also has a football ground named for him in Pisa.

Perhaps the most interesting plaque to Garibaldi was one I didn't expect to find. I had gone to the National Archaeological Museum, one of the finest in the world, which holds an immense collection of finds from Pompeii. On the wall by a swooping marble staircase up to first floor there was a huge plaque which said that 'Garibaldi, the dictator, dedicated this museum to the people of the new nation of Italy.' It also said that he ordered archaeologists to speed up excavations of Pompeii, and that he demanded a re-opening of the doors of a secret room on the first floor.

Until 1860, this museum had been a private collection of the Bourbons, and there was one room where erotic art was housed, and only 'men of the world' had been allowed through its doors. Now it was by far the busiest place in this prestigious home to stupendous finds from the ancient world. Marble statues of Julius Caesar and many others, for example, were displayed on four levels, and mostly admired in awed silence by visitors – certainly when I was there. Then, turning round one corner, there was suddenly the sound of laughing and joking. Everyone was smiling, even though they were standing in the longest queue of the museum. Yes, they were waiting to enter the secret room. Nobody forgets going there. The laughter became louder the nearer I approached. At the entrance a noticeboard told the story of the room being opened 'within the context of Garibaldi's insurrection of 1860... it was reorganised according to scientific criteria, excluding any irrelevant objects, and was defined as pornographic.'

The context was that, for a couple of months, Garibaldi was Dictator of Naples and could do what he wished. Another decision he made, as the plaque mentioned, was to begin a new era at Pompeii. It had previously belonged to the Bourbon royal family, but on the advice of his friend Alexandre Dumas, the greatest archaeological site of ancient Rome was made the property of the state. Garibaldi went to visit on 22 October 1860 and was photographed alongside the eminent archaeologist Giuseppe Fiorelli, who had been a political prisoner until then because of his strong nationalist views and would become the major figure in the transformation of Pompeii during the next two decades. It is a hazy picture, but the first known photograph of Garibaldi, who was wearing a red shirt and a bowler hat. Garibaldi put Dumas in charge initially, with the title of Honorary Director of Museums and Excavations, even though the writer had no qualifications for the role. It didn't last long. Following street protests in Naples about a foreigner as boss, Dumas resigned.

Dumas had been with Garibaldi in Palermo and then, working as a French journalist, had taken a boat to Naples to assess the situation. Garibaldi and his Red Shirts did not have that luxury. After the battle of Milazzo, they had to decide where best to land on the shores of Calabria and continue the crusade against the Bourbons. The shortest route, the way the modern ferry goes, was heavily guarded, so they sailed from the town of Taormina across to the southern coast of Calabria – underneath the big toe of Italy. Garibaldi landed at night on a beach just outside Melito di Porto Salvo, staying one night at Casa Ramirez, a building still there sporting the usual plaque. The little port is mighty proud of this, and in 2011 a new monument was created to remember the event – a sleek white obelisk with a museum next to it. The town's official website it declared this to be 'the starting point of the unification of Italy'. It's a boast, that would be fiercely disputed by maybe twenty-five or thirty other towns.

Many of the well-trained and disciplined Bourbon soldiers were still ready to fight against the Red Shirts, and Casa Ramirez shows the marks to this day of when it was bombarded the night Garibaldi was there. The generals and King Francesco II were more cautious, shaken by the series of defeats inflicted by Garibaldi's forces, who now appeared to be invincible. They immediately marched northwards and took the regional capital of Reggio Calabria in less than a day of fighting. His speed of action, typical of the guerrilla style, was invaluable, a stark contrast to the slow reactions of the Bourbon leaders.

Another group of Red Shirts landed further north in Calabria four days later at Marinella, close to the town of Palmi, and when Garibaldi joined them they inflicted a further crushing defeat against the Bourbons, despite having far fewer numbers on the battlefield. Garibaldi's 3,600 men had trounced opponents with 16,000 troops at their disposal, and now they had a virtually unopposed journey north through the region on the road to Naples.

One of several places in which he stopped overnight was the small town of Castrovillari. The main avenue through the centre is Corso Garibaldi, and here the Hero of Two Worlds lodged at the home of Colonel Giuseppe Pace, a local dignitary who joined the march of the Red Shirts and later became a deputy in the early Italian parliaments. There was a plaque commemorating the stay on a building above a kitchenware shop, although it was easy to miss high up shaded by the leaves of a plane tree. I was taking a photo of the plaque when the shop owner, Carmine Mirabelli, came out to chat. He was joyfully enthusiastic when I told him I was interested in Garibaldi, and he invited me into the house through a courtyard, past his two sleepy truffle-hunting dogs, and up some wide stone steps to the second-floor rooms where Garibaldi had lodged for a night. The house was gently decaying now, paint peeling everywhere, but his pride was beyond measure – and the counterpoint to the many people who have told me that nobody likes Garibaldi now in the south of Italy, what they call the *Mezzogiorno*.

I have encountered just as many people in the south who revere the name of Garibaldi as those who loathe it. There was the time, for example, when I was in the coastal town of Gallipoli in the region of Puglia, in the stilleto heel of Italy, a place with a vibrant beach culture and summer nightlife which attracts thousands of young people. Here, opposite the Teatro Garibaldi, which stands in Via Garibaldi, there was a restaurant that was the obvious place for me to eat. It was early evening, the tables were all empty, and the grumpy owner was sitting outside. He told me they were all reserved, which they were – but only for people arriving two hours later. Then I asked him about the name of his restaurant – *Le Garibaldine* – and suddenly he was alive with conversation, and as if by magic the perfect table was available.

Le Garibaldine is the name given to the women who fought alongside the Red Shirts, and the front page of the menu told the story of Antonietta De Pace, who had been working underground for many years in the cause of Italian freedom and was in Salerno, just south of Naples in the region of Campania, when Garibaldi arrived there in September 1860. He was so impressed with her story and her courage that he asked De Pace to join him on the train for the liberation of the Bourbon capital. She was one of only thirty people beside Garibaldi as he arrived in Naples.

As I was reading, the restaurant owner's wife came out. She wanted to talk as well, telling me the restaurant was named in honour of all the women who fought for Italy. Her passion was infectious and the food was good. I took the local speciality, *orecchiette con cime di rapa* (ear-shaped pasta with turnip tops). It's a dish that sounds much better in Italian and tastes fine.

If there is a mixed modern-day verdict in the *Mezzogiorno* about Garibaldi, there is no doubt the excitement was at fever pitch as he travelled up through Calabria and Campania in the late summer of 1860. One local politician described the scenes:

> When Garibaldi passed through a village you would not have said he was a general, but the head of a new religion. The women were no less enthusiastic than the men, bringing their babies to Garibaldi so that he should bless and even baptise them. It was delirium when he spoke with that beautiful voice of his.

The British military attaché George Cadogan witnessed the fervour, too, and wrote: 'He could make his followers go anywhere and do anything.'

Several times on this march north Colonel Peard was sent ahead with a few soldiers to assess the mood in an approaching town. The locals usually mobbed him, believing he was Garibaldi because there was a reasonably strong resemblance between the two men, with their flowing robes and long beards. Peard recalled one such incident: 'At Postiglione everyone was mad with excitement. One of the priests went on his knees and called me a second Jesus Christ. I was not prepared for so excessive a bit of blasphemy.'

The next major town they reached was Eboli, where the locals refused to believe that Peard was not actually Garibaldi – and so did the Bourbon generals. Peard, acting as if were Garibaldi, demanded that local officials in Eboli send a telegram to the Bourbon minister of war in Naples saying there were already thousands of Red Shirts in the town and many more were expected shortly. In fact, there were very few, but the bluff helped to persuade King Francesco II not to stand and fight for his capital, Naples.

Almost every Italian knows the name of Eboli, although not for this episode. One of the most important and famous books of this nation is *Christ Stopped at Eboli*, written by Carlo Levi, an author who was exiled to the barren southern region of Basilicata in the 1930s for his opposition to the fascist regime of Mussolini. In the book he describes the appalling poverty he found across the south of Italy, the result of appalling neglect by many successive national governments. 'No message, human or divine, has reached this stubborn poverty, this shadowy land,' wrote Levi. 'Christ did not come. Christ stopped at Eboli.'

Garibaldi stopped at Eboli, too, the day after Peard had tricked the Bourbons there. He stayed for a few hours before heading north to Naples, as testified by the obligatory plaque on the wall of the house at which he rested. Garibaldi also did not go to Basilicata. He bypassed that region, and Levi described in his book how the Hero of Two Worlds was scorned by the people there. 'Garibaldi was not popular in these parts.' One character that Levi encountered, says: 'Of course they pass off a lot of tall tales in the schoolbooks about his exploits, but Garibaldi was a fake.'

There was nothing unreal about the triumphant progress of the Red Shirts in 1860. The next stop was Salerno, and by this time Francesco II and the bulk of his army had abandoned Naples, leaving the city open for Garibaldi to move in. He travelled immediately on the specially commissioned train that trundled past the ruins of Pompeii on the way. The happy crowds who greeted him in the city dissuaded the remaining Bourbon soldiers from action.

'When the people greet us like this there are no cannons,' said Garibaldi to some fearful companions as they rode in a carriage down to the harbour and along the quayside. Hundreds of thousands of Neapolitans filled the streets around the long seafront. Today this is Via Caracciolo, which has barely any traffic and is a perfect place for a *Passeggiata*. Vesuvius dominates the skyline across the water, a brooding menace, and its top covered by clouds on the day I took this stroll. The volcano which destroyed ancient Pompeii has long been dormant, but it is not extinct. (Some have described it as 'Europe's ticking time bomb'.) I could also see the outline of islands on the horizon, Capri the most visible. Most of all there was the view of the sea. This must have thrilled Garibaldi as his procession made its way. The sea was his natural habitat.

At this time Naples was the largest city on the Italian peninsula and third largest in Europe, and Garibaldi ruled it as a dictator for two months. He stated an ambition to bring in social reform and free education, declared a desire to abolish gambling and build more railways, but there wasn't enough time for anything of significance to be achieved. Letting prisoners out of jail was a serious mistake, the level of crime swiftly increased. His main focus, in any case, was the final decisive battle of the whole Expedition of The Thousand in this momentous summer of 1860. The Bourbons had retreated to a strong position at the River Volturno, north of Naples on the road to Rome, which was Garibaldi's ultimate aim. They had 50,000 men compared to 20,000 Red Shirts, a number bolstered from the initial 1,089 by volunteer recruits collected on the march through Sicily and up the mainland.

Before the battle, Garibaldi set up his headquarters at the palace of Caserta, built by the Bourbons to resemble the glory of Versailles just outside Paris. Caserta may be the grandest palace in all of Italy, and it is reckoned to be the largest palace in the world measured by volume. It was undoubtedly a symbolic choice as well as a practical one with abundant space for his men. Garibaldi, typically for him, lodged in one of the smallest rooms he could find. Dumas also came with him from Naples, and he took the royal bedrooms.

At the same time as Garibaldi was conquering the south, the initiative was finally taken in the north of Italy by the Piedmontese army of King Vittorio Emanuele II and his Prime Minister, Cavour. With the diplomatic acquiescence of France, they invaded the Papal states of Umbria and Le Marche in the centre of Italy, a move that prompted the Bourbons to delay a possible attack on the Red Shirts. It was another stroke of luck for Garibaldi.

The first skirmish of the battle was actually initiated by one of Garibaldi's top commanders, General Turr, who captured the small hilltop town of Caiazzo just north of Caserta. It was a freelance effort, and the town was quickly retaken by Bourbon soldiers in their first and only victory against the Red Shirts. It's a minor detail of history, but today many thousands of people make a pilgrimage to the town ever year. Caiazzo, they will tell you, is home to the best pizzeria in Italy, and therefore probably the whole world. The best of the best? I know, we should all be sceptical about such claims, particularly here in Italy where locals are forever eager to claim superiority in all things. In the hilltop town of San Gimignano in Tuscany, for example, the main square has an ice cream shop on one side that is 'No. 1 in the world' with a certificate on the wall to prove it. On the other side of the square is another ice cream parlour, which also claims to be 'No. 1 in the world', also certified.

I went to Caiazzo for the history, which consisted of a small column in the main square dedicated to those who died fighting in the town for Italian unity. And I went for the pizza, which I can only say was divine. The pizzeria was called Pepe in Grano, there was a three-month waiting list for a table (military planning required), and it was worth it. Everything about the pizza was incredible – the perfect sourdough base, the sweetest tomatoes I have tasted, and *mozzarella da bufala* cheese that squeaked in the mouth just as it should. It's not so surprising, however, that this tiny town in Campania is home to what must be a contender for No. 1 pizza in the world. Naples, the capital of the region, is the acknowledged birthplace of modern pizza.

Italians everywhere will also tell you the exact moment it was born – in the summer of 1889 when Margherita, then queen of the newly unified Italy, went on a visit to Naples and was presented with a special new dish to eat, named in her honour. This was a pizza topped with tomatoes, mozzarella and basil leaves, designed to represent the three colours of the new Italian national flag. It was called, obviously, *pizza margherita*, and to this day is by far the most popular version in the country. Most people I know choose only a *margherita*, even though the pizzeria will have a wide range of options. It's plain, simple and patriotic. When you read into the history of pizza, there will be experts who say this story is just a myth, and that the dish was already becoming widespread. But whisper it quietly to Italians. This is a legend they love to believe, just like the invincibility of Garibaldi in battle.

What nobody can deny is the importance of pizza to everyday life in Italy. An example of this was illustrated when Italy played in the 2006 football World Cup, and faced a semi-final showdown against Germany, where the tournament was being held. The day before the match, the German newspaper *Bild* printed what it considered a humorous front-page headline declaring: 'Arrivederci Pizza'. There was outrage among Italian supporters and media. Italy won the game, and afterwards *La Gazzetta dello Sport* told the world: 'Mock anything you like about us, but don't touch mothers, pizza, pasta and Garibaldi.'

Pizza is ubiquitous, even more than pasta and Garibaldi. Pizzerias are like the beaches, an integral and classless part of social life where everybody goes to chat. The best of them are noisy and exuberant, like one I visited in the old working-class district of Testaccio in Rome where Oscar-winning actor Roberto Benigni wandered by without anyone troubling him for a selfie or an autograph. Eating pizza comes along with one of the strongest unwritten rules of Italian dining – that with it you drink only beer or cola, and never wine. And don't even think about mentioning the possibility of putting pineapple on a pizza. That is considered an abomination. There is also a common question asked of an outsider like myself. Do you prefer Neapolitan pizza, with its thicker, chewy dough or Roman pizza, which is thin and crispier? In Naples they have no doubts and corroborate this unimpeachable truth by telling you that in 2017 their style of pizza was put on the official UNESCO cultural heritage list.

Anyhow, I'm very glad I made the pilgrimage to Caiazzo – and the Bourbon generals were very wrong in believing they had turned the tide of war against Garibaldi with their recapture of the town. It was just a precursor to a titanic battle that ended their regime and opened the final door to the unification of Italy. This was the Battle of Volturno, where the Bourbons attacked the heavily outnumbered Red Shirts but were defied by a brilliant defensive campaign from Garibaldi.

He was inspirational once more by personal example, leading charges from the front against the enemy, sword in hand, oblivious to the danger and ready to die for Italy. In one area of the battle there was a vast aqueduct that spans a gorge – still there today and known as The Arches of the Valley, an impressive sight on the road towards Caiazzo. Garibaldi's men controlled this, running across a path on top to keep information flowing between various arenas of the battle. The outcome of the conflict was in the balance until Garibaldi ordered a decisive attack led by volunteers who had joined him from Hungary. Many argue this was the moment that created Italy. It came at a heavy cost. 1,400 Red Shirts were killed or wounded, while the Bourbons lost nearly 1,100 men. This was Garibaldi's last great victory on a battlefield.

It is remembered by the Volturno memorial, where the bones of the many who died lie behind an imposing iron door at the foot of a 20-metre high stone obelisk topped by the star of Italy, a bleak as well as solemn place. On the front of the memorial was a carving of some of the main characters of the battle, where half of Garibaldi's face was missing. Either it had weathered away, although others were intact, or this was another case of vandalism. Two other heads of Red

Shirts were completely missing, looking as if they had been deliberately knocked off. Certainly, there was no urgency for any restoration work.

As the Battle of Volturno was unfolding, the Piedmont army swept south through the Papal States, although they avoided Rome following a diplomatic accord with France that the Pope should remain in control of the Eternal City. What would happen now? It was unconceivable that the Red Shirt liberators would fight the Piedmontese, whose goal now was also a united Italy. And It had become impractical for Garibaldi to press on ahead for Rome. It might have been possible for him to remain as Dictator of the whole of the southern region of Italy he had conquered in several mighty battles. But Garibaldi had been consistent in always declaring that he was fighting for a united Italy – and the only way that would happen was to hand over the south to King Vittorio Emanuele II.

Legend has it that he met the King on a picturesque hillside at Teano, a small town roughly halfway between Rome and Naples. There are several famous paintings of both men on horseback at the scene, which symbolises for many Italians the moment their nation was created. There is also a statue depicting it in the town of Fiesole just outside Florence. Every person in Italy knows the name of Teano, and almost every Italian is taught in school about this crucial moment of their history. Almost.

There is one town which begs to differ, where a different story is told in the classroom. This is Vairano, a few miles north of Teano. I visited on a hot summer's day and the place had a sleepy air, most people were indoors and the few who were out sat in the shade of the terraces of the local bars. Many Italian flags were flying, which was the first hint of something unusual. Then I began to see other flags decorated with notices, which were all about the local pride of Vairano.

Here, they said, at the Taverna Catena on 26 October 1860, Garibaldi met King Vittorio Emanuele II to agree the transfer of the south to a new united Italy, of which he would be the monarch. This was stated on a big tricolour flag attached to the post for a CCTV camera. Nearby there was a stone monument in the main square, named Piazza Unita D'Italia, which declared that here the two men concluded the unity of Italy. Next to this was an old-fashioned town noticeboard, of fancy ironwork, with a red background and a painting of Garibaldi meeting the King.

Round the corner I found a second stone monument, put up in 1967. A long statement in legalese was inscribed on this, which said Vairano is officially the place where the unity of Italy was concluded. A few steps away was the Taverna Catena itself. It was empty, the tavern long since closed, but with several signs saying renovation was now in process. For those visitors still not convinced about Vairano's claim to fame, there was yet another marble notice on a wall declaring: 'With this plaque we recover for our territory the legitimate glory of the event of Garibaldi meeting the King.' I found a further four plaques emphasising this obscure and unremarkable town's special place in the history of Italy. They don't want you to leave with any doubts.

As for Teano itself? That's a different story. Its monument to history is located well outside town on a road where it was almost impossible to stop safely to take a look. I parked in a perilous position on the kerb, getting a couple of angry horn blasts from cars speeding past. The place was surrounded by a locked fence, and less than lovingly maintained. The grass was knee high and there were only some decaying weeds in two flowerpots by a stone column, at the bottom of which read: 'Salute the King of Italy, Giuseppe Garibaldi.' A tattered Italian flag hung limply behind.

A second headstone lay behind the fence, this one to celebrate the twinning in 2010 of Teano with Calatafimi in Sicily and the town of Camogli near to Quarto in Genoa. This was to link the start of the Expedition of The Thousand to its first major battle in Sicily and its finishing point here in the rolling countryside between Naples and Rome. In the town of Teano itself I found a colourful mural of Garibaldi and the King meeting on horseback, but little else of note. Maybe Teano is confident enough of its legend not to boast too much. Or maybe it's a sign of squeamishness, because it knows it doesn't really deserve its fame.

All of Italy was now united except for Rome, still ruled by the Pope, and the region around and including Venice, which remained under the control of Austria. Garibaldi had achieved his dream, his job was done, and he was now redundant. It seems he was glad to exit the stage and return to his farm on the island of Caprera. He was a warrior, not a politician, and departed on a ship with no grand farewell from the authorities after six months of intense struggle which had totally transformed his homeland. The only salute was from guns of British Royal Navy ships moored in the harbour at Naples.

The legacy of this moment has forever been debated in Italy and will continue to be a matter of fervent contention. Did Garibaldi wantonly give away the south to the north and condemn it to poverty and servitude? Or was unity with the Piedmont regime of Vittorio Emanuele II the only rational and practical choice? The most pressing question asked is could Garibaldi have remained in charge of the south and created a separate radical and republican nation state? The answer to this final question is surely no. That wasn't his aim, and nor was he suited to political leadership. As a long-term dictator, even a president, Garibaldi would almost certainly have been a disaster.

This is a classic 'what if' conundrum. What if he'd done this? What if he'd done that? History will not be the judge, because there are many different versions of history, and opinions alter back and forth with time and fashion, moulded by ideology and intransigence.

Personally, I'm inclined towards the verdict of British historian G.M .Trevelyan, given 110 years ago:

> Garibaldi will be the symbol of Italia to her children in all ages to come. As the centuries slip by, carrying into oblivion almost all that was once noble or renowned, Mazzini's soul and Cavour's wisdom will be forgotten by the Italian who tends the vine or sweats beside the furnace. They will be forgotten sooner than the old grey cloak and the red shirt and that face of simple faith and love. Garibaldi will live as the incarnate symbol of two passions ... the love of country and the love of freedom.

That's what I have seen so often travelling around Italy – an instant and instinctive enthusiasm to talk about Garibaldi when his name is mentioned, like the shopkeeper in Castrovillari and the restaurant owner in Gallipoli. And even for those who disparage Garibaldi across the *Mezzogiorno*, he is the symbol of Italy, the symbol of what they feel is wrong about their country.

11

TURIN/TORINO

'Garibaldi has rendered to Italy the greatest service a man could: he has given the Italians confidence in themselves.'

Camillo Cavour

The long march of Giuseppe Garibaldi and Expedition of The Thousand from Marsala to Palermo and Naples had paved the way for the new country of Italy. This was officially proclaimed in February 1861 by King Vittorio Emmanuele II in his home city of Turin, which became the nation's first capital. I wanted to see the exact spot where the declaration occurred, and that meant marching along the longest pedestrian street in Europe. It could have only one name – Via Garibaldi – which is 1.3 kilometres from end to end, and as straight as the crow flies because it was the first ancient Roman road into the city. These days it's a temple to modern consumerism, full of mobile phone stores, jewellers, ice cream parlours and designer clothes shops amid the splendour of five-storey nineteenth-century buildings. I spurned the chance to eat in the *Gari* sushi restaurant, opting instead for a coffee and panino halfway along the street at *Caffe Garibaldi*. Inside was a temple to the Hero of Two Worlds, with paintings and memorabilia decorating every wall. Sitting outside I could look far down the street and see in the distance my target, the Palazzo Madama.

It is one of the myriad treasures of Turin. Two thousand years ago this was the location of Porta Decumana, the old Roman gateway into the city, but now there is a fifteenth-century grey stone castle with the addition of a baroque façade visible all the way down Via Garibaldi. Behind the entrance here I discovered two majestic marble staircases that ascended to the Senate chamber of the first Italian parliament created in 1861. An information sign told me this was where the new nation of Italy was proclaimed, although it failed to say anything about the turmoil and strife already brewing in Turin and beyond. The seats of the Senate, the upper house of parliament, have long since gone; it moved within a few years to Florence and then to Rome's very own Palazzo Madama. Today, this place is an exhibition hall and the Palazzo Madama houses the Turin Museum of Ancient Art.

A short stroll from here was where the real political action of the early days of Italy occurred, in the heart of the Palazzo Carignano, which houses the monumental *Museo Nazionale di Risorgimento*, the largest of them all. Its showpiece is the perfectly preserved previous chamber of deputies of the old Piedmont parliament. It has an intimate circular design, much like the old anatomical theatres used for public dissections, with high banks of seats overlooking the middle. The analogy is apt. The dissections of policy could be fierce here, not least when Garibaldi got himself elected to this parliament for the seat of Nizza in March 1860 to try to prevent his home city being given to France in a secret deal negotiated by Camillo Cavour. This chamber is too fragile to allow hordes of visitors, but every couple of years they open it up for a weekend so you can sit in the seats of Garibaldi and Cavour.

Despite his eloquence, Garibaldi failed to save Nizza, and its seat in this parliament disappeared. Garibaldi responded by putting himself up for symbolic election in two different locations at the next ballot held in July 1860. By this time he was leading the Expedition of The Thousand on the battlefields of Sicily, moving between the triumphs at Palermo and Milazzo, yet his popularity ensured he was easily elected in both the city of Milan and the tiny hilltop village of Corniglio in the region of Emilia Romagna. Needless to say, he did not attend the last days of the Piedmont chamber of deputies.

Garibaldi only returned to active parliamentary duty in Turin in April 1861, when he was elected to the new Italian lower house as a representative for Naples, where he had been the Dictator a few months earlier. The old chamber was too small for a national parliament, and a temporary one was built in the courtyard of the Palazzo Carignano. It no longer exists, although a marble plaque on the wall tells of how it was commissioned by Cavour and completed in just 113 days. Blink, and you would miss this information, which is kept curiously hidden by the museum – perhaps because they don't wish to take the spotlight away from their pride and joy, the old chamber.

This is a pity because the most historic confrontation of all happened in the temporary parliament when Garibaldi launched a ferocious verbal attack on Cavour, accusing him and the northern deputies of provoking a civil war in the south of the new Italy with a harsh punishment regime and too little financial assistance. He also clashed with Cavour about the disbandment of the Red Shirt soldiers left behind after the unification battles, and about their poor treatment. All the deputies in the chamber were in formal dress except for Garibaldi, who entered wearing a red shirt, white cloak and Spanish sombrero. His speech caused uproar; deputies fought each other like boxers and the session was suspended.

Garibaldi refused to back down from his strong views, and although he agreed to meet Cavour at the Royal Palace, the two giants of the age did not shake hands. General Ciadini, a friend of Cavour, publicly challenged Garibaldi to a duel because of his behaviour, prompting further fury among the rival deputies. Garibaldi swerved that folly with, for him, a rare moment of diplomacy. All this was political theatre, too easily descending into pantomime. Cavour had the reins of power, but he knew Garibaldi commanded the loyalty of the people in the streets, and he knew why, saying: 'Public opinion would be right. Garibaldi has rendered to Italy the greatest service a man could: he has given the Italians confidence in themselves.'

For all his faults, the psychological impact of Garibaldi's swashbuckling style and courage is a crucial part of his nation's story. Even though the pair had become political foes, Cavour admired this aspect of his accuser. By this time, however, Cavour was already ill, and he died a few weeks later. It was reported that on his deathbed he said: 'Brave Garibaldi. I bear him no grudge. He wants to go to Venice and Rome, and so do I.' To the end they shared the vision of a completely united nation.

Although the temporary parliamentary chamber no longer exists, the wooden seat with Garibaldi's name on the back survives and is on display in Rome's Central Risorgimento museum. Here in Turin they have the National Risorgimento museum, which houses even more memorabilia than its rival in the Eternal City. Walking around here was a delight. On display was one of Garibaldi's saddles from his days fighting in South America, a gorgeous object of leather and iron. More people stopped to look at this than anything else. I was particularly taken by his famous Turkish style cap, and also what was described as the 'Parliamentary medal of the Honourable Garibaldi'. There was a fine old black carriage given to Garibaldi late in his life by King Vittorio Emanuele II when he was stricken by arthritis. The caption read: 'The carriage, and no longer the horse, for the elderly hero.'

The most emotional relic for Italians is the scrap of paper on which in 1847 Goffredo Mameli wrote the lyrics of their national anthem, which he entitled *Canto Nazionale* – the National Song. As with every Risorgimento museum, there were also many paintings, including the original by Giralomo Induno of the moment Garibaldi planted the Italian flag on landing at Marsala. In the final room I found a wonderful painting that depicted Garibaldi returning to Mandriole in 1859 to see the place where Anita died. This was in a big hall designed to become the new permanent chamber of deputies for the Italian parliament, a project never completed because the capital switched to Florence in 1865 and eventually to Rome in 1871.

Caprera was the immediate destination for Garibaldi after the tumultuous spring of 1861. It was a haven from the Turin parliament, but there was little rest from politics. A swarm of visitors came to see him, among them European revolutionaries and fellow Italians agitating for assaults on Venice and/or Rome to bring these cities into the new united nation. There were also Americans, intrigued by the exploits of Garibaldi, and wondering if he could be of use to them. US minister George Perkins Marsh went to Caprera and sent this message back across the Atlantic: 'Though Garibaldi is but a solitary and private individual, he is at this moment one of the Great Powers of the world.'

The US Civil War had just begun in April 1861, and Garibaldi received an offer from President Abraham Lincoln to join the conflict on the side of the Union as a Major-General. It was a genuine proposal, and an attractive idea for the Hero of Two Worlds, who had once lived in New York. Several elements, though, conspired to thwart the sight of Garibaldi on the battlefield against the Confederates. He told the Americans he wished to be the Supreme Commander of Lincoln's army, which was never going to happen. He also sent word that he would not go to the Civil War unless the President committed to abolishing slavery. Garibaldi had proudly freed slaves when he came across them during his years in South America, and he was always a humanitarian at heart. All his battles, he felt, were in the cause of freedom and justice. At this time, for example, he was campaigning for the abolition of the death penalty. Lincoln would not give the guarantee Garibaldi required.

Politics in Italy also played a significant part. Scores of petitions were published in newspapers urging Garibaldi not to leave. The Turin journal *L'Armonia* wrote: 'What will become of Italy if Garibaldi and his staff go to America?' The Milan-based paper *L'Unita Italiana* addressed an open letter to Garibaldi:

> General, do not go to America. The people here have faith in you, and you must have faith in them. The unity of Italy is far from being accomplished. You have laid its foundation. You alone can complete the work. We are waiting for you, General, to lead us to Rome.

Long-term friends and allies like Francesco Crispi and Nino Bixio also fought hard to persuade him to stay. This is another of those delicious 'what ifs' of history. What if Garibaldi had gone to the Civil War? He is remembered nevertheless with two statues in the United States. One is located in Washington Square in the Manhattan district of New York, not far from the museum on Staten Island. The other statue is in Garibaldi Park in Chicago. The town of Garibaldi lies on the Pacific coast just west of Portland in Oregon, founded in 1860 and so named because the first postmaster was an admirer of Garibaldi's adventures. And during the civil war the 39th New York Infantry Regiment, fighting on the Union side, gave themselves the nickname of the Garibaldi Guard.

We will never know how Cavour would have reacted to the American offer. We do know that he and Garibaldi met several times in Turin, which was Cavour's town. Certainly they did so at *Farmacia Del Cambio*, which is not a chemist shop but a splendid coffee bar across the square from *Museo Nazionale di Risorgimento* and the old chamber of deputies. It's still there, and still looks the same, with polished wood panelling, exquisite crockery, old-school service and charm. Only the prices are modern. Cavour would often wait there, ready to be called when needed for a vote in the chamber.

If Turin is the town of Cavour, it is also a coffee town, perhaps the coffee town of Italy – although that accolade would be strongly contested by Naples and Trieste. Nobody, however, can dispute the fundamental place of coffee across the whole of the country. More than 90 per cent of Italians drink at least one coffee a day, and the majority several more. It is a ritual of daily life that binds people together, and it comes with strict methods, curious traditions and strongly observed unwritten rules. I discovered this very quickly, falling into the trap of ordering a cappuccino for an Italian friend in the afternoon. I knew she adored cappuccino, but when it arrived she looked at the cup with pure disgust and refused point blank to consider taking even one sip. It was sent back to the hell from which it came. Cappuccino is a drink only for breakfast in Italy, rarely taken after 11am, and never after midday. Never. Well, only by pitiful visitors who don't know the rules, and don't realise the truth of which every Italian is convinced – that drinking hot milk in coffee following a hot meal is very bad for digestion.

Another rule is that at mealtimes coffee is never drunk during lunch or dinner, only afterwards. I happily continue to ignore this one, taking coffee with my sandwich, a mild offence tolerated by the owner of my local bar because I'm a *straniero* – a foreigner. He always gives me a glass of water as well, which is part of the ritual, and occasionally I do the correct thing and drink the water first so that you can taste the coffee with a clean palate.

Everybody has their local bar, or the place where they stop to have breakfast on the way to work. Coffee starts early. Many bars open at six in the morning, some even earlier, to cater for commuters who will probably have a pastry of some kind with their cappuccino. Most people stand at the bar, *al banco*, because it's quicker and because it's cheaper. You pay more if you sit at a table, considerably more in a tourist hotspot, but prices are generally low by international standards. The morning ritual is to read the paper with breakfast, most often one of the three national sports newspapers published every day in Italy. Most bars have several papers available for customers, it's part of the service.

The bar is like the beach – a truly democratic space where everyone goes: businessmen in smart suits, old ladies out with their dogs, tradesmen, university professors, taxi drivers, film directors and schoolkids doing their homework. It's a meeting place, a talking shop, the hub of social life through the day. It's a second home. It was also a slightly intimidating place at first for me when I could speak little Italian, especially when the bar was noisy and crowded. How do you manoeuvre your way to the bar without the required words, and with the uncertain body language of an outsider? With time I discovered a gentle push here, and a not so gentle shove there and saying *permesso* (excuse me) with just the right amount of authority did the trick. This is particularly important during the mad rush when Italians take the essential and obligatory *pausa caffe* in mid-morning, usually drinking a strong espresso served in a tiny cup.

If cappuccino is the queen of coffees at breakfast, then espresso is the emperor for the rest of the day. The first effort at making something like the modern espresso, which means 'pressed out', was unveiled at the Turin Expo of 1884. What we think of as espresso now came with an invention by Achille Gaggia in 1938, a system which forces hot water through coffee grounds at very high pressure to produce a strong coffee. Gaggia's name is still on many of the espresso machines in coffee bars today around the world. There is, of course, in this highly bureaucratic nation, an organisation called the Italian Espresso Institute, and it proclaims that a 'Certified Italian Espresso has a hazel-brown to dark brown colour and a foam characterised by tawny reflexes.' I bet you didn't know your coffee was supposed to have tawny reflexes, but after much deliberation with Italian friends, this probably means it should have some colour similar to that of a lion's mane.

Another historic coffee invention had been made a few years earlier in 1933 by Alfonso Bialetti – the stove-top Moka *caffettiera* used by millions in Italy to make high-quality and intensely strong coffee. More than ninety per cent of households in Italy have a Moka, and if someone doesn't stop for coffee on the way to work, they will invariably have it at home. This will be made in a Moka, even if they also own a modern capsule machine. It's another cherished rule. It's Moka for breakfast at home, and capsule coffee later on, if you don't go out to the bar instead. As for instant coffee? A mere thirteen per cent of Italians admit to having drunk a cup of instant coffee even once in their lives, and they probably did so only as a last resort, and almost certainly when they were abroad.

Coffee's place in everyday life here is beyond question, and people nod in happy agreement as I read them the words of one-time agriculture minister Gian Marco Centinaio: 'In Italy coffee is much more than a simple drink. It is an integral part of our national identity, and an expression of our sociality that distinguishes us in the world.' The politician made this proud declaration when talking about a campaign in 2022 to gain UNESCO cultural heritage recognition for espresso coffee. Given how many other similar requests are approved around the world, this should have been like knocking on an open door. Instead, it stirred up local pride and the eternal rivalries within Italy. Two separate groups were determined to lead the way, one of them the region of Campania, representing Naples, which believes it is the home of coffee as well as pizza. It does have perhaps the best coffee tradition of all, called the *Caffe Sospeso* – where a person buys two cups of espresso when they go to a bar, one for themselves, and one for the next person who comes in who can't afford a coffee. This practice remains as strong as ever, and for my money should have given Naples the edge.

The rival group was fronted by the pompously titled Consortium for the Protection of Traditional Italian Espresso Coffee, which is based in the smart town of Treviso, just north of Venice. Its desire to be in charge was declared 'an act of war by the north against the south' by the Campania campaign, reflecting deep-rooted distrust and animosity going back to Garibaldi's day, and which some say Garibaldi is most responsible for. Neither side won this battle. Italy's internal UNESCO committee became so fed up with the feuding that it disallowed both applications. Twelve months later, the city of Trieste decided to have a go at winning cultural heritage status for the espresso, but they were also rejected. Nobody has yet succeeded as I write, but expect more attempts in the future.

One other thing has been evident about coffee in Italy along my journey – that every town seems to have its own particular coffee brand. There are hundreds, if not thousands. The two names most famous across the world are probably Lavazza and Illy, based in Turin and Trieste respectively. Verganano, Danesi, Kimbo, Segafredo Zanetti, Borbone, Hausbrandt and Pellini are just a few other great coffees. When I stopped for lunch in *Caffe Garibaldi* in Turin they served a brand from the city called simply Il Caffe. There is also (how could there not be?) a brand named Gran Caffe Garibaldi, which is based in Milan. They sell capsules as well.

All the different brands give a clue to why Italian coffee is so good. The answer, many people have told me, is the quality of the way the coffee beans are toasted by each company, and the balance chosen between arabica and robusta varieties of bean. Every brand has its own method and balance and will claim its superiority.

The *Tazza d'Oro* coffee bar near the Pantheon in central Rome claims to be the best in the world, and its espresso is excellent. But here in Turin, they proclaim the glory of a bar called Caffe Al Bicerin, which was the favourite of Cavour, and where you can sit in his lovingly preserved seat. This is a tourist attraction in its own right, and you are encouraged to drink Bicerin, a mixture of hot chocolate, coffee and cream.

Walking through Turin was a joy. It is a city of handsome squares, classical colonnades, magnificent museums and the royal palace of the Piedmont kings where Garibaldi had his confrontation with Cavour. Another jewel was the Mole Antonelliana tower that was begun in 1863, just after the unification of Italy, and which for 30 years housed the Risorgimento museum before it transferred to Palazzo Carignano. The tower is now Italy's national museum of cinema. The brightest diamond, though, is the Egyptian museum, widely considered to be the most important in Europe.

My focus was elsewhere. I wandered down to the banks of the river Po where cars and lorries drove by on the embankment road and a steady *Passeggiata* of pedestrians stopped to look at a statue and take photos. They decided to put their stone Garibaldi by the river in this city. The inscriptions are plain. *I Mille* is carved on one side, and it says simply 'To Garibaldi. Torino' on the front. There was also an information board which said the statue was erected in 1887 to encourage political togetherness among warring parties amid the struggle to make a new Italy. In this depiction Garibaldi was wearing the cap displayed in the museum and had a sword in both hands held horizontally across his midriff. The symbolism was clear enough; Garibaldi was at peace rather than ready for conflict.

There is always a strong symbolic element to the statues and the plaques and the road names. They were used to promote the idea of the new united Italy, as a deliberate and monumental method of nation-building. When you stroll down a Via Garibaldi anywhere across Italy, you are in effect walking along a weapon of national propaganda. Francesco Crispi, when he became Prime Minister in the 1880s, was quite explicit about this, saying he wished to make Garibaldi 'a sacred symbol of the unity of the nation, of the people bound in selfless faith and duty to Italy'. Other notable characters of the Risorgimento, like Mazzini, Cavour and Vittorio Emanuele II, were also used in this fashion, but none of them on the scale of Garibaldi. Even as I write, two messages have come from friends containing photos of a Garibaldi plaque where they happen to be: one in the tiny village of Candela in Puglia, the other from the city of Bologna where a chapel in a church has been dedicated to the memory of Garibaldi's red shirt warriors who died in battle. The scope and reach of the legend of Garibaldi is almost limitless.

The statue here in Turin had Garibaldi standing with his back to the river. Over his shoulder I could see the Superga hill and its Basilica. Why was he facing that way? Wouldn't it have been more natural to have him looking out over the Po to the landscape beyond? The answer was another symbol. Garibaldi had been planted in this exact position so that he was looking up another long straight road that led into the centre of the city. This was the Via Dei Mille. I walked up alongside cars locked in a traffic jam and noticed a crowd of people ahead. They had stopped to gawp at a bright red Ferrari trapped in the mess.

If Turin was Cavour's town and it's a coffee town, it is also a car town – home to Italy's most popular brand, Fiat, which is an acronym for *Fabbrica Italiana Automobili di Torino*. It was founded in 1899, and the rival Lancia car company also started in Turin in 1906. Both are still going strong, and the Fiat headquarters in the Lingotto district in the south of the city has become a major tourist attraction. Visitors flock to see the testing track on top of the old factory, made famous by the 1960s movie, *The Italian Job*, where the Minis of Michael Caine and company are chased by police cars around the track. For anyone like me who adores that movie, this is an evocative place to visit, and it now has the added attraction of a small *pinocateca* art gallery in the centre featuring works by Picasso,

Renoir, Matisse and Manet. These days it is known as the Pista 500 in honour of the company's most beloved car, the Fiat 500, or as the Italians call it – the *Cinquecento*. The old ones feel impossibly tiny, yet I have still seen many all across Italy, some lovingly preserved or renovated, and others being driven around in a battered state. The modern *Cinquecento*, a stylish reinvention, is one of the most popular cars in the country, certainly among city dwellers, along with the Fiat Panda and the Smart.

Italy and Italians played a crucial role in the development of the motor car, and the obsession with engines, oil and speed goes right back to the days of Garibaldi. In fact, there is a curious link between the early development of cars and the Red Shirt fighters. The first man to invent a liquid fuel engine, in 1836, and who later invented the first carburettor, was an engineer from Milan called Luigi de Cristoforis, who was the cousin of two men closely involved with Garibaldi. One of these was Carlo de Cristoforis, a general who died at the battle of San Fermo, and is honoured with a crypt in the village. The other was Malachia de Cristoforis, who worked as a doctor to the Red Shirts amid the battles of Milazzo and the Volturno, and who stood as a candidate for the first Turin parliament alongside Garibaldi.

The obsession with cars manifests itself in many ways, for example at the funeral of a close friend in Padova. After the service, the coffin was carried outside to the hearse. And what a hearse it was – a sleek grey Maserati, a beautiful car that turned the heads of everyone in the street, not just those of us attending the funeral. '*Che macchina*' – what a car! This, apparently, is quite usual, and my old friend would have appreciated the scene – his favourite car had been an Alfa Romeo. Alfa, by the way, is an acronym for *Anonima Lombarda Fabbrica Automobili* – which translates as the anonymous car factory of Lombardy.

Alfas are hardly anonymous now, instead synonymous with speed and style. Most police cars in Italy are Alfa Romeos, and a taxi ride in an Alfa can be a hair-raising experience. One took me from Fiumicino airport to the centre of Rome as if the roads were a grand prix race track. He zig-zagged madly on the ring motorway, sometimes talking on his mobile. Suddenly, though, he came to a halt with a screech of brakes as if practising an emergency stop for a driving test. He had noticed a well-dressed young woman waiting to cross the road, and the gallant Alfa knight of the road had to deliver the final piece of the stereotype jigsaw. She barely turned her head in acknowledgement. He would have needed a Supercar for that – a Ferrari, Maserati or a Lamborghini.

Another symbol of the Italian attachment to cars is that youngsters are allowed to drive specially made mini-cars or *macchinette* from the age of fourteen, with merely the same licence required for a moped. No, this is not a joke. Fourteen-year-olds are allowed to zip around in the traffic alongside proper cars, buses and lorries – instantly assimilating the dark arts of overtaking, undertaking, jumping red lights and aggravating fellow drivers. These machines cost anything up to 15,000 Euros each, are legally obliged to have engines no bigger than 50cc, and a top speed of 28mph. As anyone who drives a car in any Italian city knows, however, that is a nonsense. Souped-up engines are a routine sight and sound. Even more astounding is that adults who have their regular driving licences revoked for multiple traffic offences can still go around in these *macchinette* with a moped licence. Many older people simply choose to drive them because they are easier to park and are allowed into city centre zones where ordinary cars are banned.

Most of them are made by French companies like Ligier and Aixam, but Fiat have moved into the market with their own electric version, which they call the *Topolino*. This is also the Italian name for Mickey Mouse – and, no, I am still not joking. You don't make fun of cars in Turin.

The city is the centre of the Italian car industry, and was still the first capital of Italy when Garibaldi made a visit in December 1861 for a private audience with King Vittorio Emanuele II to talk about the possibility of completing the new nation by liberating the cities of Venice and Rome, ruled by the Austrians and the Pope respectively. Garibaldi spoke at meetings of nationalist groups in Genoa and campaigned across Lombardy for immediate action. He sparked strong emotions and enthusiasm wherever he went, and he was convinced that the time was right for another mighty adventure. There was a first crucial question to be addressed. Which city should be the next target – Venice or Rome? He decided on the Eternal City, a choice which led to one of the most famous episodes of his life.

12

ASPROMONTE

'He is a noble human being, and his manners have a certain divine simplicity in them.'

Alfred, Lord Tennyson

A thick carpet of pine cones crackled under my feet as I wandered into a forest on the slopes of the beautiful, treacherous, evocative Aspromonte mountain. It was the only sound to be heard in this remote wilderness, otherwise a place of silence and maybe a few ghosts. It was also a place of wonder, because hidden amid the dauntingly tall pine trees I found a slice of history immortalised for all Italians in a simple nursery rhyme. The words are learned by children in every school and sung with instinctive delight by adults whenever I mention the name of Aspromonte. The first line is *Garibaldi fu ferito* – Garibaldi was wounded – and records the moment in August 1862 when he was shot by government troops during a futile attempt to liberate Rome from the Pope and deliver the Eternal City to the new nation of Italy.

People cannot help themselves when they sing, because Aspromonte is a crucial part of the legend of Giuseppe Garibaldi. It is the first story every Italian learns about their national hero; everyone but everyone in the country knows that Garibaldi was wounded here. The tree where it happened is a place of pilgrimage, and even in this dense forest it didn't take me too long to find it after parking my car at the end of a long and winding road up the north-west edge of the mountain. There was only one tree with a small iron fence around it, only one with a stone plaque in the ground next to it like a tombstone. There are many other pines with hollows at the bottom of their trunks, but only this one was the very spot where Garibaldi sat and lit a cigar after being severely injured in the ankle and calmly told a doctor to amputate the leg if necessary. It has no rival as Italy's most historic tree. It was where he rested until being carried down the mountainside on a stretcher, a tortuous journey that took fifteen hours. The stone plaque had a simple message – that while he sat here wounded Garibaldi once more declared: *O Roma O Morte*. It is not some ancient relic; this stone was placed there in 2007 on the bicentenary of his birth. The legend is forever being replenished for new generations.

The road up this side of Aspromonte, a mountain that climbs to 6,414 feet was little more than a track really, but plenty of people make the journey to see the spot marked as Cippo di Garibaldi on maps. It felt like the edge of civilisation. Beyond lay only an immense area of uninhabited forest, while the nearest town of Gambarie, a ski resort in winter, was four kilometres away. My trip was in August, when the temperature was 38°C on the coast close by, but even in high summer

I needed a jumper and jacket to visit the mountain. There was a distinct chill in the air up by the tree.

On the map it said there was also a *Mausoleo di Giuseppe Garibaldi* in the area. I walked 100 metres through the forest to a clearing where a small museum has been built which contains memorabilia from the events of 29 August 1862. I have to take that on trust because the building was closed on the day I went and apparently is rarely open. What did impress was a vivid battle scene sculpted above the museum door, with Garibaldi standing in the centre, arms splayed wide, about to be fired at.

Outside there was also a plaque with words attributed to Giouse Carducci, who is regarded as the official national poet of modern Italy and was the first Italian to win the Nobel Prize for literature: 'Long live you magnanimous rebel. The forests of Aspromonte grew more sacred laurels on your forehead.'

Carducci lionised Garibaldi with reams of florid poetry, one of which was about Aspromonte. Some years ago, this plaque was badly cracked, with pieces falling off. A new one was fashioned, along with two other plaques – just to make sure any visitor knows what occurred here. Yet nobody comes without wishing to. It is too remote for the accidental tourist, and the magical aura of the scene does not require an excess of explanation. You cannot be here without hearing in your head the nursery rhyme celebrating Aspromonte.

Garibaldi fu ferito
Fu ferito a una gamba
Garibaldi che commanda
Che commanda un battaglion

'Garibaldi was wounded / he was wounded in the leg / Garibaldi who commands / who commands a battalion' – and this is the verse sung to me so many times with joyful gusto, the best-known version of the nursery rhyme. There are many others, however, the words altered to suit the groups or organisations involved. The scout movement has its own *Garibaldi fu ferito*, as do the Bersagliere soldiers of Italy. It was turned into a pop song by Bruno Lauzi, a crooner from the 1960s and 70s, who called it 'Garibaldi Blues' and reworked the words again. Who first sang or wrote the words to *Garibaldi fu ferito*? Nobody knows. The origins are obscure, lost in the mists of time, or maybe deep in the heart of the forest.

Aspromonte is much more than merely the place where Garibaldi was wounded, though. Its rugged isolation long made it a refuge from the scourge of malaria, a disease which racked the southern half of Italy for hundreds of years. It has also been a natural home to bandits and mafia groups for many generations. The name itself translates as Bitter Mountain, or Tough Mountain, and it can be both. It is also spectacularly beautiful, a national park since 1989, and garlanded with UNESCO status for its unique landscape where pine forests suddenly become impassable rocky ravines. You can go skiing on a mountainside with a view of the sea, which is a rare combination. There are also many abandoned villages, mostly because they were too isolated, but some of which are beginning to be revived.

The mountain was also off limits for several decades because it was the heart of mafia territory, a haven for the 'Ndrangheta clan. Some historians say they were active from the start of the 1860s, at the time of Garibaldi's escapade here. They were first widely mentioned in Calabrian police reports of the 1880s and were notorious for hundreds of kidnappings for three decades at the end of the twentieth century. Many of the hostages taken for ransom were hidden in the wilderness of Aspromonte. The most famous victim was John Paul Getty III, who was kept in the region of Campania further north, but it is believed the proceeds from his ransom helped to pay for houses in the town of Bovalino on the edge of Aspromonte. The particular district is supposedly still known informally as 'Paul Getty'.

Brigands have always roamed the mountain, making it a perilous place for travellers. The evolution into mafia came following the early years of Italian unification, starting in Sicily as unofficial private armies, or *mafie*, hired by absentee landlords to protect their estates during a period of immense instability. The mafia, known on the island as *Cosa Nostra*, became so powerful they could extort money from these same landlords, and then acted as a corrupt irregular police force, keeping order where the often-despised public authorities could not. Similar groups emerged in Naples called the *Camorra*, in Calabria known as the *'Ndrangheta*, and in Puglia where they name themselves the *Sacra corona unita* (sacred crown united). Through the twentieth century they branched out into criminal areas like drugs-running, into mainstream economic spheres such as the construction industry, and consolidated their strength through corruption of government officials and ministers.

The fascist dictator Benito Mussolini tried with limited success to eradicate them before the Second World War, and they flourished again afterwards when the American occupation authorities released many mafiosi from prison.

There has been another fightback in recent times from the worst days of the 1990s when two anti-mafia magistrates, Giovanni Falcone and Paolo Borsellino, were assassinated in the early summer of 1992, murders that shocked the nation and marked a clear turning point in attitudes.

The mafia in Italy may have less power and influence than three decades ago, but they are still there, affecting the daily life of too many people in the shadows. Who are they? Where do they operate? These are million-dollar questions in modern Italy. I have never had any knowing contact, but I don't own a shop or trade goods or frequent places that invite obvious danger. 'No, you will never see them,' one friend told me, 'but hopefully you will never be unlucky enough to be in the wrong place at the wrong moment and witness something you shouldn't.' There was also the conversation I had with another acquaintance in Rome who runs a market stall. I mentioned that I had to go to the pharmacy down the road to buy some painkillers and she said: 'Why do you go there? That's a pharmacy run by the mafia.' It turned out to be a piece of information most people knew, but nobody talked about. The place remains very popular because of its myriad special offers.

Another question is how much mafia infiltration remains in the present political culture and systems. In early 2025, the European Court of Human Rights ruled that Italy was guilty of violating citizens' rights by failing to deal with illegal toxic waste dumped by the mafia in the region of Campania. The court reprimanded Italy for its inaction 'despite having known about the problem for many years'. Knowing is one thing, but doing something about an issue where the mafia is concerned is quite another. In most countries such a damning public verdict would have been the number one item on the TV evening news. In Italy, that night, it was buried at the end of the programme. Who can blame ordinary Italians for being sceptical rather than optimistic about any battle to curb the mafia, and for being convinced that intrigue will never end? I wouldn't. Politics, of course, is rarely free of intrigue and plotting and double-dealing. It was certainly rife in the early years of the Italian nation, when Garibaldi was at the heart of public debate and secret plans about capturing Venice and Rome to complete the process of unification.

In the early months of 1862, he conducted a congress of all the country's democratic nationalist groups to promote the cause, and he made a series of emotional speeches across northern Italy that stirred popular fervour for action. In the same period Garibaldi also held clandestine meetings in Turin with the king and two prime ministers, first Bettino Ricasoli and then his successor Urbano Rattazzi. The real intentions of the government in their dealings with the Hero of Two Worlds has never been clarified. It seems that, in private, they told Garibaldi they wanted to co-operate with him and promised money for an expedition to the Balkans that would pave the way to Venice. But they offered no open public support. Some historians think the government hoped that Garibaldi would perish in the Balkans. Others contend they wanted to let Garibaldi loose and see what happened – so that if he were to be successful they could take the credit, and if not they would disown him. It was a recipe for chaos.

Garibaldi enjoyed the intrigue, but not the vacuum into which he had been plunged. He decided a mission through the Balkans was too risky, and took matters into his own hands, opting instead for a march on Rome. This would start in Sicily, just like the Expedition of The Thousand two years earlier, and it would be undertaken with his own new volunteer army. The government dithered again. They did not prevent him from travelling south, and nor did they intervene when Garibaldi proclaimed he had the King's support during fiery speeches in Palermo. This only encouraged his belief that he did have official backing. He also went to Marsala, and for the first time Garibaldi declared that for him it was now 'Rome or Death'. The effect was powerful as 3,000 volunteers signed up for a new Red Shirts campaign and they began to move across Sicily. Whenever a local official questioned their motives, an ornate metal box containing a document with a red seal was produced by Garibaldi, which he said was a personal mandate for action from King Vittorio Emanuele II. It was never challenged, and if it was a bluff it was a good one. The King privately admitted that Garibaldi had been following his orders to 'a certain extent'.

After reaching Catania they seized two merchant ships, again with no hindrance from government soldiers, and landed at Porto Salvo on the southern coast of Calabria in the same place where the Expedition of The Thousand had arrived on the mainland. This time it was different. The decisive moment came when Napoleon III demanded a halt, telling the Italian government he would send French soldiers to defend Rome if the city was attacked and the Pope was threatened.

Vittorio Emanuele II desperately wanted Rome, but could not countenance a fight with France, so the Italian army was now ordered to prevent Garibaldi marching north – not that they were doing much marching. They found his volunteer Red Shirts in a bedraggled state, eating raw potatoes, having lost their way in the mysterious depths of the Aspromonte mountain. They had been walking round in circles for 24 hours. And so, on 29 August 1862 a troop of Italian government soldiers stood in the way of Garibaldi. He did not wish to fight them; he had assumed they would be on his side. He had no desire for a civil war. A brief skirmish led to five Red Shirts and seven soldiers being killed. Garibaldi rushed to the front to prevent further bloodshed and was wounded by shots fired by Lieutenant Luigi Ferrari of the Bersaglieri, who in all probability deliberately aimed at Garibaldi's legs. The Hero of Two Worlds had been defenceless, an easy target. Once again, in remarkable circumstances, he had defied death in action.

How many times was he hit? Where was he struck? In many years working as a sportswriter I learned it was vital to be accurate about the details of an injury to an athlete. So, I checked the history books about Garibaldi's wound. The first very well-regarded biography I consulted said he was hit in the right ankle. The next book, equally renowned, said it was the left ankle. The third book said he was struck a glancing blow on the left thigh and severely wounded in the right ankle.

So, of course, I leafed through some more. The next two, one old, one modern, both brilliant, decided to play safe and just say he was hit in the foot. I have another book called *Lo Stivale Di Garibaldi* (The Boot of Garibaldi). It is a collection of Risorgimento era photographs, with the boot adorning the front cover. This, too, declines to identify whether it is a right boot or left boot. From the photo it looks more like the left than the right, but it's impossible to tell. Another tome, the *Life of Garibaldi* written by Jesse White Mario, who nursed him personally, agreed with the version that there was a glancing blow to the left thigh and bad damage to the right ankle. Garibaldi's own memoir concurs with this account, but many scholars say his memory wasn't sound and that his account is full of exaggeration and errors. The only way to be sure was to look at the boot itself, which is on permanent display in the Central Museum of the Risorgimento in Rome.

The fifteen euros ticket to enter the museum was a small price to pay for accuracy – and the boot was there, and it was definitely a right-footed boot. I can say that with 100 per cent confidence. There was a bullet-sized hole on the inside of this boot at ankle height. That was clear as well. So, there you are, a job well done? Well, maybe not. To one side of the display case was an information board about the events at Aspromonte. It declared, and I kid you not: 'A brief skirmish finished when Garibaldi was hit by two shots, one in the hip, and one in his left foot.'

I couldn't help but laugh out loud. The whole thing is a theatre of the absurd worthy of Luigi Pirandello, whose uncle you may remember collected the boot from Garibaldi himself and kept it in his home for many years before donating it to the museum. The legend of the boot also lends itself, and by now you cannot be surprised, to modern marketing. It is possible to buy Garibaldi boots which are purpose-made for dressage riders. They come from a specialist shop in Milan at the princely sum of 600 euros. The Helly Hansen clothing brand from Norway sells Garibaldi snow boots with a sheepskin lining for 160 euros.

Whether it was the right boot or the left boot, there is no disputing that Garibaldi sat in the hollow of the pine tree smoking a cigar as he waited for assistance. 'Rome or Death' had been his rallying cry, but he had neither. Instead, he was forced to endure an agonising fifteen-hour journey down the mountainside on a wooden stretcher, wrapped only in a woollen blanket. The stretcher was rudimentary, two long slats of wood bound together by rope and two wooden poles on each side.

This and the blanket were on display in the museum next to the boot, and an inscription in English was sewn into the cloth afterwards by Jesse White Mario. It read: 'The blanket of General Garibaldi in which when wounded at Aspromonte he was carried off the field' – making him sound rather like an injured superstar footballer taken away to a dressing room.

In fact, he was treated like a common criminal and transported by boat north to a military hospital prison in the Varignano fortress near La Spezia on the coast of Liguria. Some ministers in the Italian government wanted Garibaldi put on trial and charged with treason, either in a court of law, or by a military tribunal. The possibility sparked outrage and protests across Italy and Europe. There was a demonstration of 100,000 people in Hyde Park in London, where a group of Royal Guards' officers shouted 'Long live Garibaldi' as they dealt with the crowds. Newspapers and writers leapt to his defence. An English poet, Menella Bute Smedley, a relative of Lewis Carroll, was particularly obsessed with the Hero of Two Worlds. She wrote a series of poems about him, including 'Garibaldi Impeached' – a stirring cry from the heart against putting him on trial after Aspromonte.

> Where shall we try Garibaldi?
> Find us some Italian town
> Not alive with his renown,

> Where the air is not on flame
> With the splendour of his name,
> Where the pavement of the street
> Would not rise to kiss his feet,
> Not till such a place is found,
> Try him on Italian ground!

Her passion is obvious enough, and her instincts were correct. Widespread anger among the people of Italy meant it was politically imprudent for Garibaldi to be punished by the authorities. It would be impossible to find a jury that would pronounce him guilty, and he was eventually freed from jail with no sanction or condemnation. The British connection did not end there. When Garibaldi was released, he was carried out of Varignano on a special bed sent by Lady Palmerston, wife of the Prime Minister.

Never mind the boot, what about the bullet? This became an object of international curiosity and concern. Six Italian doctors could not diagnose where it was lodged in his ankle, and five of them thought it wasn't there at all. Two weeks later, they changed their mind. A surgeon from Vienna was pessimistic and said that amputation should take place immediately. Money was raised in London for an English surgeon, Richard Partridge, to visit Garibaldi for another inspection. He said there was no need for an operation, and that time and rest would be the cure. This was wrong. A few weeks later sepsis set in, and amputation now seemed probable. Finally, a French surgeon called Auguste Nelaton arrived, and using new instruments discovered where the bullet was lodged and declared that it could safely be removed from Garibaldi's ankle.

The operation was performed in Pisa some eighty-seven days after the shooting by Ferdinando Zanetti, a surgeon from Tuscany. The scalpel he used is now an exhibit in the Risorgimento museum in Rome, sitting alongside the fabled boot. A fragment of Garibaldi's ankle bone hit by the bullet is also there, as well as bandages from the wound. No detail is too small to be ignored, including the wooden crutch he now had to lean on to get around. In the city famous for its Leaning Tower, this episode of history is celebrated with another statue of Garibaldi, where he is depicted standing tall. There are three scenes in relief on the base of the statue – the General departing for Aspromonte, being wounded at Aspromonte, and arriving at Pisa after his release from jail, being carried by friends off a boat. The bullet itself? That was on display at the Risorgimento museum in Turin, while there is a cast of the bullet at the Caprera museum.

A period of convalescence followed as Garibaldi returned to his refuge on Caprera. The injury to both his ankle and his morale had been profound, and it took more than a year to fully recover. He also had rheumatism in his right hand that prevented him from writing. Nevertheless, a stream of visitors continued to arrive at his remote White House, including an English gardener, Robert Webster, who came to help give life to the barren, rocky land and brought seeds and plants from Britain. The farm was gradually transformed, and Garibaldi later wrote a letter of thanks to Webster: 'My dear Robert, among these granite rocks we used the same tool – the hoe. I am only happy when using it. Your country is free and therefore you are not obliged to change the hoe for the sword.'

There was an intense fascination in England for the adventures and the legends of Garibaldi, and he received a string of invitations to visit following the trauma of Aspromonte. By early 1864 he felt revived enough to finally accept and arrived at Southampton in April of that year to a tumultuous welcome. Among the politicians at the scene was a Member of Parliament, Charles Seely, whose home was nearby on the Isle of Wight. He and his wife Mary almost kidnapped Garibaldi off the boat and took him to stay at their house. It was a matter of prestige for the MP; it was a matter of sexual attraction for Mary Seely. She and Garibaldi had an affair, and they wrote to each other for the following ten years.

Another person who lived on the Isle of Wight was Alfred, Lord Tennyson, the poet laureate. Garibaldi went to his home, Farringford House, and they recited poems to each other. Garibaldi did so in Italian to Tennyson, probably reading some of the poems of patriot Ugo Foscolo, who was exiled and died in London and whose grave Garibaldi visited at Chiswick cemetery. Then Tennyson read some of his poems in English. Garibaldi also planted a pine tree in the garden, part of which is still there today outside the house that is now a museum. This tree was immortalised in Tennyson's poem *To Ulysses*:

> Or watch the waving pine which here
> The warrior of Caprera set
> A name that earth will not forget
> Till earth has roll'd her latest year

Garibaldi wanted a tranquil domestic life, rather like Tennyson. In later years he would write *agricoltore*, or farmer, as his status on official documents. Tennyson recognised this aspect of his famous visitor's character: 'He has a certain divine simplicity such as I have never witnessed in a native of these islands – among men at least.'

Other English poets, mostly women, became besotted with Garibaldi. The most famous of these was Elizabeth Barrett Browning, who had been a rival to Tennyson to be named poet laureate. She moved to Italy in 1846, living there for fifteen years until her death in Florence, and became a strong supporter of the Risorgimento. In 1860 she wrote a poem called simply *Garibaldi*, celebrating his victories in the battles of Varese and Como in 1859 during the Second War of Italian Independence. Another poem entitled *Garibaldi* was written in 1861 by the English poet and novelist Mary Elizabeth Braddon. This was an epic, ninety pages long with 158 verses, describing the battles at Calatafimi, Palermo and Milazzo which captured Sicily. It is an extraordinarily overwrought work, but indicative of the general mood.

In the same year the Peek Freans company invented their new biscuit – and calling it Garibaldi guaranteed its success. As mentioned in the prologue, a few years later the Nottingham Forest football team chose Garibaldi red for their colours, and continue to celebrate this fact at every match now with a banner behind one goal which reads: 'The Garibaldi that we wear with pride was made in 1865'. Sometimes, a giant flag featuring a picture of Italy's national hero is also displayed before kick-off. It covers thousands of supporters sitting in the same stand as the banner, and it seems to me rather magical.

There are various stories which also link Garibaldi to the shirt colours of major Italian football clubs such as AC Milan. They were co-founded by Herbert Kilpin, who had started a junior Garibaldi Nottingham team when he was a teenager and which played in red. He then played for a team called Notts Olympic, whose colours were red and black. Like Garibaldi, he was certain that red was a good colour for battle, and when AC Milan was created he said: 'We will be a team of devils. Our colours will be red like fire and black like the fear we will instil in our opponents.' This history is certain.

Another tale, which may be only myth, although many Juventus fans hope it's true, is about the creation of their kit. Juventus turned out originally in pink shirts, but one of their team, an Englishman from Nottingham called John Savage, thought the faded strip made them look like 'a gang of war survivors'. He sent one of the shirts to a friend in a clothing company in Nottingham, asking for a new set of red shirts like Nottingham Forest. The story goes that the pink looked as if it was white, and the clothing company thought it must be a mistake, and that they actually wanted the black and white stripes of another team from the city, Notts County. Ever since, Juventus have played in these zebra colours, when it should have been Garibaldi red. Or maybe not. John Savage was previously a Notts County footballer, and quite possibly ordered the black and white stripes directly.

What can never be doubted is the importance of football in Italy. *La Gazzetta dello Sport* is the best-selling and most widely read newspaper in the country. There are also two other national sports papers, mostly devoted to football. The game is a mirror of society. It reflects, for sure, the north-south economic and cultural divide, with the rich north dominant. At the time of writing there were just three clubs geographically below Rome in the top league, *Serie A*. There is also widespread fear that matches and seasons are manipulated by corruption and conspiracy, with several scandals uncovered through the years. The Juventus club was run for many decades by the same Agnelli family who own the Fiat car company, and with the same market dominance. Calcio, as the Italians call the sport, is an almost religious obsession for the vast majority of the country, men and women, factory workers and entrepreneurs, craftsmen and intellectuals. The film-maker Pier Paolo Pasolini remarked: 'Football is the last sacred representation of our time.'

The rituals, the passion and the cynicism are eternal. There is a positive power to this. Many people have told me that Italy feels most united when watching its national football team play, especially when they are winning – and the national anthem written by Garibaldi's young adjutant Goffredo Mameli is always sung with particular fervour before matches. In one history of Italian football, the author writes: 'In a young and regionally divided nation, football has been a powerful glue around which national identity has been able to form.' I saw the multiplication of national flags hung from many homes during the European Championships played in the summer of 2021 as Italy began to play well. I also remember an article in *La Gazzetta* previewing a tough quarter-final match against Belgium. The writer exhorted the Italian team 'to struggle with all their blood, with heroic resistance and Garibaldian resolve'. Yes, they were victorious in that game, and went on to win the tournament by beating England in the final – and the carnival madness in the streets at midnight was a sight to behold.

There must been a similar wonder in April 1864 when Garibaldi arrived in central London after his stay on the Isle of Wight and was acclaimed on the streets of the city by a crowd estimated at half a million people. This was a private visit without precedent or probably equal. On the first night there was a dinner in his honour at Stafford House, where he was staying with the Duke of Sutherland. Most of the British Government were in attendance along with Prime Minister Lord Palmerston. In the following days Garibaldi met other notable Victorian characters like Florence Nightingale, Charles Dickens and William Gladstone. He went to the opera but also to a steam-roller factory in Bedford and a brewery in Southwark. He had talks with Mazzini and the Russian revolutionary leader Alexander Herzen in Teddington, and he spoke at two major rallies of working men at Crystal Palace. He was given the freedom of the City of London by the Lord Mayor in a ceremony at Guildhall.

All of this was deeply alarming to Queen Victoria, to whom the Dowager Duchess of Sutherland was an intimate companion. In a letter to the Foreign Secretary Lord Russell, she wrote:

> The Queen very much regrets the extravagant excitement respecting Garibaldi, which shows little dignity and discrimination in the nation and is not very flattering to others who are similarly received. The Queen fears the Government may find Garibaldi's views and connections no little cause of inconvenience with foreign governments hereafter, and trusts they will be cautious in what they do for him in their official capacity.

She wanted him out of the country.

The concern was shared by Italian royalty. King Vittorio Emanuele II was worried the popularity of Garibaldi in England was detrimental to his country, and also that it was overshadowing everyone else, including himself. He knew the way to tempt Garibaldi home, and he sent a message that he needed the General for a new attempt to wrestle Venice away from rule by Austria. This was bound to interest Garibaldi, who had also become weary of the relentless dinners, rallies and meetings during his time in London. After a short stay in Cornwall with his friend Colonel John Peard, the English *garibaldino* who had fought with him during the Expedition of The Thousand, he sailed home to Caprera on a boat owned by the Duke of Sutherland. This then took him on further to the island of Ischia in the bay of Naples, a place famed for its thermal spas.

Garibaldi's health was still fragile, and Ischia was an ideal spot for further recuperation. The island, of course, trades on this. On the 150th anniversary of a united Italy in 2011, Ischia held a month-long cultural celebration, which it entitled: 'The thermal waters – and Garibaldi's wound'. The island was also more convenient to reach than Caprera, and he had a deluge of visitors there; people who wanted to make plans and dream up new plots to liberate Venice and/or Rome. This time the target would be Venice.

13

VENICE/FLORENCE

'Here he was wounded and people reverently kissed the clods of earth bathed in the blood of the great hero of the world.'
Memorial stone close to the shores of Lake Garda.

A fierce wind was blowing hard in my face on a chill winter morning as I walked down the longest and widest paved street in Venice. I'd come from the glory of St Mark's Square, strolling along the waterfront where every building seemed to have a dedication on its walls to people who had lived or worked there, among them the composers Tchaikovsky and Vivaldi, the physicist Christian Doppler, and the writer Franz Kafka. The road I was looking for was at an angle to the quayside and the first house here was the family home of Giovani Caboto, the explorer John Cabot, who discovered Newfoundland. The road was almost empty, most of the shops and bars closed for the season in an area where few tourists came at this time of year. There were hundreds of pigeons pecking away for scraps of food on the tarmac. Suddenly,

Via Garibaldi

presumably on some kind of secret pigeon signal, they all took wing, flying low and fast at human head level with the wind behind them. For a moment it felt like being in a Hitchcock film, under attack from a flock of cruel birds until they swooped past and out onto the lagoon beyond.

Thus, I was introduced to Via Garibaldi, a proper road in Venice, the city of canals. In any other location it would be unremarkable. Here it seems huge and never-ending, and Google maps describes it as 'a notable street' although in fact it is barely 400 metres long and without distinction. Almost at the end there was a tall iron gate leading into a pleasant avenue of trees where people take their dogs for walks. Close to this entrance was my target – one of the most interesting statues of Garibaldi anywhere in Italy. Inevitably, there was a massive seagull standing on his head, which was coloured white from the attentions of painter/decorator pigeons and gulls. Much of the statue was affected, and the lack of care was evident. Garibaldi, standing on top of a rock, resting on his sword, was looking very weathered, perhaps also because the bronze and marble used by the sculptor had not aged well. The rock was supposed to represent the stony hillside of his home island Caprera – and I can tell you that because I looked it up. There wasn't a single piece of information anywhere around the statue, not even an inscription to say it was Giuseppe Garibaldi. Nothing. This is more than a pity; it seems to me a dereliction of civic duty when the place is much more than the usual commemorative statue.

One peculiarity is that the rock was positioned in a small pond or moat, and home to five turtles swimming in the murky brown water as well as a couple of hefty-looking goldfish.

At the front of the monument erected in 1885 there was a lion perched below Garibaldi, placed there as a symbol of Venice. Around the back, at the foot of the rock, I found another sculpture, the smaller figure of a soldier with a rifle slung over his shoulder. This represented Giuseppe Zolli, a volunteer Red Shirt fighter from Venice, one of those involved from the start in the Expedition of The Thousand. He was one of the most passionate followers of Garibaldi and vowed to protect him forever. After the unification of Italy was complete, Zolli returned to his home city and when he died in 1921 the story is that strange events began in the area of the statue. One man said he had been hit powerfully on the arm by something in a red shirt when he was standing close to the bronze figure of Garibaldi. Other people said similar things had occurred to them, and the locals decided this could only be the ghost of Zolli still trying to protect his hero, and that the place was now haunted. Their solution was to commission a statue of Zolli below the Hero of Two Worlds, and as soon as this was in place all the strange occurrences immediately ended. It's a wonderful tale, so why not tell visitors when they pass by?

Only a few people were there on this winter morning, but many thousands pass by when the world-renowned Biennale arts festival is held in this area of the city. And maybe most people will recognise Garibaldi, certainly Italians, but not necessarily the large number of tourists. Tourism is vital to Italy, a significant contributor to the nation's economy. The latest estimate is that this industry makes up thirteen per cent of Italy's GDP, thanks to 57 million arriving each year from other countries. Italy is a magnet for visitors with its spectacular scenery, rich art galleries, myriad UNESCO world heritage sites, thousands of hilltop villages, incredible history and inimitable cuisine. The so-called Grand Tour of cities like Venice, Florence and Rome was a feature of international travel long before Garibaldi's adventures and political unity.

Now, though, and despite its economic benefits, many Italians are beginning to resent the overcrowding that makes daily life more difficult in the most popular spots, and the issue of over-tourism is causing a backlash. A protest group in Rome attacked and destroyed many key boxes outside holiday rental properties, leaving behind Robin Hood stickers. In some central districts there is almost no housing available for young families in Rome, while rents in previously cheaper areas have risen in consequence. Activists in Venice have started squatting in abandoned buildings to protest against the unaffordability of renting in the city. Graffiti declaring 'tourists go home' have started to appear in many places.

It can be an uncomfortable balance between income gained and life inconvenienced. I know of a couple of people in Rome who own a second apartment which they rent out lucratively to tourists, but at the same time complain bitterly about the noisy visitors who stay awake until two am in the holiday rental next door to the flat they actually live in.

Many places in Italy are trying to find an equitable way forward. Florence and Rome are both trying to curb short-term rentals, while the national government decided to outlaw key boxes at the start of 2025 and sent operatives to remove them with heavy duty wire-cutters where necessary. They said this was to prevent terrorists renting flats anonymously, but the Robin Hood protests were probably also a factor. Other measures have been taken. Tourist buses are not allowed on the

Amalfi coast seafront, for example, and in Rome visitors can be given a 250 Euros fine if they sit down on the Spanish Steps. In the Eternal City they have enacted the 'urban decorum law', under which you can be punished with a 500 Euros fine for stopping to eat at tourist sites like the Trevi Fountain. This is not just an idle threat – the police in Rome control this strictly.

Venice, the most beautiful and haunting city with its canals, narrow lanes and historic buildings, has the worst problem. It is known as *La Serenissima*, and its official title is The Most Serene Republic of Venice, but the mood has been anything but calm in recent times. The city has 50,000 permanent residents and 140,000 visitors every day. Apparently, the first question many Americans ask when they arrive is 'What time does Venice close?' – as if it's just another museum to tick off their visiting list. The city was forced to ban cruise ships from its centre in 2021 when UNESCO threatened to put Venice on its endangered list because of damage the giant vessels were causing to the lagoon. Another over-tourism measure introduced in 2024 was a system of charging day-trippers five Euros to enter the city on the busiest days of the year. There were sanctions, too, for feeding the pigeons, and what a good idea that was.

Internal tourism is also big business. Italian friends are forever eager to show off their country, particularly their own home region. I've been told that I simply *had* to go and stay in Lecce, Matera, Treviso, Spoleto, Benevento, Cagliari, Noto, Siena and Lake Garda, just a few examples. I took the advice, and each one of these varied spots was delightful – even though they are all some way down the list of must-see places in this country. Lake Garda was essential for me anyhow, because it was the backdrop to Garibaldi's involvement in the Third War of Italian Independence in 1866 and another major step forward to achieving his ultimate dream of seeing Italy complete.

The two years following his trip to England had been a deliberately quiet period for Garibaldi, who needed time at his island home to continue physical recovery from the severe trauma of the Aspromonte wounding. However, he continued to receive visitors at Caprera, and to talk endlessly about the need to capture Venice and Rome. At one point he considered travelling to Mexico to assist the revolutionaries fighting for independence there. In despair at the way the southern half of the new Italy was being badly treated by the politicians in Turin, he asked King Vittorio Emanuele II to be given full powers to govern the *Mezzogiorno* as a benevolent dictator. This idea was instantly rejected, but the request by Garibaldi reveals he was aware of, and sympathetic to, the rebellious and angry mood in the regions he had conquered a few years before.

As with so many governments through the ages, when the scene at home looks bleak, the leaders of the young Italian nation decided a war to capture Venice would provide a morale boost and divert attention away from their domestic struggles. They made a secret deal with the Prussian leader Otto Von Bismarck, who also had eyes on Austrian territory and whom it suited to have Italy fighting against Austria on a second front. Various plans were conceived and altered through the spring of 1866, including what role Garibaldi could or should take. The Italian government knew that people would demand he was involved in the action, but once more they did not want him at the centre of things. Eventually, on 10 June, he sailed from Caprera to take command of a volunteer force of 35,000 men to fight the Austrians. They were allowed to wear Red Shirts and although they had outdated weapons, they still won two battles while the main Italian army suffered defeats.

Garibaldi's initial headquarters was at Salò on the shores of Lake Garda, and the first skirmish against their opponents was the battle of Monte Suello a few kilometres to the west. The Austrians were beaten there on 3 July, and among the Red Shirts was another future Italian prime minister, Alessandro Fortis. Once again, Garibaldi was injured, this time struck in the left thigh by a misplaced shot from one of his own men. A shrine was placed to those who died there and close by a memorial stone commemorating the spot where Garibaldi was hit. 'Here he was wounded and people reverently kissed the clods of earth bathed in the blood of the great hero of the world.'

The second and more famous battle was at Bezzecca, where Garibaldi had to direct operations while sitting in a carriage because his injuries prevented him from riding on horseback. I saw a painting of this remarkable scene in Milan's Risorgimento museum. Bezzecca today is a village of 700 people nestled in the wooded hills and tranquil valleys above Lake Garda, but back then it was one of the first places where the Red Cross, created in the wake of the Solferino horror of 1859, operated amid the destruction of a battlefield.

It was another windy day, the air crisp and clear at 2,300 feet when I walked around the centre of Bezzecca, which has a small but excellent museum containing red shirts, flags, guns, medals and a bugle. There was a map of Italy on the wall indicating how many Red Shirt volunteers from each region had taken part in the conflict, and also a list of the number of foreign fighters inspired to join by the legend of Garibaldi. They had come from 29 countries, including fifteen men from Egypt, five from England, four from Turkey, two from Brazil and one from Uruguay.

The main monument to the Battle of Bezzecca was outside the village on the Santa Stefano hill, and I took the direct route rather than the scenic one. This was a slightly claustrophobic but wonderfully evocative path through a series of brick and concrete tunnels built for soldiers during fighting here in World War One. At the top I emerged blinking into the sunlight to find a stupendous view towards the Dolomite mountains and a well-kept memorial area inside and outside the Santa Stefano church. There was a robust cross made from pure white marble with a simple inscription below: 'To the memory of the Austrian and Italian fighters who died here on 21 July 1866'. Close to this was an old cannon with rotting wooden wheels and rusty ironwork. Another well preserved cannon was inside the church, along with more plaques and dedications to the fallen.

This was to be Garibaldi's final victory on Italian soil, one in which his sons Menotti and Ricciotti both took part. The Austrians were pushing forward here, having won a decisive triumph against the main Italian army at Custoza, south of Lake Garda. Their attack was repulsed by the Red Shirts, as Garibaldi took command from his carriage, and then the Austrian troops were driven out of the strategic stronghold of Bezzecca. It was a further example of Garibaldi's tactical awareness in battle, and he was chasing eastwards after the enemy when an armistice was called on 9 August. Prussia had stopped its war against Austria after several victories, and the Italian government had no desire to fight alone after the humiliation of Custoza.

A telegram was sent to Garibaldi when the armistice was agreed, telling him to stop fighting and withdraw his Red Shirt volunteers back to Bezzecca. He replied with a one-word message: *Obbedisco*, 'I obey'. It is a reply that is legendary still in modern Italy. When a wife or husband tells their partner to do something, very often the instant reply, with or without a smile, will be *Obbedisco*. Each year in July the village of Bezzecca holds a celebration weekend to remember the events of 1866. Its title is *Bezzecca Obbedisco*.

In the village museum there was a fascinating display which added some substance to the moment. It reported the words of the telegraph operator Respicio Bilancioni:

> Garibaldi asked for a telegram module and a pen and looked very worried. He sighed, and slumped on a seat holding his head in his hands. Suddenly he wrote on the paper *Obbedisco*, and signed it. I read this and had a moment of hesitation. So, Garibaldi asked me brusquely, 'What do you think of this voluntary stop?' I said I thought it would demoralise the volunteer corps and therefore the whole nation. 'You're right' said Garibaldi. 'Unfortunately, Italy is a country in disgrace. We are betrayed.' But the telegram had been sent.

Back up the hill at the memorial site I had seen a stone column which was given to the village by the city of Rome. The words carved into the base said: 'Warning of war. Warning of Peace. I obey.' With the armistice came negotiations and a diplomatic deal that handed Venice to the new Italy. It did not happen directly because Austria would not concede the territory to a nation it had defeated in conflict at Custoza. So, the city of Venice was ceded to France, who then handed it over to Italy. It was a humiliating way to claim *La Serenissima* – for Garibaldi in particular after his own successes. He said it was like being given 'second-hand goods'.

The feelings of betrayal and humiliation did not linger too long. Venice was now part of Italy and free to be visited for the first time in Garibaldi's life. Everybody should go at least once to this unique city, and to the glory of St Mark's Square with its formidable bell tower and the Byzantine-style Basilica which dates from the eleventh century and features astonishing golden mosaics on the domes inside. I marvelled at these like so many tourists, but my eyes were more taken by another jewel of history in the vast square outside. This was a plaque on the *Procuratie Vecchie*, a vast renaissance building which stands on one side of the square and read: 'Garibaldi here saluted a free Venice and proclaimed his hope that Rome will become the capital of Italy.' It is a reminder of a speech he gave from a balcony on this building in February 1867 – and it is the only plaque which has been allowed in one of the world's most famous and beautiful squares.

Fifty metres away I was able to see another Risorgimento treasure, although again it was one you have to know about, both to find and then to appreciate. This was a tomb located on the edge of a side wall of St Mark's Basilica. It is the final resting place of Daniele Manin, one of the great figures of the drive to Italian unity, but the most neglected in the history books. He led the rebellion in Venice in 1849 and created an independent republic similar to the one in Rome in the same year. Garibaldi had been aiming to join Manin's struggle in Venice when he had to flee the Eternal City after the collapse of the *Repubblica Romana*, and he was a profound admirer.

Manin went into exile after his republic was crushed by the Austrians, and he died in Paris in 1857. His son, Giorgio Manin, took up the reins of family radicalism, and he was one of the volunteers who sailed on the Expedition of The Thousand with Garibaldi in 1860. The younger Manin was wounded at the battle of Calatafimi, but demanded to continue and was then injured even more severely during the capture of Palermo. The body of Daniele Manin was returned to Venice when the city became part of the new Italy and was placed in the impressive black marble tomb at St Mark's. His son Giorgio was also laid to rest there when he died in 1882.

The prominent and prestigious location of the tomb will gladden the heart of anyone interested in the history of Venice and the Risorgimento in general. It is an indication of the respect that Manin and his son deserve. But there was no information board to explain the story and its significance. This seems to me a great pity. Venice possesses many treasures, of course, from the Grand Canal to the Doge's Palace and the Rialto bridge – but this is one of them, too.

While I was in Venice a new film was released in cinemas across Italy called *L'abbaglio*, recounting actual events amid the battles of the Expedition of The Thousand. I had to see it, of course, and the movie was visually striking with a fine balance of comedy and serious history to keep a modern audience enthralled. Garibaldi was portrayed as an empathetic leader of men, attuned to the horrors faced in war by soldiers, and came across as an admirable hero of the Risorgimento. The movie was an instant success at the box office in Italy, with more than half a million people watching it in the first three weeks of its release. Several films about the Hero of Two Worlds have been made, the finest probably in 1961 called simply *Garibaldi*, although originally released as *Viva l'Italia*, directed by one of international cinema's most influential figures, Roberto Rossellini, the father of neo-realism. Rossellini said the movie he was most proud of was *Garibaldi*.

Cinema is another of the aspects of everyday that unites Italians. Going to the movies remains very popular, whether it's to see the serious, artistic films of highly respected modern directors like Nanni Moretti, Matteo Garrone and Paolo Sorrentino, or the vast numbers of comedy movies made each year, or even the mostly silly Christmas films known as *cinepanettone*.

There is huge pride in Italy's place in the history of cinema established by directors like Federico Fellini, Luchino Visconti and Sergio Leone, and in the fact they have won the Oscar for the best foreign film 14 times, more than any other nation. Italian cinema also produced one of the most memorable movie moments of all time, when Anita Ekberg waded into the Trevi fountain in *La Dolce Vita*.

The Venice Film Festival is the oldest in the world, founded in the 1930s, and still enticing glamorous stars to the city every autumn. I took the vaporetto water bus across the lagoon to where the festival is held on the Lido, a long thin strip of land that acts as a barrier to the city from the Adriatic. It's home to excellent sands and smart beach clubs, and it's easy to understand why the name lido was appropriated in England as a descriptor for outdoor swimming pools.

At the heart of the film festival is a gleaming-white huge art deco building on the seafront called the *Mostra Internazionale D'Arte Cinematografica*. Next door was the *Palazzo del Cinema*, art deco too, and across the road the five-star Hotel Excelsior where the film stars stay. This is a different kind of Venice; normal in some senses with proper tree-lined streets, roundabouts, bicycle lanes, and buses with four wheels. But not that normal. This is an exclusive and wealthy area to live, contented and relaxed all year round, the kind of place where money doesn't have to talk back to have its say.

Garibaldi still had a lot to say – remaining utterly obsessed with Rome, the final piece of the Italian jigsaw. After his big speech in St Mark's Square and an obligatory ride on a gondola, he went to Florence to continue the crusade and make ever more fiery speeches demanding the capture of the Eternal City. The choice of Florence was no accident. It had become the capital of Italy instead of Turin in 1865 as part of a diplomatic deal with France whereby the Italian government renounced any ambition to incorporate Rome into its territory, and the French agreed to withdraw their soldiers from the city who were protecting the Pope. There were violent protests on the streets by the people of Turin about this move, but Italy wanted and needed a more central capital. Garibaldi was outraged that Italy was apparently giving up on Rome, and he made his speeches and got himself elected to the new parliament in Florence.

Although there is no record of Garibaldi actually attending this parliament, we do know that he was elected to it as a deputy in two places on the same day in March 1867, winning the vote in Andria, a town in the southern region of Puglia, and at Ozieri in northern Sardinia. He campaigned only so that he had another platform to shout about the issue of Rome, although in Ozieri they remain proud that Garibaldi did also push for the creation of one of the first technical schools in Italy.

The noisy calls to action by Garibaldi were a public embarrassment to the politicians, but at the same time they were conspiring privately to create the conditions for unrest and a rebellion within Rome. They could not support an open assault by Garibaldi and a new band of Red Shirt volunteers on the Eternal City, but they knew he still had huge popular support, and they hedged their bets as they had before the episode of Aspromonte. In September 1867, Garibaldi decided it was time to act, but before he could reach the borders of the Papal State he was once more arrested by the Italian authorities. They could not and would not put him on trial, so he was sent back to Caprera and effectively imprisoned on his own island, which was under quarantine due to an outbreak of cholera. Just to be sure, the Italian government sent warships to patrol the perimeter of the island and prevent his exit.

Garibaldi was not welcome in Florence – then or now it seems. There is a statue of him in the city, the design virtually identical to the one in Venice, but it is located away from the historic centre along banks of the River Arno in a small square next to the American consulate. The place was almost deserted when I arrived, but when I took my camera out for a photo a stern security guard materialised from thin air, shouting, in English: 'No pictures, no pictures.' He then marched over with a menacing air that clearly meant he wanted no debate.

'No pictures, no pictures,' he repeated, and when I asked why he just pointed to the consulate building and said: 'Security risk, security risk.' I lingered for maybe twenty seconds to read the inscriptions on this public monument to Italy's great national hero, and he shouted: 'Move on, move on.' What could be the security risk? An image of the consulate building in public view, a building which was not cordoned off? The number plates of the few cars parked in the vicinity? There was no other living soul in the square – only the bronze likeness of Giuseppe Garibaldi.

He was named on this statue, so the security guard could not claim ignorance of who was standing on the plinth, which also featured the names of four of his battles – those at Montevideo, Rome, Marsala and Dijon. I saw this, and moved on, walking right in front of the Consulate because I knew that the road on the other side leading away from the river was the city's Via Garibaldi. This was a short, rather nondescript street, but still under highly visible protection. There was an armoured jeep at the river end entrance flanked by soldiers with assault rifles. Their body language screamed 'move on, move on'. They didn't need to speak. You see this kind of scene all around Italy close to embassies, official buildings and some private residences. Close to where I live there are always two armed policemen or soldiers standing guard outside a normal apartment block, which means someone significant lives there, perhaps an anti-mafia prosecutor.

The nine warships sailing in the waters of La Maddalena had not been sent to protect Garibaldi, but to keep him blockaded on Caprera. Meanwhile, the government was still, as always, plotting privately – giving money to help organise volunteers if they were needed for an attack on Rome. Amid this turbulent and complicated situation, Garibaldi decided he had to find a way back to Florence. He was now sixty years old and plagued by rheumatism and arthritis, yet he did so. The first stage of the escape was to silently pass by the Navy vessels in a rowing boat on a night of helpful fog to reach the island of La Maddalena. He stayed the night there at the house of Claire Collins and then slipped onto Sardinia itself. All the time, a friend was impersonating him back home on Caprera, walking round the outdoor terrace on crutches. Garibaldi then dyed his beard black and rode across Sardinia on horseback, a gruelling journey that took seventeen hours. Finally, he sailed under his old alias of Joseph Pane on a boat to Livorno and then took a carriage to Florence.

This escape gave him more satisfaction than many of the battles he won, and that is little wonder. It was an incredible achievement which only added to the lustre of his legend. Who could keep him down? Certainly not the dithering Italian government which changed prime ministers with bewildering regularity. Only one of them, Bettino Ricasoli, known as the Iron Baron, appeared to have any of the political craft of Cavour. He was in power from June 1861 to March 1862, and it was in the aftermath of his exit that the events of Aspromonte occurred. Ricasoli was in charge again from June 1866 to April 1867, through the time of the Third War of Italian Independence and the deal that claimed Venice. It was after his exit this time that Garibaldi headed towards another disaster. Maybe this is just coincidence, maybe not.

Ricasoli remained a deputy in parliament until his death in 1880 at his Brolio castle in the little town of Gaiole-in-Chianti, and although he was one of the more noteworthy figures of the Risorgimento he is now most famous for creating the modern blend of Chianti wine. His idea was to use predominantly Sangiovese grapes, and his family still make fine wines to this day, bearing his name and that of Brolio.

Italy has been the world's biggest producer of wine through the last two decades, even ahead of France. The island of Sicily alone produces a greater volume of wine annually than Australia. There are excellent wines found in all twenty regions of Italy, and it is unusual to find any from other countries sold in supermarkets here. Whereas in Britain supermarkets and wine merchants will display bottles by country of origin, in Italy they are ordered by region – from Puglia and Calabria in the south to Veneto and Trentino Alto-Adige in the north.

There are more than 2,000 distinct grape varieties. Popular ones include the *Sangiovese* grape for Chianti, the *Nebbiolo* grape for Barolo, and the *Corvina* grape for Valpolicella. Many varieties are being revived from near extinction, together with their tongue-twister names: *Schioppettino, Carricante, Susumaniello*. There is one from the north-eastern region of Friuli called *Tazzelenghe*, which in the local dialect means tongue-cutting or tongue-stinging. Not surprisingly, this has a sharp, acidic taste. On one restaurant wine list I saw in Venice it said that you should only try this if you're an experienced wine drinker. There's a reason why it's a very rare option.

Living in Italy I learned immediately that wine plays a fundamental role in everyday life. As coffee flows abundantly through the conviviality of mornings, so wine takes the the baton from late afternoon. Red, white, pink or prosecco, it is an essential element of early evening aperitivo culture, the *struscio*, and dinner at home. Italy is at heart a conservative and traditional country, and wine is just what they drink. It's a glass or two for most people, but rarely more. Every time, wherever you are, whoever you're with, there is a timeless ritual at the table when a bottle is opened. The wine is poured, there is the first taste, always followed by a pause for a few seconds of deliberation and appreciation. Then comes a slight nod of the head – and if people say *buono* (good) all is well. If not, just smile politely and make sure you try harder and spend a little more next time.

You won't be surprised to discover that wine doesn't escape the Garibaldi touch. Nothing escapes the Garibaldi touch. The most well-known is the marsala fortified wine from Sicily that is called Garibaldi, but there are others. The best sparkling wine made in Brazil is a Garibaldi, and there is a range of Garibaldi Cellars wines in Oregon, US. A company calling themselves Vini Garibaldi makes red wines from Sangiovese grapes at a vineyard near Livorno. There is also a *Grignolino D'Asti* Garibaldi wine produced by the Mura Mura firm in Piedmont, close to the town of Alessandria where the Hero of Two Worlds was put in a notorious prison after his arrest in Florence in September 1867.

The grape was important back then as well, and not just for Ricasoli. His predecessor Camillo Cavour had his own vineyard that produced Barolo wines, while King Vittorio Emanuele II created the *Fontanafredda* winery that continues to this day. Garibaldi also grew his own grapes on Caprera to produce a home-made style of sweet wine that he preferred. These were a variety called *Malvasia di Maiatico*, which he acquired after a visit in 1861 to stay with friends in the tiny village of Maiatico, close to the city of Parma. He enjoyed their wine so much he took home some plants to Caprera and had 8,000 vines in the end. There is, naturally, a plaque in Maiatico to record this fact.

The litmus test of what really matters to people in this country was on display during the tough 'red zone' lockdown period of the Covid pandemic when only essential shops could stay open. The categories were, in no particular order: florists, children's clothes, ironmongers, perfume shops, picture-framers, electricals, bookshops, chemists, stationers, chocolatiers, mobile phone outlets, grocers, and last but not least, wine shops. These necessities of life may seem a curious mixture, but that's how it was during the time of the pandemic, and that's how it is in Italy. Flowers, wine, books, medicine, phones and chocolate. What more could you need?

When Garibaldi avoided the quarantine on Caprera with his daring escape, the absolute necessity for him was to march on Rome. The Italian government dared not arrest him again on his return to Florence, where he gave a provocative speech to a big crowd outside the Basilica of Santa Maria Novella in the heart of the city. I found the plaque which commemorates this moment outside what is now the Garibaldi Blu hotel in the square:

> From this house Giuseppe Garibaldi, constant soldier for Italy and humanity, on 22 October 1867 to a cheering crowd, said the memorable words, Rome or Death, before departing on the expedition to Mentana to restore Rome as the capital of Italy.

Garibaldi stayed in Florence for the next eight days while the government dithered about whether to support him or not.

It seemed to him this constituted a green light to head for Rome, which is the only feasible explanation for continuing with a plan that looked like folly. A special train was arranged to take him to the Papal border where a volunteer force of Red Shirts would be waiting. As the locomotive left the station at Florence the government issued orders to arrest Garibaldi again, but it was too late. He was gone, and when he reached the hilltop town of Mentana, the Hero of Two Worlds was just twenty-nine kilometres away from the Eternal City.

14

ROME/MENTANA

'This very important work will change the river, so that instead of the devastating Tiber which scares two-thirds of the people of Rome, it will give new life to the city and improve public health.'

Giuseppe Garibaldi

The big bunch of keys was the kind that jailers always have in the movies, and the man holding them picked out the longest, chunkiest one as we stood in front of a robust wooden door with a steel grille on the top half. It clanked into the lock and the key needed a strong twist and tug before the door creaked open to reveal a tiny room behind. The space was all but filled by a rough stone box without a lid. We squeezed in next to it, and the man with the keys didn't need to say a word. The box was a sarcophagus full of bones and skulls, the remains of Red Shirt volunteers who had been killed in the battle of Mentana on 3 November 1867, the final day of combat on Italian soil for Giuseppe Garibaldi. One of the thigh bones had a name written on it, Giovanni Ricci, who was among more than 150 soldiers who perished here. It was a solemn, unsettling and very unexpected moment on the trail of the General. The skulls and bones weren't covered by glass but left exposed as a powerful reminder of the reality of war. All these men had died very quickly and on a hopeless mission, because the French army defending the Pope's leadership of Rome had new chassepot guns that fired twelve times a minute and overwhelmed the Red Shirts. It had been an ignominious end to Garibaldi's dream of capturing the Eternal City.

I had been invited inside the *Ara-ossario Garibaldino*, a national monument erected as a memorial to those who lost their lives in this brief battle, both the Red Shirts and the French soldiers, some of whose bones were also in the sarcophagus. The man with the keys was a young museum officer from the town, working as a volunteer at the weekends while studying for a history degree. His passion and enthusiasm to tell the story was infectious, and it revealed the obvious pride that Mentana continues to feel for its place in the making of Italy. It is a modest spot in the hills north-east of Rome, but the mood was just the same as I had found at Salemi, Cesenatico, Vairano and San Fermo di Battaglia. It seems to me greatly to Italy's credit that history matters so much to local people in so many cities, towns and villages.

The story here in Mentana was one of horror and humiliation, but perhaps that makes it even more important to retain knowledge of the past. There was clearly an enduring affection for the Hero of Two Worlds. On the main street I passed the town's best restaurant, the *Antica Trattoria Garibaldi*, first opened in 1908, which was full and had no place for a casual visitor without a reservation. A little way along I turned right onto a wide set of steps that led up to the memorial. On one side a mural had been painted on the walls of houses that depicted the battle of Mentana, with Garibaldi sitting astride his familiar white horse. This was only begun in 2017, and work remains in progress. At the top of the steps, I turned to look the other way and had a view across to hills on the other side of a valley covered in olive trees.

The memorial itself was made of bleak, brownish-grey stone planted in the middle of well-kept gardens full of cypress trees and umbrella pines. By the door into the little vault room was a plaque dedicated to the 'brave men who fought with Garibaldi and died for the liberty and independence of their people. We remember them with affection and admiration.' There were several other plaques around the gardens, but I took a path across the grass to a small but perfectly formed museum that details the history of this battle, and also one that occurred at the nearby hill town of Monterotondo a few days earlier. In the centre of the museum was a delightful bust of Garibaldi – made entirely of Lego bricks. The events of autumn 1867 are brilliantly told, with just the right amount of information displayed with clarity and intelligence – which is not always the case in Italian museums. There were also some worthwhile memorabilia, including Garibaldi's black scarf he wore in the battle.

I was heading out when the museum officer asked if I would like to see another exhibition room. Of course, I did. So he locked the door to the museum, put up a sign saying, 'Back in 10 minutes' and we walked down the street and around a corner. Then he needed his bunch of keys again. One opened a

Via Garibaldi

courtyard gate, another the door to a building, and finally one inside to the additional exhibition. Inside was the finest and largest collection of Garibaldini red shirts, numbering forty in total. For context, other museums in Italy are overjoyed to be able to display one red shirt. The man with the keys happily told me this was the best collection in all the world. Most of them were displayed on mannequins, others kept in wooden drawers that could be opened by visitors. The holes in some of the shirts, he told me, were rarely the result of gunshots from battle, but mostly because they had been moth-eaten through years of being stored poorly.

Most of these historic red shirts had been donated by the families of men who fought at Mentana, and each one was identified with the name of their volunteer. There was also a handsome collection of red caps and rifles, including several of the French chassepots which were the decisive factor. The difference to the guns used by Garibaldi's men was clear enough. I had seen many museums on my travels around Italy, and this was one of the most impressive. The man with the keys told me it had fallen into disrepair for some years, but the red shirts had been restored and the entire museum revamped in 2017, on the 150th anniversary of the battle, at the direction of a new independent political mayor. They did a superb job.

Mentana is another name that everyone knows in Italy, even if they have never been anywhere near the town. The battle has been commemorated elsewhere, too, as I had already seen in Milan, and also in Florence, where Piazza Mentana was located right next to the Uffizi museum, one of the finest art galleries in the world. The statue in the centre of this square was particularly vivid, depicting a Red Shirt soldier firing a pistol with his right hand while a mortally wounded colleague lay slumped over his left shoulder. The inscription read: 'To the strong ones who fell at Mentana.'

The prologue to the battle was in Florence where Garibaldi had given a series of fiery speeches about the need to march on Rome. During them his animosity towards the Pope spilled out, as he spoke of his belief that a new 'natural religion of Christ' could evolve which would be without altars and priests and Papal control. It would be, in Garibaldi's words, 'a religion of truth and reason, of science and intelligence'. When the crowds cheered wildly, it fuelled Garibaldi's illusion that he was a modern prophet, not least when he was asked by people to baptise their babies, which he did.

Fame, celebrity and power have always turned the heads of people through history, and Garibaldi was not an exception. Half a million people had packed the streets of London to see him. He encountered public adoration everywhere he travelled in Italy. This all convinced him of his genius and invincibility, whereas in reality he was now an old man being given the runaround by politicians and a general with a poorly armed volunteer force likely to be heavily outnumbered. The heroism of those who fought and died at Mentana should not obscure the culpability of Garibaldi for insisting on pushing ahead with a doomed mission.

When he arrived at the border of Papal territory on the train from Florence, his eldest son Menotti was waiting with a group of volunteer soldiers. They moved forward to take the town of Monterotondo in a brief skirmish on 27 October 1867, but events moved swiftly against Garibaldi. French soldiers returned to Rome to protect the Pope and Garibaldi was then formally disowned by the Italian government. The final showdown came at Mentana, and when he knew that a superior French force had marched out of Rome towards them, the sensible option for Garibaldi would have been to order a retreat. But he was too close to the Eternal City, less than thirty kilometres away, and could draw on memories of overcoming impossible odds in previous victories like the Battle of Calatafimi in 1860. He would not give up his lifelong dream without a fight. It was a case of so near, and yet so far. The battle at Mentana lasted only a few hours despite the heroism of his fighters. It was a day of needless bloodshed as the chassepot guns gave the French troops an unbeatable advantage. Defeat was swift and total. Garibaldi disbanded his surviving troops and he left the way he had arrived, on a train. He was arrested at Figline station and jailed once more. Figline, just south of Florence, is still a railway town, its pride and joy today the Garibaldi Theatre.

Another significant part of this story in November 1867, one filled with equal sorrow, concerned various groups of rebels who had organised themselves inside Rome, trying to create conditions for a people's uprising against the Pope in the knowledge that Garibaldi, the supposedly invincible liberator, was on his way. The most famous battle within the city in 1867 occurred at Villa Glori, a park in the Parioli district, where seventy Red Shirts, who had arrived in Rome as an advance guard of Garibaldi volunteers, fought against Papal troops. Among them were two brothers, Enrico and Giovanni Cairoli, who had also been involved in the Expedition of The Thousand. On a day of heroic action, the Red Shirts fought off an attack by Papal troops, a battle in which Enrico Cairoli was killed and brother Giovanni badly wounded. The next day a larger brigade of Papal soldiers returned and ended the resistance. In the centre of Villa Glori is a stone column standing in a rocky outcrop erected as a monument to those who died. It was situated close to an almond tree where Enrico Cairoli fell, and it is said that a dry branch of the almond tree was laid within the rocks.

Giovanni Cairoli survived this battle, but his wounds were so severe that he died two years later at the age of twenty-seven. He is immortalised in a statue on the terrace of the Pincio hill in Rome, which I reached by climbing the Spanish Steps. This depicted Giovanni shooting at the enemy as Enrico lay dying at his side. There were five Cairoli brothers in total, all of them dedicated followers of Garibaldi. The second eldest, Ernesto, died in the battle of Varese in 1859. The next, Luigi, was killed during the Expedition of The Thousand, while the eldest, Benedetto Cairoli, had been severely wounded at Palermo in 1860. He recovered and was among those who fought at the battle of Mentana. Eleven years later he became Prime Minister of Italy, a post he held for three years.

Villa Glori is also known as the Park of Remembrance, dedicated to all Romans who died fighting for their country. That doesn't mean it has been cared for as it should. 'The park is unfortunately currently in conditions of neglect, the fault of politicians who run the artistic heritage of Rome,' was the scathing comment of the *Romapedia* website.

In 1867 a second rebel group in Rome was based in the Trastevere district at a woollen mill called Casa Anjani, where the heroine was a *garabaldina* called Giuditta Tavani Arquati. She was a committed radical, the daughter of one of the fighters who survived the battles of 1849. Arquati, heavily pregnant with her fourth child, was in charge of storing weapons at the mill in Via Lungaretta. When Papal troops attacked she stood at the door allowing many others to escape, before being brutally killed by a bayonet stab along with her husband and two sons. Her three-year-old daughter Adelaide survived, hidden in a basket of linen.

Via Lungaretta is still there today, one of the main streets of Trastevere, and I was one among thousands of people taking a stroll when I visited, but perhaps the only one who noticed that a square along the road had been named in honour of Arquati. Where the mill once stood there was now an ice cream parlour, a shoe shop, and a store selling replica football kits for Fourth Division football team Trastevere Calcio. On the wall high above was a bust of this heroine of the Risorgimento, with a detailed inscription below. It said it had been placed 'To show new generations the virtues of sacrifice fighting strongly for the people'. Crowds of youngsters fill this street every night; it is one of the prime venues for what young Italians call the *Movida* – nightlife in bars and clubs that spills out onto pavements and roads. Few, if any, stop in Via Lungaretta to look up and consider a woman who was one of the 'mothers of the nation'. It doesn't help, of course, that the bust has been placed too high to catch people's attention as they pass by.

The district of Trastevere was where Garibaldi lodged during the time of the *Repubblica Romana* in 1849. It is one of the most atmospheric parts of the city, full of old lanes, the fabulous Basilica of Santa Maria with thirteenth-century mosaics, the city's botanical gardens which sweep up the hill towards the Garibaldi statue, and Villa Farnesina, one of the most beautiful buildings in Rome, some of the walls decorated with frescoes by Raphael, including the Triumph of Galatea which features instantly recognisable cherubs flying in the sky with bows and arrows.

Trastevere is also home to hundreds of restaurants, most of them serving the traditional cuisine of Rome: pasta dishes like *cacio e pepe, amatriciana,* and *carbonara,* and vegetables such as *puntarelle* (a feathery, weed-like type of Italian chicory, according to the Cambridge dictionary, but in reality untranslatable) and *carciofi alla romana* (artichokes cooked Roman style). This is not Italian food; it is Roman food. Every city around the world has enticing Italian restaurants. Italy does not. It has restaurants which reflect the particular region of their owners and chefs. In my district of Rome, within a few hundred square metres, there are places devotedly serving dishes from Tuscany, Puglia, Abruzzo, Sardinia, Campania, Sicily, and Calabria. This concentration of so many various regional cuisines is unusual in Italy, a reflection of the fact that Rome is a melting pot of the people of this nation, the place where the country feels most unified – the bridge between north and south, between religion and republic, the bridge to history.

I walked along the road from Trastevere to the ancient centre of Rome, which takes you across the Ponte Garibaldi. The four corners of this bridge over the Tiber all had a column, and each one was inscribed with the name of two of Garibaldi's battles: Montevideo, Rome, Varese, Marsala, Volturno, Bezzecca, Dijon and Mentana. I was heading for the Vittoriano, the huge white monument to King Vittorio Emanuele II, which was hosting a special exhibition of paintings by Silvestro Lega, one of the finest Italian artists of the nineteenth century. Several of his works hang in the Uffizi gallery in Florence, and others in Rome's excellent National Gallery of Modern Art.

Lega had fought in the Second War of Italian Independence during 1859, and the next year he painted one of the best portraits of Garibaldi, just after the meeting with the King which clinched the unification of the country. The Hero is portrayed in an immaculate red shirt, his hair and beard still flame red, a rifle held loosely under his arm. Is there a look of regret in his eyes? Many people see that in this painting and note the dark clouds looming in the sky behind. It was on loan for this exhibition from the *Pinacoteca Comunale*, a gallery in the tiny village of Modigliana in the region of Emilia Romagna, the village where Lega was born, and where the local priest hid Garibaldi for a night during his escape from Cesenatico and Ravenna after the death of Anita. There was another fabulous Lega painting on show, entitled 'The Last Moments of Giuseppe Mazzini', depicting the intellectual inspiration of the Risorgimento on his deathbed. This was on loan from a gallery in Rhode Island, US. There was more emotion in this work and the portrait of Garibaldi than any photograph could provide.

There are many fine paintings of Garibaldi and the events of the Risorgimento, which is not so surprising given the prominence of art in Italy. It is the home of Da Vinci and Michelangelo, and the land of the *pinacoteca*. This is a useful word to know in Italy, which in rough translation means 'picture gallery'. Most villages and towns have one, and they are mostly small, though not always. Modigliana, for example, is place of just 4,400 inhabitants, yet has its *pinacoteca*.

The gallery at the Lingotto rooftop racing track in Turin is also a *pinacoteca*.

Garibaldi's lifelong obsession was to unify the country, but Italy's fractured history is a crucial reason why it has produced a legion of great painters and why there is so much extraordinary artistic output. For hundreds of years there was intense competition between rich men and between cities like Rome, Milan, Florence and Venice to have the best of everything – castles, palaces, food, art, music and cathedrals. Artistic endeavour flourished most of all in the Renaissance of the fifteenth and sixteenth centuries. Another factor in the astounding quality and volume of art was the rivalry between the painters themselves. They continually had to prove themselves in their own heat of battle.

Who was the greatest of them all? An impossible question. At one moment in history, incredibly, two giants were pitted head-to-head in a painting 'competition'. It occurred in 1504 when Leonardo and Michelangelo were each commissioned to paint a huge battle scene, side by side, on a wall in the Palazzo Vecchio in Florence. Leonardo was fifty-three, Michelangelo only twenty-nine. The former had just finished painting the *Mona Lisa*, while the *Statue of David* by Michelangelo had recently been unveiled in Florence. Sadly, neither man finished painting their battle scene, but initial drawings remained on the walls for many decades, only to be painted over by another artist, Giorgio Vasari, in 1560. A unique treasure was lost forever, to the immense chagrin of historians of art.

Another intense artistic rivalry was between Gian Lorenzo Bernini and Francesco Borromini, the Baroque blockbusters of sculpture and architecture. Bernini was commissioned by the

Pope to create the Four Rivers Fountain in the centre of Piazza Navona, one of the most-loved squares of Rome to this day. The four rivers were the Danube, the Ganges, the Nile and the River Plate, and it was unveiled in 1651. At the same time Borromini was commissioned to build the Church of St'Agnese in Agone on one side of Piazza Navona, close to the fountain. The story goes that Bernini had his figure on the Nile cover its eyes to avoid looking at the disgrace of the church façade, while the figure on the River Plate was fashioned with its arm out to stop the church from falling on the fountain. In response, it is said Borromini's figure of St Agnes, with her head to one side, is placed that way in contempt for the ugliness of the fountain. Whether or not this is myth, it's certain that Bernini and Borromini detested each other. It was of an intensity that matched Garibaldi's hatred for the Pope, and vice versa.

The fountain and the façade are examples of magnificent art that cost nothing to see. Go to the major galleries and the delightful *pinacotecas*, of course, but also revel in what's all around. A striking joy of Italy is how masterpieces decorate thousands of churches up and down the land – astonishing, spellbinding works which are either completely free to view, or with only a minimal fee. Yes, it's true that Michelangelo's most famous fresco, the ceiling of the Sistine chapel in the Vatican, comes with a twenty Euro ticket and quite often a queue of many hours. But his extraordinary *Pieta* sculpture in St Peter's Basilica has easy access, and another Michelangelo delight for me was simply a pavement – the geometric floor of the Piazza del Campidoglio in central Rome.

I went to the Basilica of St Francis in the town of Assisi and saw glorious frescoes by the medieval maestro Giotto. Even more impressive were Giotto's paintings on the walls of the Scrovegni chapel in Padova, completed in 1305. They are sublime, but now so fragile that you have to first pass into a room outside, which is locked for a period so that the microclimate inside the chapel is maintained at the appropriate level. Once inside the chapel you can only stay for fifteen minutes, but it's worth it. Another wonder was the small Umbrian hilltop town of Spello. This had a lovely *pinacoteca*, but its star attraction was the Baglioni Chapel inside the town's main church with bewitching frescoes by the fifteenth-century painter Pinturicchio.

I saw frescoes by Raphael in Santa Maria della Pace, but for me the most magnificent were two works by Caravaggio in the Church of Santa Maria which stands at one edge of Piazza Del Popolo – the people's square, the traditional venue for left-wing political demonstrations. One painting portrayed The *Crucifixion of St Peter*, while opposite it was The *Conversion of Paul on the Road to Damascus*. They hung in a dark corner at the end of the left-hand aisle, but I put two Euros into a box and the lights went on. They shone a light on genius, and two Euros were never better spent.

There is also one final work to mention. It is far from a masterpiece, but in the church of St Paul Within-the-Walls in Rome, a multi-cultural and multi-lingual episcopal church built in 1873, I discovered a mosaic depicting various saints riding into battle. Curiously, the figures of these saints were represented by men of the time and so St Andrew became Abraham Lincoln, while St James galloped along in the guise, very recognisably, of Giuseppe Garibaldi.

When this mosaic was created Rome had finally been liberated from Papal control. The capture of the Eternal City, by force, occurred in 1870, but Garibaldi was not there to take part in the action and witness the final step in unifying his country. He was at home on Caprera, prevented from leaving by a fleet of warships ordered by the Italian Government to surround the island. There was no daring escape this time for an arthritic old man. Even though he was still revered by the ordinary people of Italy as the hero of the nation, the authorities effectively put him under house arrest as government troops stormed through the gate of Porta Pia on 20 September 1870 to take command of the city. There were no French soldiers to defend Rome now – they had left the Eternal City to fight in the Franco-Prussian war, which had begun that year. Italy was finally complete.

Garibaldi hadn't set foot in Rome since 1849 and didn't again until he attended the new national parliament as an elected representative, winning ballots in the Roma 1 and Roma 5 districts on the same day in 1874. The man of the people never in his life lost an election he contested, and he simply had to take his place in the parliament once Rome had become the capital of Italy. Before this, however, there had been one last battle to fight. It was a deep irony, given his long history of combat against French soldiers, that this last call to action was in the cause of France in their war against Prussia.

In 1870 he was thoroughly disenchanted with the conservative royalists who dominated Italian politics and looked to the new Republic of France as a better model. He was bitter about being kept away from the capture of Rome, he had also heard alarming tales of Prussian brutality in their war with France, and he believed this was a fight for justice and common humanity. A final factor, probably, was that

Garibaldi was simply bored with his enforced exile on Caprera and wanted to experience the thrill of combat again. He sailed to Marseille, receiving a rapturous reception from the crowds. The French government had hesitated in accepting Garibaldi's offer of help in their war, but they now put him in charge of a force of 5,000 men, called the Army of the Vosges.

He was sixty-three, walking with a stick or crutches, and barely able to mount a horse. But his mind was still sharp, and he enjoyed one success against the Prussians in a battle at Dijon on 23 January 1871 – repelling an attack by 4,000 enemy troops and capturing a flag from the 61st Pomeranian regiment. It was almost the only victory on the French side, and less than a week later an armistice was called to end the war. The legend of Garibaldi the mighty general had been burnished a little more, and he was elected to the French parliament in Bordeaux, winning the popular vote in six separate places.

There was just one appearance at the chamber in Bordeaux, in February 1871, where Garibaldi was treated as a hostile, foreign revolutionary presence by most of the other deputies and shouted down when he tried to speak – to plead the case of Italians who had been wounded in the conflict while fighting for France. He left immediately for Caprera. Three weeks later, Victor Hugo gave a fierce speech in the parliament defending the honour of his friend and telling unimpressed deputies: 'Garibaldi was the only one of the generals who fought for France who was not defeated.' It caused uproar in the chamber and Hugo resigned in disgust.

The politics of the new Italy was, if anything, even more combustible. Governments were in constant flux with a revolving door for Prime Ministers. There were nine changes of leadership within the first eight years of national unity, and for many Italians there has been a sense of eternal crisis ever since. Within the last fifteen years in Italy there has twice been a 'technical government', led by respected men from outside political parties brought in to provide temporary stability to the system at particular moments of stress. It happened during the Covid pandemic, for example, when Mario Draghi, the economist and former President of the European Central Bank, a man born and bred in Rome, came riding to the rescue to popular acclaim. Italy is forever searching for heroes and none has been more enduring than Garibaldi, even though (or perhaps partly because) he was hopeless at politics.

A perfect illustration of this is the story of a piece of political graffiti in the Garbatella district of Rome, which friends told me I had to see. So I went to Via Basilio Brollo and there it was in bold red paint: 'Vote Garibaldi. List No. 1'. This was first seen on the wall during the 1948 general election when the Italian Communist Party and Italian Socialist Party decided to join forces and list themselves together as the Popular Democratic front, with the face of Garibaldi imposed on a green star as their political symbol. It was said to be the dirtiest election in Italy's history, with American money backing the centre-right Christian Democrats who won the day. The graffiti saying Vote Garibaldi remained in place and has become a cause célèbre. It was painted over in 2004 but quickly restored, with a plaque placed there to explain its historical significance. It was covered over again in 2019, this time, according to officials 'in error by an employee of the company contracted for the service of urban decorum' – a worker who hadn't seen the plaque. This provoked another outcry, and the graffiti was back in place within a couple of days.

Three years earlier it was partisans from the 52nd Garibaldi Brigade, members of the Italian Communist Party, who had captured Mussolini at the end of the Second World War and executed him on the shores of Lake Como. They chose the name Garibaldi because of its national-patriotic symbolism, just as Italian anti-fascist volunteers in the Spanish Civil War had called themselves the Garibaldi Brigade. Another reason was to reclaim the spirit of the Hero of Two Worlds for the left-wing of politics after Mussolini had spent years declaring that Garibaldi was his inspiration and had commissioned statues such as the one of Anita on the Gianicolo hill.

The legacy of Garibaldi is still fought over. In 2023, the right-wing Prime Minister Giorgia Meloni, who grew up in Garbatella, borrowed the famous phrase, 'Here we make Italy or we die,' to tell the public that her government was not afraid to make tough choices. When Meloni again referenced Garibaldi in October 2024, the opposition leader Elly Schlein immediately responded with an emotional speech, saying: 'Leave him alone. Garibaldi is our great hero of the republic.'

Garibaldi's published views during his own lifetime would suggest he stood more on the left wing of politics than the right, and although he was never bound to any particular party he admired the socialist International movement. In the couple of years after the French episode he spoke for universal suffrage, the introduction of free and universal education, for income tax paid according to wealth, for equality of opportunity, and for the abolition of taxes on essential household items like salt and flour. He was an idealist and a dreamer in many ways, but also had one practical obsession that dominated his life after being elected to the parliament in Rome in November 1874. This was a mission to improve the health of the Eternal City, which had been bedevilled for centuries by malaria, poor sanitation and widespread poverty. The central plank was a scheme to re-route the River Tiber and take it around the city towards the coast at Fiumicino, now the site of Rome's major international airport, rather than keep it flowing in the centre close to the Colosseum, St Peter's and Trastevere. The river was prone to extensive flooding, making lakes of squares like Piazza Navona, and in December 1870 had caused widespread damage and loss of life. The river was a stagnant and putrid mess, full of the detritus of the city. Malaria, in particular, was a huge issue.

London and Vienna had similar problems during the nineteenth century and their answer was to build new embankments. Rome set up a commission to assess its options and the plan of diverting the river, the idea of two engineers Paolo Molini and Alessandro Castellani, was a cause taken up by Garibaldi. He travelled to Rome in 1875 to give an impassioned speech at Parliament: 'This very important work will change the river, so that instead of the threatening and devastating Tiber which scares two-thirds of the people of Rome, it will give new life to the city and improve public health and hygiene.' His vision was for a huge modern avenue to be created where the Tiber flowed, similar to that which now exists in the Spanish city of Valencia. Huge crowds cheered Garibaldi throughout his stay, and there was applause in Parliament for his plan. It was too costly, though, to have any chance of being implemented, and the Italian government eventually opted for the solution of embankments. Garibaldi had lost another battle.

Critics of the embankments in modern Rome say that the river is effectively divorced from the people due to their height. Under the Garibaldi plan the area would have become an integral part of the working and living city. The response of the majority is probably that great cities have great rivers; and that the Tiber is surely where it should be, snaking through the hills of Rome. There is a fine cycle path on the riverbank, and in the summer one section has a festival of bars, stalls and restaurants in a long tented village. The river remains dirty, and I often see volunteers trying to clean it up on weekends, fishing plastic bottles and other rubbish from the water. It's not a river you want to fall into.

The embankments have done their job of preventing flooding, and the tidal waves of malaria affecting the people of Rome are long gone. But there is one legacy from Garibaldi's desire to improve public health. His obsession is now one of the national obsessions of Italy. There is a pharmacy on every street, and sometimes two or three. In every TV advert break at least half the commercials are for medicines. At a dinner party you will be lucky if the conversation is not dominated by talk about health, particularly about a curious malady known as *la cervicale*. Almost every Italian worries about suffering *cervicale*, a condition which does not exist anywhere else in the world. It is something akin to neck-ache (but definitely not the same as), which many believe can be caused just by being hit by a puff of cold air at the wrong moment. People talk endlessly about getting *cervicale*, the problems it causes, and there are even medicines sold specifically to deal with it.

For many months I expressed scepticism about *cervicale* to Italian friends, and they scoffed at my ignorance. 'You British just don't understand anatomy.' Eventually, I asked a pharmacist in Rome and she told me that *cervicale* is just a myth, and that an eminent neurologist had confirmed this to her. But she said people really believe it exists and buy painkillers advertised to deal with *cervicale* even though they are no different to any other painkiller. She also told me how effective the TV commercials are. There is always a rush the next day for products when they have been on television the previous evening, and it's crucial for her to liaise with the pharmaceutical companies to know when commercials will run, so that she can stock up and be ready. Perhaps it's not so surprising that the mafia have entered the business.

In some places pharmacies have become social arenas. The one at the bottom of my road (there are also two at the top) has put in a table and chairs for people to sit and chat with each other. The prevalence of pharmacies is not just an impression – the stats confirm it. There are approximately 24,000 pharmacies in Italy, compared to 14,300 in the UK – even though Italy has population of 10 million fewer people. This makes it one pharmacy in Italy for every 2,500 people, whereas in the UK it is one chemist for every 4,780.

This is a vast difference. One reason is that Italian supermarkets are not allowed to sell basic medicines like painkillers. You can't just pick them off a shelf, you have to buy at a pharmacy. The difference, though, also reflects the reality that Italy and Italians take health (and anatomy) very seriously. Another example is that a percentage of the cost of medicines and dental treatment can be deducted off your income tax bill. I know because I've done it.

One likely consequence of this obsession is that life expectancy in Italy is one of the longest in the world at an average of almost 84 years. The nation was full of pride a few years back when the fishing village of Acciaroli, on the coast south of Naples, made worldwide headlines because eighty-one people among the population of 600 were aged in their 90s or had turned 100. Why were they so long-lived? The residents gleefully gave their answers, saying it was a combination of factors – climbing stairs, drinking a glass of red wine, having sex, and eating lots of rosemary. They all had a smile on their faces.

Garibaldi, who by then was seventy-two years old, made a final visit to Rome in 1879, this time on a personal mission, to try to gain an annulment of his marriage in 1860 to the Marchesina Raimondi. This proved to be one more battle. Both the king and the prime minister refused, and it took much behind-the-scenes persuasion by his old friend and lawyer Francesco Crispi to prompt the court of appeal to grant Garibaldi's wish at a second time of asking. This allowed him to marry Francesca Armosina, who had been his companion at Caprera for his final twenty years and with whom he had two children, Clelia and Manlio.

The Hero had become plagued by arthritis in both his feet and hands in his final years, and could move around only in a wheelchair. Yet he insisted on a trip to Milan in November 1880 to personally inaugurate the city's monument to the Red Shirts who were killed at Mentana. He made another journey to Naples in the hope the weather there would improve his health. Then there was a final visit to Sicily in spring 1882 when Garibaldi was carried through the streets of Palermo amid silent crowds, shocked by his poor state. It was ten kinds of miracles, in truth, that he had lived so long given the adventures of his life – wounded so many times as he led from the front in fierce combat.

The end came for Giuseppe Garibaldi on 2 June 1882, just shy of his seventy-fifth birthday. He died peacefully in bed at his home on Caprera, looking out of the window towards Nizza.

15

EPILOGUE: CAPRERA

'The only hero the world has ever needed is Giuseppe Garibaldi.'

Che Guevara

The sky was a perfect blue and the stillness broken only by birdsong and a slight rustling of leaves amid the gentle breeze as I walked in the garden of Giuseppe Garibaldi's house on the island of Caprera. I had travelled there for a second time because this was the only possible place to end a journey on the trail of the Hero of Two Worlds – at his final resting place. Once again, the serenity was enchanting, such a contrast to his tumultuous life of revolutions, momentous battles and sailing the world's oceans. The path down the garden was still full of lizards and geckos darting this way and that as I walked to the private cemetery area where he was laid to rest. The tomb was up against a low white wall alongside those of other family members, including some of his children. It was made of granite from the island's local stone – it was rough, natural, unpolished, which seemed entirely fitting. GARIBALDI was inscribed on top in capital letters. No more was required.

It has been a place of pilgrimage ever since, from princes and presidents to schoolchildren and countless tourists. One of the first things that Sergio Mattarella, the much-loved current President of Italy, did after his accession was to visit Caprera and stand alone in front of the tomb in contemplation. This was a private trip, not a formal state occasion. Mattarella didn't have to go, he wanted to – just like so many Italians through the generations since Garibaldi died on 2 June 1882.

In another part of the garden I came across an umbrella pine tree that had fallen down, probably in a storm, and I wasn't there by accident. This is thought to be the spot where Garibaldi had requested a funeral pyre to be made. He had not wanted to be buried in a tomb, however appropriate this now looks, but instead had left strict instructions in his will that his body should be burnt on a pyre and the ashes placed in a crystal glass bottle and buried under his favourite juniper tree. The inspiration was the example of the English poet Percy Bysshe Shelley, whose body had been burnt on a beach at Viareggio in Tuscany some sixty years earlier, after he died in a storm at sea – this ceremony observed by his wife Mary Shelley, the author of *Frankenstein*, by Lord Byron, and by a Captain Daniel Roberts who subsequently went to live on La Maddalena and told Garibaldi about it.

This is not a tale of legend. It was confirmed by Jesse White Mario, the long-time friend and occasional nurse of Garibaldi. 'Tell me the exact story of your poet's fire-burial,' he asked Jesse. After she did, Garibaldi responded: 'That is the right way. It is a beautiful and healthy thing too. Only the priests oppose it. It hurts their trade.' Throughout his life there had been an English influence on the Hero of Two Worlds, and this was another. In the will, Garibaldi ordered his wife Francesca Armosina not to tell anyone in authority about his death until he had been cremated. He said the pyre should be made with wood such as acacia and myrtle that was abundant on the island, and said his body should be clothed in a red shirt and burned under the open sky.

Garibaldi did not get his way. The Italian government insisted that a State funeral was required for the hero of the new nation, the greatest hero of his age. Some said he should be buried in Rome on the Gianicolo hill, or in the Pantheon alongside the artist Raphael and King Vittorio Emanuele II, who had died four years earlier. Eventually, the funeral was held at Caprera, attended by members of the royal family along with politicians and military chiefs. The coffin was carried by survivors from the Expedition of The Thousand. It seems to me the proper place for Garibaldi's tomb, even though he will forever be in the pantheon of Italian heroes. At rest alongside him now are his last wife Francesca, and the three children they had together: Clelia, Rosita and Manlio.

Another tombstone was also placed in the Chateau Cemetery in Nice where his mother Rosa was buried. On this he is called Joseph Garibaldi, to match the name on his birth certificate.

Funeral processions to honour him took place all over Italy in the days following his death. The largest and most ostentatious was in Rome, starting amid a vast crowd in the Piazza del Popolo before moving down Via del Corso and ending at the Campidoglio. A giant image of Garibaldi was created, crowned with a laurel wreath held by a statue of liberty at his side. It was drawn along in a large carriage by eight white horses, and carved into the side of the carriage were images of triumph at Palermo, Naples and Rome.

Of course it was Rome. All roads lead to Rome. It couldn't have been a properly united Italy without Rome, the obsession for Garibaldi since his first visit as a young man and then his radicalisation by the Young Italy movement of Giuseppe Mazzini. For many years he lived by the slogan Rome or Death, declared from balconies in towns and cities all round the country to noisy audiences. I've lost count of how many times I've seen *O Roma O Morte* inscribed on statues and plaques and monuments.

One of the many things I have learned on this journey is that there is an enduring obsession in modern Italy with Garibaldi, not least in Rome, which has been my home for the past few years. When I mentioned to people that I was writing this book the reward was a cascade of interest and joy. One evening I went to see an acquaintance playing in his band, and halfway through the gig he suddenly announced he was dedicating the next song to me and they launched into a rendition of *Il Garibaldi Innamorato*, a 1987 samba-style hit for Italian singer Sergio Caputo whose title translates as 'Garibaldi in Love':

There's Garibaldi in love on the streets of Rio,
Wide-brimmed hat under a brown poncho,
And under the poncho, my Anita, a heart beats.

Who goes there? Super Garibaldi,
Ooh-la-la the conquistador,

Epilogue: Caprera

Who goes there? Long Live Garibaldi,
Ooh-la-la the conquistador.

Another friend bought me a little bottle of Garibaldi cologne, absurdly delighted with the discovery that such an article existed. Many sent links to newspaper articles and books they'd found, as well as a stream of photos of Garibaldi plaques and statues around Italy. Then there was my next-door neighbour who told me that her ninety-three-year-old uncle was a devoted admirer of the Hero of Two Worlds. That led to a wonderful conversation over lunch with a chap who had been an Italian army General for many years and whose own great grandfather had been one of the fighters among the Expedition of The Thousand. The General, as everybody called him, was a very sprightly ninety-something, and often still attended Garibaldi commemorations wearing his red shirt and neckerchief.

I was welcomed in by the American Academy in Rome, where many writers have worked and lived down the years. It lies in the heart of Gianicolo and has its administration section in the Villa Aurelia, which was the headquarters of Garibaldi during the 1849 battle to defend the *Repubblica Romana*. In another grand building on the opposite side of the street was the Academy's extensive library, where I was able to do invaluable research and do much of my writing. There was nowhere more appropriate.

Even closer to Villa Aurelia was Porta San Pancrazio, which housed the *Museo Della Repubblica Romana and Memoria Garibaldina*. The director of the museum, Mara Minasi, responded with enthusiasm and a waterfall of words to my request for information, and then kindly invited me to deliver a talk about *Garibaldi and England*. It was a happy and very unexpected privilege to stand in the museum next to a bust of the Hero of Two Worlds and tell an audience of Italians about the biscuit, the football shirts, the poetry and the 1864 visit to London.

Dottoressa Minasi also filled in details about the massive red arch at the entrance of Villa Pamphili, built in the wake of the *Repubblica Romana* battles which destroyed the Casino Dei Quattro Venti building that previously stood there. After the conflict, the area was sold in 1856 by the Corsini family to the Pamphili family, who owned most of the land beyond, in what is now the biggest public park in Rome. Until 1856 there were only small side gates into the Pamphili grounds, on the Via Aurelia Antica road, but the purchase allowed them to commission the big arch and create an imposing entrance to match their wealth and status.

The wife of the owner, Filippo Doria Pamphili, was Mary Talbot, the daughter of the Earl of Shrewsbury, the most prominent Catholic in nineteenth-century England. She built a conservatory and a fountain in another part of the park that still exists, and together they planned the red arch in the style of the triumphal arches of ancient Rome. It was designed by the Pope's architect Andrea Busiri Vici, but this was a private building rather than a public monument when completed in 1859. Only after Rome became part of a united Italy was a plaque put up on the inside wall of the left-hand leg of the arch in 1873, which read: 'Garibaldi and his brave men fought here courageously for the freedom of Rome and Italy.'

Epilogue: Caprera

When I went to take a look, I had to put a camera through the rails of rusty fencing to take a picture of this hidden plaque. The arch had long been left in ruin, and is too dangerous to allow visitors inside. However, planning for a restoration project using money from the European Union's post-covid Recovery Fund began in late 2024. This may cost anything up to one million Euros, and it immediately provoked a very modern conflict between rival visions for the future of the arch. A family in Rome had offered to donate its collection of Garibaldi memorabilia for display inside the arch once the renovation is finished, and the historians of the city authorities were supportive of this idea. Another more commercial faction was arguing for a café/bar to be created inside the arch to attract visitors. The first group reckoned that would be extremely insensitive on the site of one of the bloodiest battlegrounds of the Risorgimento. For me, it still felt like the most cheerless chunk of stone in the Eternal City.

The dispute about the arch illustrates how history continues to engage and sometimes to enrage the people of Italy. I learned that the name of the path leading up to the arch, the *Viale del Battaglione della Speranza* (Avenue of the Battalion of Hope) was only altered to reflect its heroic past in the 1990s. A few hundred metres away on the Gianicolo hill there were two more changes. Finally, in the autumn of 2024, the most important statue of Garibaldi was repaired, five years after it had been severely damaged when struck by a bolt of lightning. The protests by campaigners had not been in vain, and when the restoration happened they did it properly. Garibaldi and his horse are now surrounded by an invisible Faraday cage which protects it from being hit by lightning in future.

Anita's statue was also renovated in the early months of 2025, and a friend was overjoyed to tell me she was involved in the project, which cleaned the bronze surface of the statue along with its travertine base, and also 'installed a system to monitor the microclimatic condition of the bronze and regulation of the surrounding environment'. A new support structure was placed under the galloping horse as well. My friend told me that the statue seen and loved by the people of Rome since 1932 was not the original design. This had depicted Anita holding a gun in either hand as she rode side-saddle on the horse, but Mussolini, whose regime had commissioned the statue, vetoed this version. To his fascist way of thinking the strong woman also had to be a motherly woman, and so he demanded it be changed to show Anita holding only one gun and carrying her baby under the other. It's a clear example of a wider truth, that Garibaldi and his story is so often the prism through which different factions try to assert their idea of Italian history and society.

I have learned so much, and one vital lesson is that things are not always as they seem. Rome has many problems – the crazy traffic, the stifling bureaucracy, the frustrating public transport system and the parlous rubbish collection, although that was beginning to improve as I write (we'll see if it lasts). All these are as easy to see for a visitor as the Colosseum and the Pantheon. What I could only discover by living in the Eternal City is the friendliness of the Roman people, its vital sense of community, and how very quickly one is accepted by the locals. There is a culture of everyday common sense and patience, very rare in a major global city, that lifts the spirit. It comes with a touch of romance, too. There are public hydrants all over the city where potable water flows out of the tap 24 hours a day, and close to many of them are flower stalls which almost fill the pavement. These block the path for pedestrians, but nobody minds. There's a flower stall at the top of my road and another at the bottom, just like the pharmacies. Another example is what they call the *kiss and go* section right outside the doors to the departures section of Fiumicino airport – an area of fifteen minutes free parking for people dropping off loved ones. It's an illuminating contrast to the rapacious and draconian parking systems operating at British airports.

Just about the only thing in Italy that doesn't have the name Garibaldi attached to it is an airport (although there is one in Brazil) but rarely a day passes without a mention of his name somewhere. When the great Scottish footballer Denis Law died in early 2025, in an admiring obituary to him in *La Gazzetta dello Sport*, they wrote: 'A Garibaldini spirit coursed through his play and his life.' For the sports newspaper there could be no finer tribute.

One of the reasons for the legion of streets, statues and plaques commemorating his exploits was the nation-building mania of the late nineteenth century. But it's not merely that. Several modern statues have been commissioned and erected in our more sceptical twenty-first century age, and many festivals and events are held every year throughout Italy. Another honour is also being mooted – that if a road bridge is finally built to link Calabria and Sicily, it should be called the Garibaldi Bridge. Even through all the academic and social media debates about him, the spirit of Garibaldi endures.

There are always more questions than answers when considering the lives of the significant figures of history, but it's worth asking a few here. To begin with: What kind of man was Giuseppe Garibaldi, and did he deserve the admiration that accompanied him through his lifetime and beyond?

It seems to me his mighty reputation was not only the result of winning many crucial against-all-the-odds battles through thirty-five years across Europe and South America. It was not only because he possessed the glamour of a revolutionary figure. It was not only down to his charismatic personality, brilliant tactics and fearless leading from the front that inspired absolute dedication from soldiers. An essential ingredient of his fame was that all these factors were combined with a personal nobility and innate humility. Garibaldi rejected gifts of money all his life, so as not to be corrupted. This element of his character and his legend was what captivated observers from Tennyson to Alexandre Dumas and Giuseppe Verdi. In later life, when he was the most famous man in the world, Garibaldi always declared his profession to be *agricoltore* (farmer) on official documents and when he arrived to sit in Parliament. He was a farmer on Caprera, whose land flourished with fruit and vines, sheep and goats, and his favourite flowerbed of red carnations. He was quite often compared to the ancient Roman statesman and military leader Cincinnatus, who was a model of public virtue and then retired to work on a farm. When Cincinnatus was called back for combat, he won a major battle in sixteen days and then returned to his quiet life working the land. The similarities with Garibaldi are clear.

There are many paintings of Garibaldi at home on the island. In most of them he is wearing a red shirt, and in some there is a melancholy that suggests loneliness. However, others picture him as thoughtful, sitting at ease on the rocks, considering which cause to fight for next. His tendency to idealism was reflected in his political views, which although not always coherent were often way ahead of their time. He was an internationalist who argued for a community of European nations working together, many decades before the creation of the EU. He spoke for women's suffrage, even though to contemporary eyes this can seem at odds with his brusque and selfish attitude to relationships with women in his private life. Flawed or not, this idealism inspired many in his wake on both sides of the Atlantic. Perhaps the most famous was Che Guevara, the revolutionary icon of the 1950s and 60s, who said: 'The only hero the world has ever needed is Giuseppe Garibaldi.'

Another important question is what did Garibaldi think of Italy in the years between unification and his death? At his house on Caprera he wrote in 1880: 'It was a different Italy that I had dreamed of all my life – not this miserable, poverty-stricken, humiliated Italy that we now see governed by the dregs of the nation.' The south he had conquered during the Expedition of The Thousand was horribly neglected by a series of inept and corrupt governments. Conditions were so bad that thirteen million Italians emigrated between 1880 and 1914, most leaving behind a bleak existence for the dream of riches in the US, while Argentina and Brazil were also popular destinations. Today, the vast metropolis of Sao Paulo in Brazil is the city outside Italy with the highest population of people of Italian descent. Garibaldi himself, of course, was exiled in both the US and Brazil during his life, as well as Uruguay. This process of emigration speeded up after unification, but it had begun as early as 1820 due to rural poverty under the

Bourbon regime. Garibaldi was convinced the early years of unification were ruined by the self-interest of the rich and their exploitation of the poor. One bad regime had changed for another. Garibaldi's idealistic hope for a prosperous, proud new Italy would not happen anywhere close to his lifetime. He told a friend

> Human beings are divided into two types – the selfish ones who never sacrifice anything for the common good, and the true patriots who freely sacrifice what is most dear to them for the benefit of others. The latter are always misunderstood, insulted and dragged through the dirt, while the former rule the world.

Throughout my journey the most significant question has been this: What does Italy, and what do Italians, think of Garibaldi today? Everybody has a view. Nobody is neutral. I have found that the majority of people mostly admire and cherish him, telling me that nobody is perfect, but he was the man who did most to make modern Italy a reality. Some people are sceptical about the legend, saying that other figures were equally or more important to the Risorgimento, particularly the radical intellectual inspiration of Giuseppe Mazzini. They wonder if Garibaldi could have made better choices, but generally give no answer as to what these would have been. A minority of people are actively hostile to Garibaldi, convinced by the historical revisionism which paints him as a useful idiot manipulated by Piedmont and almost a traitor for handing the south to the north in September 1860.

Each to his own, of course, but I find it fascinating that Garibaldi is a symbol for everyone, whether they are positive or negative about him. It seems to me, also, highly significant that every political party wants to claim his legacy even now, as they have since his death in 1882. Nobody else from the Risorgimento era attracts this attention – not Mazzini, Cavour, Vittorio Emanuele II, or any of the others. Why? It's surely the same reason that he inspired so many people in his own time. He was a charismatic, swashbuckling figure whom people identified with and were attracted to. Whether myth or reality, and the legend doesn't matter here, he had a worldwide renown for making things happen and getting things done. He was a man of action. It was, and still is, better to have him on your side than against you. I believe this is why his name still reverberates through this land and why it will continue to do so. It's plain enough that Italy, for better or worse, would not exist as it does today but for Giuseppe Garibaldi.

There is one final question. What would Garibaldi think of Italy today? I believe he would be delighted that it's a united country, one which is more at peace with itself than when he was alive. He would be happy that it's a republic whose constitution is founded on the one he helped to forge for the *Repubblica Romana* in 1849. I suspect he would be impressed that in 2025 both of the two most popular political parties had female leaders – and he would be overjoyed that his wife Anita had become a symbolic heroine of the Italian nation, known to everyone in the land.

He would surely be full of pride when the Mameli national anthem is played, remembering how it was sung when his men went into battle, and would appreciate the words of a former President of Italy, Carlo Azeglio Ciampi, who said: 'It is a hymn that makes you vibrate inside, it is a song of freedom of a united people who have risen again after centuries of divisions and humiliations.' He would be amazed that the first nursery rhyme every child in Italy learns is *Garibaldi fu ferito*, about the moment he was wounded at Aspromonte.

He would be content that Rome is the capital of his country, and as a farmer he would be happy to see that local produce is still cherished across the land in this era of globalisation. He would probably be astounded at the statues found in almost every town, that new ones are being commissioned nearly 150 years after his death, and that more than 6,000 roads across his land are called Via Garibaldi.

He might roll a quizzical eye at the sight of Italy playing against France at rugby union to win the Garibaldi trophy – and that the English are still eating the biscuit named in his honour. And he would be humbled that tens of thousands of people come each year to visit Caprera, to walk round his house and climb the hill to the museum that tells the story of his tumultuous life, to look over the glistening waters around his island and discover on a sunny day of blue skies and a slight breeze that here is a slice of paradise.

BIBLIOGRAPHY

Addis, Ferdinand, *Rome: Eternal City* (London: Head Zeus, 2018)
Alajmo, Roberto, *Palermo* (London: Armchair Traveller, 2005)
Balzani, Roberto, *I Luoghi del Risorgimento* (Bologna: Mulino, 2024)
Barzini, Luigi, *The Italians* (London: Penguin, 1964)
Baudinelli, Riccardo, *Seguendo Garibaldi* (Fidenza: Mattioli, 2011)
Beales, Derek, and Biagini, Eugenio, *The Risorgimento and the Unification of Italy* (Abingdon: Routledge, 1971)
Brignoli, Marziano, *I Mille di Garibaldi* (Milan: Rusconi immagini, 1981)
Camilleri, Andrea, *Lo Stivale di Garibaldi* (Rome: La Repubblica, 2021)
Ciotta, Antonio, *La Maddalena* (Olbia: Innocenti, 2018)
Costacurta, Angelo and Tazzer, Sergio, *Marsala: Il vino di Garibaldi che piaceva agli Inglese* (Vittorio Veneto: Kellerman, 2019)
Dickie, John, *Delizia: The Epic History of the Italians and Their Food* (New York: Free Press, 2008)
D'Epiro, Peter and Pinkowish, Mary Desmond, *Sprezzatura: 50 Ways Italian Genius Shaped the World* (New York: Anchor Books, 2001)

Foot, John, *Calcio: A History of Italian Football* (London: Harper Perennial, 2007)

Gallo, Max, *Garibaldi: La forza di un destino* (Milan: Bompani, 1981)

Garibaldi, Erika, *Qui Sostò Garibaldi* (Rome: Schena Editore, 1989)

Garibaldi, Giuseppe, *My Life* (London: Hesperus, 1932)

Garibaldi in Parlamento (Rome: Camera dei deputati, Archivico storico, 2007)

Gilmour, David, *The Pursuit of Italy* (London: Penguin, 2011)

Hales, Dianne, *La Bella Lingua* (New York: Broadway Books, 2009)

Hero: Garibaldi Icona Pop (Turin: Azzurra publishing, 2002)

Hibbert, Christopher, *Garibaldi: Hero of Italian Unification* (London: St Martin's Press Griffin, 1965)

Hooper, John *The Italians* (London: Penguin, 2015)

Kneale, Matthew, *Rome: A History in Seven Sackings* (London: Atlantic Books, 2017)

La Casa di Garibaldi a Caprera (Olbia: Paolo Sorba Editore, 2015)

Levi, Carlo, *Christ Stopped at Eboli* (London: Penguin, 2000)

Levy, Shawn, *Dolce Vita Confidential* (London: Weidenfeld and Nicolson, 2017)

Mack Smith, Denis, *Garibaldi* (London: Hutchinson and Co, 1957)

Mack Smith, Denis, *Garibaldi: A Portrait in Documents* (Florence: Passigli Editori, 1982)

Mari, Maurizio, *Il Passaggio di Garibaldi in Romagna* (Ravenna: Società Conservatrice del Capanno Garibaldi, 2015)

Mascilli Migliorni, Luigi, *11 Maggio 1860* (Bari: Laterza), 2023)

Mazzocca, Fernandi and Villari, Anna, *Garibaldi Il Mito* (Genoa: Giunti, 2007)

Minasi, Mara, *Guida Museo della Repubblica Romana e della Memoria Garibaldini* (Rome: Rubbettino, 2020)

Norwich, John Julius, *Sicily* (London: John Murray, 2015)

Petacco, Arrigo, *O Roma O Morte* (Milan: Mondadori, 2010)

Pick, Daniel, *Rome or Death* (London: Jonathan Cape, 2005)
Pirandello, Luigi, *The Old and the Young* (Oxford: Benediction Classics, 2011)
Pizzo, Marco, *Lo Stivale di Garibaldi* (Milan: Mondadori, 2011)
Riall, Lucy, *Garibaldi: Invention of a Hero* (New Haven: Yale University Press, 2007)
Richards, Charles, *The New Italians* (London: Penguin, 1994)
Ridley, Jasper, *Garibaldi* (London: Constable and Company 1974)
Sacerdote, Gustavo, *La Vita di Giuseppe Garibaldi* (Milan: Rizzoli, 1933)
Saviano, Roberto, *My Italians* (London: Penguin, 2016)
Scardigli, Marco, *Le Grande Battaglie del Risorgimento* (Milan: Rizzoli, 2010)
Sciascia, Leonardo, *Il Quarantotto* (Milan: Adelphi, 1997)
Severgnini, Beppe, *An Italian in Italy* (Milan: BUR saggi, 2005)
Severgnini, Beppe, *Italian Lessons* (New York: Vintage, 2022)
Spreafico, Eugenio, *Ritratti di pietra e di bronzo* (Ravenna: Società Conservatrice del Capanno Garibaldi, 2019)
Tomasi di Lampedusa, Giuseppe, *The Leopard* (London: Vintage, 2007)
Trevelyan, GM, *Garibaldi and the Making of Italy.* (London: Longmans, 1926)
Trevelyan, GM, *Garibaldi and The Thousand* (London: Phoenix Press, 1909)
Trevelyan, GM, *Garibaldi's Defence of the Roman Republic* (London: Phoenix Press, 1907)
Valerio, Anthony, *Anita Garibaldi: A Biography* (Westport: Praeger, 2001)
Various authors, *Donne del Risorgimento* (Bologna: Mulino, 2011)
Verga, Giovanni, *Little Novels of Sicily* (London: Esprios, 2005)
Walton, Nicholas, *Genoa 'La Superba'* (London: Hurst, 2015)
White Mario, Jesse, *Vita di Garibaldi* (Pordenone: Studio Tesi, 1986)

ACKNOWLEDGEMENTS

So many people, and so many new friends, helped me along this journey of discovery from the tumult of London to the secluded glory of Caprera. I would like to say a special *grazie mille* to Claudia Cecamore, Raul Grisolia, Betty Garbarino, Paquita Taddei, Raimonda Pianomortari, Maurizia Garzia, Livio Quagliata, Eleonara Ronchetti, Dru Burtz, Andrea D'Epifanio, Susanna Piccirillo, Massimo Chierechin, Daniela Cappa, Stefano Boldrini, Guido Martinelli, Patrizia De Salazar, Roberto Amorosino, Guido Palmieri Crispi, Laura Marcalli, Kenneth Riis, and the fabulous fratelli Zacchetti – Cristina, Guido, Filippo and Andrea.

Staff at museums and exhibitions around Italy gladly took the time to share their enthusiasm for the story and legend of Giuseppe Garibaldi. I thank them all. I owe a huge debt of gratitude to Mara Minasi, director of the *Museo della Repubblica Romana e della Memoria Garibaldina* in Rome, who so generously answered a multitude of questions and steered me away from mistakes and misconceptions.

Acknowledgements

The museum is located on the Gianicolo hill, a place of particular magic in the Eternal City, which is also home to the American Academy in Rome. My thanks also for the kindness of its chief librarian, Sebastian Hierl, who allowed me privileged access to books and documents that proved to be a goldmine. I spent many enjoyable hours researching and writing in its perfect setting.

Nell Whiscombe, Connie Berry and Kit Holden all read the text and made invaluable suggestions. I can't thank them enough for their dedication and inspiration. I would also like to mention the unstinting support of my editor Shaun Barrington and my agent Robert Dudley, without whom *Via Garibaldi* would not have seen the light of day.

Finally, this book would have been impossible to write without the love, patience, tolerance, enthusiasm and knowledge of my partner Nicoletta Zacchetti. She walked along many of the Via Garibaldi alongside me, and didn't flinch even in the 44°C heat of Salemi. *Grazie, amore mio.*

INDEX

Abruzzo 249
AC Milan 216-217
Aegean Sea 31-32
Agrigento 158
Alfa Romeo 200
Alessandria 238
American Academy in
 Rome 62, 267, 281
Andria 234
Antonietti, Colomba 90
Appenines 67, 83, 93
Arducci, Antonio 64
Arena Garibaldi 21
Arezzo 84
Argentina 49, 51, 273
Armellini, Carlo 70
Armosina, Francesca
 261, 265
Arsenal 14, 50
Arquati, Giuditta Tavani
 247-248
Aspromonte 157, 159,
 202-206, 211-212,
 214, 226, 234, 236,
 276
Assisi 252
Australia 12, 100, 107,
 237
Austria 34, 53, 118,
 125, 127, 183, 220,
 226, 229-230

Bakunin, Mikhail 99
Barrault, Emile 32-33
Basile, Giovanni 148
Basilicata 175
Bedford 219
Bell, Alexander Graham
 106
Belo Horizonte 52
Benigni, Roberto 179
Bergamo 120, 134
Bernini, Gian Lorenzo
 251-252
Berry, Ian 38-39
Bettini, Sofia 116
Bezzecca 126, 227-229,
 249
Bialetti, Alfonso 194
Bilancioni, Respicio 229
Bismarck, Otto Von
 226
Bixio, Nino 120, 143,
 160, 191
Boer War 109
Bologna 115, 121, 198
Bonnet, Giacomo 86-87
Bordeaux 255
Borromini, Francesco
 251-252
Borsellino, Paolo 207
Boston 107, 132
Bourne End 14

Bovalino 206
Braddon, Mary
 Elizabeth 216
Bramante 64
Brazil 15, 46, 49, 52,
 60, 97, 228, 238,
 271, 273
Brescia 120, 134
British Museum 108
Brolio 236-237
Bronte 160
Browning, Elisabeth
 Barrett 216
Bucci, Marco 41
Buckingham Palace 12
Byron, Lady 133
Byron, Lord 264

Cabot, John (Giovani
 Caboto) 107, 247
Cadogan, George 174
Caesar, Julius 170
Cagliari 94, 225
Caiazzo 177-178, 180
Caine, Michael 198
Cairoli, Benedetto 135,
 247
Cairoli, Enrico 246-
 247
Cairoli, Giovanni 246-
 247

Index

Calabria 103, 163-164, 171-172, 174, 206, 209, 237, 249, 271
Calatafimi 58, 126, 142-146, 150, 162, 183, 216, 231, 246
California 14
Camilleri, Andrea 158-159
Campania 173-174, 178, 195, 206-207, 249
Caprera 20, 33, 94, 96-99, 101, 106, 110, 115, 118, 127, 183, 189-190, 214-215, 220, 222, 226, 234-236, 238-239, 254-255, 261-265, 272-273, 276
Capri 176
Caputo, Sergio 266
Caracalla, Baths of 56
Caravaggio 40, 253
Carbonari secret society 34
Cardinale, Claudia 159
Carducci, Giouse 204
Carlo Alberto, King of Piedmont 52-53
Carpaneto, Francesco 107
Caserta 177
Castellani, Alessandro 258
Castrovillari 172, 184
Catania 153, 209
Cavour, Camillo 118-120, 127-128, 133,-134, 177, 184-185, 187-188, 191-192, 196-198, 238, 275
Centinaio, GianMarco 194

Cesenatico 78-82, 85-86, 113, 120, 242, 250
Charles II, King of England 13
Chateau Cemetery, Nice 265
Chianti 236-237
Chiavari 23, 93
Chicago 191
Chile 107
China 12, 18, 107
Churchill, Winston 75
Ciadini, General 188
Ciampi, Carlo Azeglio 275
Cicagna 53
Ciceruacchio (Angelo Brunetti) 60-61, 80, 86
Cincinnatus 272
Cliveden 20
Clooney, George 114
Collins, Richard and Claire 110, 236
Colosseum 56, 169, 258, 270
Columbus, Christopher 16, 35, 45, 101, 107
Comacchio 85-86, 88, 125
Como 111-114, 116-118, 120, 123, 125, 216, 257
Constantinople 31, 33, 115
Corniglio 187
Costa Smeralda 96
Cremona 127
Crispi, Francesco 128, 133-135, 140, 155, 191, 197, 261
Crystal Palace 219

Cuba 97, 107
Cuneo, Giovanni Battista 35
Curitibanos 48
Custoza 228-230

Danesi, Pirade 88, 196
Dante, Alighieri 16, 92
De Cristoforis, Carlo 113, 199
De Cristoforis, Luigi, 199
De Cristoforis, Malachia 199
De Lesseps, Ferdinand 72
De Pace, Antonietta 90, 173
Dickens, Charles 13, 40, 154, 219
Dijon 235, 249, 255
Doge of Genoa 45
Dolomite mountains 228
Doppler, Christian 221
Draghi, Mario 256
Duarte, Manoel 47
Duke of Wellington 133, 154
Dumas, Alexandre 99, 101, 127, 154-155, 170-171, 177, 272

Eastwood, Clint 122
Eboli 174-175
Egadi Islands 138
Egypt 228
Emilia Romagna 81, 83, 187, 250
Engels, Friedrich 154
England 14-15, 19-21, 45, 105, 108-109, 127, 132-133, 139,

283

154, 214, 218, 220,
226, 228, 268
Esteche, Lucia 49
European Court of
Human Rights 207
Expedition of The
Thousand (*I Mille*)
124, 131-132, 134-
136, 139, 142, 144-
145, 154, 158, 160,
163, 176, 183, 185,
187, 209, 220, 223,
231, 246-247, 265,
267, 273

Facchinetti, Fabio 80
Falcone, Giovanni 207
Fattoria Giuccioli 87
Fellini, Federico 232
Ferdinando II, King of
the Two Sicilies 133
Ferrari 55, 198, 200
Ferrari, Luigi 210
Fiat 198-199, 201, 218
Fiesole 181
Figline 246
Fino Mornasco 116
First War of Italian
Independence 52-53
Florence 9, 11, 13, 26,
92, 121, 130, 154,
181, 186, 189, 216,
219, 224, 233-234,
236, 238-240, 244-
246, 251
Foscolo, Ugo 215
France 24, 29, 32, 72,
120, 127-128, 177,
181, 209, 230, 233,
237, 254-255, 27
Francesco II, King of the
Two Sicilies 133,
153, 175

Francis I, King of
Austria 125
Franco-Prussian War
28-29, 254
French Revolution 26,
28, 32

Gaeta 72
Gaggia, Achille 194
Gallipoli 173, 184
Gallura 97
Gambarie 203
Garbatella 256-257
Garibaldi, Anita (wife
of GG)
Meets Garibaldi 46-47
A fighter 48
Marriage 48
Children 51
Statue on Gianicolo
Hill 60, 270
Joins Garibaldi in
Rome 74
Cesenatico festival
79-81
Ill with fever 83-86
Death 87-88
Legacy in Italy 89-91
Monument on La
Maddelena 104
Painting in Museo del
Risorgimento of
Milan 125
Marsala wine 139
Painting in Museo
Nazionale del
Risorgimento of
Turin 189
And *passim*
Garibaldi, Bruno
(grandson of GG) 29

Garibaldi, Clelia
(daughter of GG)
97, 261, 265
Garibaldi, Constant
(grandson of GG) 29
Garibaldi, Costanza
Ravizza (great, great
granddaughter of
GG) 78, 89
Garibaldi, Domenico
(father of GG) 23,
30
Garibaldi, Ezio
(grandson of GG)
63
Garibaldi, Manlio (son
of GG) 261, 265
Garibaldi, Menotti, (son
of GG) 29, 48, 51,
110, 120, 228, 245
Garibaldi, Peppino
(grandson of GG)
109
Garibaldi, Ricciotti (Son
of GG) 29, 51, 228
Garibaldi, Rosita
(daughter of GG)
51, 265
Garrone, Matteo 232
Gazzetta dello Sport
165, 179, 217, 271
Genoa 26-27, 37-46,
51-53, 109, 119,
125, 132-135, 151,
183, 201
Genoa Cricket and
Football Club 45
Getty III, John Paul 206
Gianicolo 9, 55-58,
60-61, 65-66, 68,
74-76, 86, 90, 113,
125, 257, 265, 267,
26

Index

Gibraltar 31
Giotto 252
Gorzowski, General Karl von 86
Gramitto, Rocco Ricci 157
Gualeguay 46
Guevara, Che 12, 52, 158, 263, 273

Hadrian's Villa 83
Hawaii 107
Hemingway, Ernest 97
Herzen, Alexander 219
Hooper, John 123
Hugo, Victor 129, 136, 255
Hungary 180
Hyde Park 212

Induno, Gerolamo 124-125, 189
Ischia 220
Isle of Wight 215
Italian Legion 49-52
Italian National Society 119, 121

Jagger, Mick 114
Johnson, Boris 21
Juventus 217

Kafka, Franz 221
Kilpin, Herbert 216
Kingdom of the Two Sicilies 132, 144

La Dolce Vita 62, 232
Laguna 52
Lake Como 111, 114, 117, 257
Lake Garda 120, 221, 225, 227-228

La Maddalena 94-97, 99-101, 103-105, 110, 235-236, 264
Lampedusa, Giuseppe Tomasi di 148, 159
Lancaster House 11-12, 21
Lanza, General Ferdinando 150-153
La Spezia 212
Law, Denis 271
Lega, Silvestro 249
Leggero (Battista Culiolo) 86, 90, 92-94, 104
Le Marche 177
Leonardo da Vinci 16, 82, 101, 126
Leone, Sergio 122, 232
Levi, Carlo 175
Liguria 23, 212
Lima 107
Lincoln, Abraham 190, 253
Lingotto 198
Liverpool 105, 109
Livorno 9, 98, 236, 238
Loana 23
Lombardy 52-53, 114, 200-201
London 11-14, 19-21, 36, 98, 105, 108, 116, 119, 124, 145, 212-213, 215, 218-220, 245, 258, 268
Luino 53

Macerata 54
Machiavelli, Niccolò 16-17
Magenta 120
Magnavacca 85

Mameli, Goffredo 63, 189, 218, 275
Mandela, Nelson 12
Mandriole 87, 121, 189
Manin, Daniele 52, 83, 230-231
Manin, Giorgio 231
Mansfield 14
Mantova 118
Maradona, Diego 169
Marconi, Guglielmo 16
Marinella 172
Marsala 97, 125, 129-132, 135-136, 138-142, 144, 148, 151, 156, 158, 160, 162, 185, 189, 209, 235, 238, 249
Marseille 32, 35, 44, 46, 255
Marsh, George Perkins 190
Marx, Karl 21
Maserati 199-200
Mattarella, Sergio 264
Mazara Del Vallo 161
Mazzini, Giuseppe 19, 34, 39, 49, 70, 72, 105, 108, 119, 132-133, 184, 197, 219, 250, 266, 274-275
Mechel, Colonel Von 153
Melito di Porto Salvo 171
Meloni, Giorgia 257
Mentana 126-127, 239-247, 249, 261
Mercantini, Luigi 119
Messina 163
Metternich, Prince 34
Meucci, Antonio 106-107

Michelangelo 16, 250-252
Milan 9, 12, 52, 113, 118, 121, 123-126, 130, 134, 151, 187, 196, 199, 211, 216-217, 227, 244, 251, 261
Mille, Francesco 104
Minasi, Mara 267-268
Mirabelli, Carmine 172
Modica 161
Modigliana 250
Mole Antonelliana 196
Molini, Paolo 251
Montalbano, Inspector 16, 158
Monte Argentario 137
Monterotondo 243, 245
Montevideo 12, 48-52, 54, 86, 105, 126, 138, 235, 249
Moore, Henry 95
Moreton Bay Fig 147
Moretti, Nanni 232
Morocco 105
Mozia 139
Mundy, Admiral 152
Murat, Joachim, King of Naples 115
Museo della Repubblica Romana e della Memoria Garibaldina 267
Museo del Risorgimento (Genoa) 38
Museo del Risorgimento (Milan) 124
Museo Nazionale del Risorgimento (Turin) 186, 191

Mussolini, Benito 16, 60, 63-64, 68, 155, 175, 206, 257, 270

Naples 72, 90, 115, 130, 132, 153, 162, 165-173, 175-179, 181, 183, 185, 187, 192, 195, 206, 220, 261, 266
Napoleon Bonaparte 24, 134
Napoleon III, Emperor of France 118, 120, 127, 209
Nelaton, Auguste 213
Nelson, Lord 12, 100, 139
Newcastle 109
New York 12, 36, 105-107, 109, 116, 119, 190-191
New Zealand 107
Nice 9, 22, 24-26, 28-31, 35-36, 38, 43, 51, 74, 93-94, 106, 127, 132, 265
Nightingale, Florence 11, 13, 154, 219
Nottingham Forest 14, 50, 216-217
Notts County 217
Obbedisco 229
Odessa 30
Olbia 97
Ortygia 131
Orvieto 84
Oudinot, General 72
Ozieri 234

Pace, Giuseppe 172
Padova 199
Paganini, Niccolo 94

Palau 95, 97
Palazzo Madama 186
Palestrina 72
Palermo 15, 18, 124, 126, 134, 138, 140, 145-159, 161-162, 171, 185, 187, 209, 216, 231, 247, 266
Pall Mall 11, 13, 19, 73
Palmerston, Lady 213
Palmerston, Lord 13, 219
Palmi 172
Pamphili, Filippo Doria 61, 63, 73, 76, 268
Panizzi, Sir Anthony 108
Pantheon 56, 196, 270
Papal States 34, 177, 181
Paris 12, 177, 231
Parma 34
Partridge, Richard 213
Pasolini, Pier Paolo 218
Patterson, Andrew 162
Peard, Colonel John 21, 163, 174-175, 220
Peek Freans 15, 216
Peru 12, 100, 107
Philippines 107
Piaggio 41
Piano, Renzo 46
Piazza Armerina 15, 156, 161
Piazza Navona 252, 258
Picasso 198
Piedmont 24, 26-29, 34, 52-53, 93-94, 107, 110, 118, 120, 127, 133, 156, 181, 183, 186-187, 196, 238, 274
Pinturicchio 253
Pisa 21, 169, 214

Index

Pirandello, Luigi 157, 211
Pirandello, Stefano 157
Pius IX, Pope 57, 59
Polo, Marco 107
Pompeii 169-171, 176
Porta Pia 254
Port Lympia 23-24
Porto Alegre 52
Porto Garibaldi 85, 87
Pra 43
Prince of Wales 13, 20
Prussia 254
Puglia 103, 173, 206, 237, 249
Pyrrhus 138

Quarto 133-137, 158, 183
Queen Victoria 11, 14, 20, 219

Raimondi, Giuseppina 116-118
Raphael 253, 265
Rattazzi, Urbano 208
Ravello, Battistina 115
Ravenna 54, 80, 82, 85, 87, 90-93, 96, 104, 121, 250
Reggio Calabria 172
Renzi, Matteo 21
Repubblica Romana 54, 57, 61, 63, 66, 73, 75-77, 86, 90, 113, 231, 248, 267-268, 27
Ribeiro da Silva, Ana Maria de Jesus (Anita) see Garibaldi, Anita
Ricasoli, Baron Bettino 208, 236, 238
Ricci, Giovanni 242
Rio de Janeiro 46

Rio Grande do Sul 46
Risorgimento 9, 34, 38-39, 83, 90, 109, 122-124, 141, 145, 147, 157, 186, 189, 191, 196-197, 210-211, 214, 216, 227, 230-232, 248, 250, 269, 274-275
Ristorante Scarpone 63-64
River Plate 46, 252
Roberts, Emma 108, 115
Robin Hood protests 224
Ronaldo, Cristiano 96
Rossellini, Roberto 232
Rossi, Pellegrino 57, 66
Russia 33, 100, 125

Saffi, Aurelio 70
Saint-Simonians 32-33, 49
Salemi 141-142, 144, 242
Salerno 90, 173, 175
Salto 50-51
San Dalmazio 93
San Fermo di Battaglia 112-113, 242
San Gimignano 178
San Marino 84-85
Santa Lucia de Los Antos 49
Sardinia 24, 26-29, 34, 52-53, 93-94, 96-97, 103, 107, 110, 118, 120, 127, 133, 234, 236, 249
Savage, John 217
Schiaffino, Simone 144
Schlein, Elly 257

Sciacca 138
Sciascia, Leonardo 159
Schwartz, Maria Esperanza Baroness Von 115
Second War of Italian Independence 110, 112, 118, 216, 250
Seely, Charles 215
Seely, Mary 215
Segesta 145-146
Shaftesbury, Lord 19
Shelley, Mary 264
Shelley, Percy Bysshe
Shrewsbury, Earl of 268
Sicily 15, 21, 39, 43, 58, 103, 128, 130-132, 134, 138-142, 148, 150-151, 153-156, 158-164, 167, 183, 187, 206, 209, 216, 237-238, 249, 271
Smedley, Menella Bute 212
Solferino 120, 127, 227
Sorrentino, Paolo 57, 232
Southampton 215
Southwark 219
Spaccanapoli 168-169
Spello 253
Stafford House 13, 20, 219
Staten Island 106, 191
St Mark's Square 221, 230-231, 233
Stourbridge 14
St Peter's Basilica 62, 75, 83, 252
Strauss, Levi 39
St Valentine 83
Superga hill 198

Sutherland, Duchess of 19-20, 219
Sutherland, Duke of 13, 20, 219-220

Taganrog 32-33, 35, 125
Talamone 137
Talbot, Mary 268
Tangier 105
Taormina 171
Tardelli, Marco 21
Tasmania 107
Taylor, A.J.P. 17
Tchaikovsky, Pyotr 221
Teano 181-183
Teatro Fossati 125
Teddington 219
Tennyson, Alfred Lord 13, 202, 215-216, 272
Terni 83
Third War of Italian Independence 236
Tiber, river 30, 56, 167, 241, 249, 258-259
Timoni, Signora 32
Tintoretto 40
Todi 84
Torre, Maria della 116
Totti, Francesco 103
Trafalgar Square 19
Trapani 43, 140
Trastevere 61, 66, 72, 247-249, 258
Trecchi, Teresa Araldi 237
Trevelyan, G.M. 184
Treviso 195, 225
Trieste 192, 195-196
Tunisia 104
Turin 27-29, 53-54, 118, 122, 128, 134, 185-187, 189-192, 196, 198-199, 201, 208, 214, 226, 233
Turkey 25, 228
Turr, General 177
Tuscany 34, 83, 93, 103, 137, 249, 264
Tynemouth 109

Uffizi Gallery 244, 250
Ukraine 30, 33
Umbria 83, 177
UNESCO 18, 40, 92, 179, 195, 205, 223, 225
Uruguay 49, 51, 97, 228, 273

Vairano 181-182, 242
Valencia 258
Varignano fortress 212-213
Varese 120, 126, 216, 247, 249
Vasari, Giorgio 251
Vecchi, Augusto 108
Velletri 72, 90
Veneto 237
Venice 26, 52-53, 83, 85, 183, 188, 190, 195, 201, 208, 220-226, 230-234, 236-237, 251
Verdi, Giuseppe 16, 34, 63, 119, 272
Verga, Giovanni 160
Verona 118
Vespucci, Amerigo 107
Vesuvius 49, 176
Vici, Andrea Busiri 268

Viel-Castel, Horace de 111
Villa Flori 117
Villa Glori 246-247
Villa Olmo 116
Villa Pamphili 61, 63, 73, 76, 268
Villa San Giovanni 163
Visconti, Luchino 232
Vittorio Emmanuele II, King of Italy 9, 133, 142, 148, 177, 181-183, 185, 189, 197, 201, 209, 220, 226, 238, 249, 265, 275
Vivaldi, Antonio 221
Volta, Alessandro 16, 114
Volterra 93
Volturno 176, 180-181, 199, 249

Washington, George 12
Washington Square, Manhattan 191
Webster, Robert 214
Whitaker family 139
White, Jesse Mario 71
Winnington-Ingram, Captain 138
Woking 14
Woodhouse, John 139

Young Italy 34-35, 40, 42, 44, 70, 125, 266

Zanetti, Fernando 196
Zingaretti, Luca 16
Zolli, Giuseppe 223
Zucchini, Marchesa Paulina 115